AN INTRODUCTION TO SPORTS COACHING

An Introduction to Sports Coaching provides students with an accessible and engaging guide to the scientific, social scientific, medical and pedagogical theories that underlie the practice of quality sports coaching. Now in a fully updated and revised second edition, it introduces students to the complex, messy, multi-faceted nature of coaching, and explores the full range of 'knowledges' that inform all successful coaching practice.

Written by a team of leading international sports coaching academics and practitioners, as well as sport scientists and social scientists, the book provides a concise guide to every key theme in sports coaching, including:

- reflective practice
- pedagogy
- skill acquisition
- psychology
- biomechanics
- physiology

- sport medicine and injury
- performance analysis
- sociology
- history
- philosophy
- sport development

Each chapter makes a clear link between theory and practice, and includes discussion of real-life coaching scenarios and insights from practising international and club coaches. The book includes clear definitions of important themes and concepts, as well as seminar and review questions in each chapter designed to confirm understanding and encourage further enquiry.

No other introductory textbook explains the importance of a holistic approach to sports coaching practice. This is an essential companion to any sports coaching course.

Robyn L. Jones is a Professor of Sport and Social Theory at the Cardiff School of Sport, Cardiff Metropolitan University (UWIC), UK, and a Visiting Professor (II) at the Norwegian School of Sport Sciences, Oslo, Norway. He has published several books on sports coaching and pedagogy, the most recent being *A Sociology of Sports Coaching* (Routledge). He also serves as the General Editor of the newly launched Taylor & Francis journal *Sports Coaching Review*.

Kieran Kingston is a Senior Lecturer in Sport Psychology at the Cardiff School of Sport, Cardiff Metropolitan University (UWIC), UK. He received his PhD in 1999 from the University of Wales. His research interests are focused broadly on the motivational aspects of sport. Recent publications involve work on goal-setting, coach/athlete motivation, confidence, treatment efficacy/adherence and performance routines. He has provided psychological support to a variety of elite and professional sports performers since 1997.

AN INTRODUCTION TO SPORTS COACHING

Connecting theory to practice

EDITED BY ROBYN L. JONES AND
KIERAN KINGSTON

Routledge
Taylor & Francis Group

LONDON AND NEW YORK

First published 2013
by Routledge
2 Park Square, Milton Park, Abingdon, Oxon OX14 4RN

Simultaneously published in the USA and Canada
by Routledge
711 Third Avenue, New York, NY 10017

*Routledge is an imprint of the Taylor & Francis Group, an
informa business*

British Library Cataloguing in Publication Data
A catalogue record for this book is available from the
British Library

Library of Congress Cataloging in Publication Data
An introduction to sports coaching: connecting theory to practice/
   edited by Robyn L. Jones and Kieran Kingston. – 2nd ed.
      p.cm.
   1. Coaching (Athletics)   I. Jones, Robyn L.   II. Kingston, Kieran.
   GV711.158147 2013
   796.07′7–dc23

                                        2012033976

ISBN: 978–0–415–69490–2 (hbk)
ISBN: 978–0–415–69491–9 (pbk)
ISBN: 978–0–203–14744–3 (ebk)

Typeset in Melior

by RefineCatch Limited, Bungay, Suffolk

CONTENTS

PART I

1 REFLECTIVE PRACTICE IN SPORTS COACHING: THOUGHTS ON PROCESS, PEDAGOGY AND RESEARCH   3

DAVID GILBOURNE, PHILLIP MARSHALL AND ZOE KNOWLES

PART II

2 PEDAGOGY FOR COACHES   15

KEVIN MORGAN AND JOHN SPROULE

V

3 SKILL ACQUISITION FOR COACHES 31

GAVIN LAWRENCE, KIERAN KINGSTON AND VICTORIA GOTTWALD

4 PSYCHOLOGY FOR COACHES 49

KIERAN KINGSTON, OWEN THOMAS AND RICHARD NEIL

vi

PART III

5 SOCIOLOGY FOR COACHES 69

NIC MATTHEWS, SCOTT FLEMING AND ROBYN L. JONES

6 HISTORY FOR COACHES 83

MALCOLM MACLEAN AND IAN PRITCHARD

7 PHILOSOPHY FOR COACHES 99

ALUN HARDMAN AND CARWYN JONES

8 ETHICS FOR COACHES   113

ALUN HARDMAN AND CARWYN JONES

9 SPORTS DEVELOPMENT FOR COACHES   131

NICOLA BOLTON AND BEV SMITH

PART IV

PART V

14 TYING IT ALL TOGETHER   **215**

ROBYN L. JONES AND KIERAN KINGSTON

ILLUSTRATIONS

TABLES

FIGURES

xiv

CONTRIBUTORS

Professor David Gilbourne, Department of Sport, Health and Exercise Science, University of Hull

Phillip Marshall, Department of Sport, Health and Exercise Science, University of Hull

Dr Zoe Knowles, School of Sport and Exercise Science, Liverpool John Moores University

Dr Kevin Morgan, Cardiff School of Sport, Cardiff Metropolitan University

Dr John Sproule, Moray House School of Education, University of Edinburgh

Dr Gavin Lawrence, School of Sport, Health and Exercise Science, Bangor University

Dr Kieran Kingston, Cardiff School of Sport, Cardiff Metropolitan University

Dr Victoria Gottwald, School of Sport, Health and Exercise Science, Bangor University

Dr Owen Thomas, Cardiff School of Sport, Cardiff Metropolitan University

Dr Richard Neil, Cardiff School of Sport, Cardiff Metropolitan University

Dr Nic Matthews, School of Leisure, University of Gloucestershire

Professor Scott Fleming, Cardiff School of Sport, Cardiff Metropolitan University

Professor Robyn L. Jones, Cardiff School of Sport, Cardiff Metropolitan University

Dr Malcolm MacLean, Department of Sport and Exercise, University of Gloucestershire

Dr Ian Pritchard, Department of Sport and Exercise Sciences, University of Chester

Dr Alun Hardman, Cardiff School of Sport, Cardiff Metropolitan University

Dr Carwyn Jones, Cardiff School of Sport, Cardiff Metropolitan University

Dr Nicola Bolton, Cardiff School of Sport, Cardiff Metropolitan University

Bev Smith, Cardiff School of Sport, Cardiff Metropolitan University

Dr Gareth Irwin, Cardiff School of Sport, Cardiff Metropolitan University

Dr Ian Bezodis, Cardiff School of Sport, Cardiff Metropolitan University

Professor David Kerwin, Cardiff School of Sport, Cardiff Metropolitan University

Dr Peter O'Donoghue, Cardiff School of Sport, Cardiff Metropolitan University

Dr Andrew Miles, Cardiff School of Sport, Cardiff Metropolitan University

Professor Richard Tong, Cardiff School of Sport, Cardiff Metropolitan University

Dr Michael G. Hughes, Cardiff School of Sport, Cardiff Metropolitan University

Dr John L. Oliver, Cardiff School of Sport, Cardiff Metropolitan University

Dr Rhodri Lloyd, Cardiff School of Sport, Cardiff Metropolitan University

PREFACE TO 2ND EDITION

BACKGROUND AND AIM

Although scholars agree that coaching is a complex, multifaceted activity involving many different forms of knowledge, the literature which has informed it, particularly at the beginner or introductory level, has been roundly criticised (e.g. Jones, 2006b, among others). The disapproval has centred on the portrayal of coaching as a simple sequential course of knowable action to be delivered and then accepted by the athlete; a picture which grossly oversimplifies the process involved. Such a portrayal has also been fragmented or splintered in nature, presenting coaching as a series of isolated, discrete and largely unrelated components. The problem with such compartmentalisation is that those parts being analysed have been de-contextualised, resulting in a very artificial account of events. As everyone who has coached or been coached can attest, coaching is just not that clear-cut. What has exacerbated the situation is that coaches and students of coaching have been left to make the links between the different theoretical strands and the thorny reality of practice for themselves; a task at which they have consistently failed. Unsurprisingly, it has left the relevancy of such work open to question. The result is that much of coaches' knowledge remains rooted in implicit assumptions as opposed to explicit research and theory. No doubt authors of such introductory texts would rightly protest that there is a need to present coaching in a way that is both accessible and understandable for students and novice coaches. We couldn't agree more. Consequently, those wishing to write a foundational book in coaching are left with a dilemma; how to pen a clear, readable text suitable for undergraduate students and beginner coaches, without dumbing-down the activity so that it lacks any perceived application to the real world.

The first edition of this book was a response to the challenge described, which to a degree was met, as we were invited by Routledge to produce a second. We were pleased to do so for a number of reasons. Principal among these was our belief in the need to improve the text, particularly in terms of strengthening the case related to the value of considered reflection in developing coaching knowledge. This was not primarily aimed at improving understanding of the content contained in the chapters (which remain grounded in differing disciplines of sport sciences), but rather to encourage considered interpretation of how the different knowledge strands presented comprise integrated coaching practice. To help develop such analysis, and consequently a more critical reading of this book, a definitive chapter borrowing, principally from the work of Donald Schön (1983, 1987) on reflective practice, now follows this Preface. This chapter, new to this second edition, encourages readers to become reflexive practitioners by recognising that interpretations of sports coaching are produced and not found (Smyth and Shacklock, 1998). Its primary aim, then, is to promote greater cognitive and creative consideration of the differing strands of knowledge presented within the book's subsequent chapters in relation to everyday coaching practice (Jones, 2000). In doing so, coaching is more firmly positioned as a personal construction where one coach may rely on his physiological or biomechanical knowledge to a greater extent to deal with a particular issue, whilst another, faced with a similar problem, would utilise her pedagogical or psychological skills.

Within this second edition, we have also tried to highlight (and encourage) this constructivist nature a little more in an amended concluding chapter. Here, we present examples of how the holistic approach we call for in the book (taking information from a range of sources) can be realised. In addition to our personal interpretations of a coaching issue (which were a popular feature of the first edition), we also present two additional real-life coaching scenarios to be engaged with. These 'exercises' further emphasise the pedagogical purpose of the book for other users, be they students, lecturers, coach educators or practitioners. Finally within this second edition, in order to take account of the burgeoning field of coaching (and sports science) research, the chapters have been both expanded and updated, often through the invited critique of additional colleagues, thus considerably enriching the original text.

Despite the changes and improvements evident, this second edition retains the three principal goals which defined the first, namely: to introduce students to the multifaceted nature of coaching and the predominant sport science knowledges which inform it; to highlight how such differing perspectives can and should be related to coaching practice; and, finally, to emphasise them as part of an integrated entirety which comprises the holistic nature of the activity. Although an introductory text, then, this is not a simple 'how-to' book of coaching comprising a list of handy hints and quick fixes. Indeed, this is where it differs from much of

what has gone before. Rather, the significance of the book lies in better defining coaching's content knowledges, and how they contribute to a collective body of understanding for beginner coaches and students of coaching. Clarifying in this way holds the potential to increase the perceived relevancy of explicit knowledge sources for readers, consequently reducing the gap between theory and practice.

CONTENT

Although not claiming to cover all the possible information sources available to coaches, the chapters included in the book examine coaching from a number of sport science related perspectives. We're aware that presenting the book in such a format can be seen as going against the argument just given in respect of fragmenting knowledge. However, taking account of the complexity of coaching as a subject and the introductory nature of the book, for the purposes of clarity and to counter fear and frustration among readers, it was decided to delineate or bracket coaches' knowledge along accepted lines within sports science. This is not to say that we have sacrificed the multifaceted and knotty nature of coaching for an easy ride as, although delivered as discrete, each chapter discusses evidence and concepts directly related to coaching's messy and interpretive character. Additionally, in line with the complexity of the subject matter examined, an inescapable element of overlap exists between the notions discussed in many of the chapters. Far from being a bad thing, however, we see this emergent conceptual blending as allowing readers to clearly identify and grasp the most illuminating and consistent ideas that underpin coaching (Jones *et al.*, 2011). For example, following an introductory chapter on reflective practice, the chapters relating to psychology (Chapter 4) and philosophy (Chapter 7) both highlight the relative importance of developing intrinsic motivation in athletes; that is, an appreciation of the game for the game's sake, to maximise performance. The same could be said of deciding what comprises appropriate interaction with athletes, which is discussed (albeit in different ways) both in Chapter 2 ('Pedagogy for coaches') and Chapter 5 ('Sociology for coaches').

To encourage readers to make the required connections between the different chapters for themselves, we have deliberately clustered them into distinct sections or parts, so that each chapter is followed by another that relates to it. For example, following Chapter 1 which comprises Part I, 'Skill acquisition for coaches' (Chapter 3) is preceded by 'Pedagogy for coaches' (Chapter 2) and followed by 'Psychology for coaches' (Chapter 4) – this cluster presented as Part II. The chapters relating to 'Sociology for coaches' (Chapter 5), 'History for coaches' (Chapter 6), 'Philosophy for coaches' (Chapter 7), 'Ethics for coaches' (Chapter 8) and 'Sports development for coaches' (Chapter 9) are similarly grouped (Part III), as are those related to 'Biomechanics for coaches' (Chapter 10), 'Match analysis for coaches' (Chapter 11), 'Sports medicine for coaches' (Chapter 12) and 'Physiology for coaches' (Chapter 13) (Part IV). Grouping in this way, however, does not imply that cross-cluster connections cannot and should not be made, as the boundaries between the clusters are inevitably flexible and permeable. Indeed, the content of the chapter groups was very much our subjective decision around which there was plenty of enthusiastic debate. The point to be made, however, is that each chapter is inherently linked (in various degrees) to every other and should be read as such.

Each of these discipline-specific chapters is based on a similar format. This comprises a clear definition of the area in question followed by a discussion of a number of important constructs or sub-areas that inform it. For example, within 'Sociology for coaches' (Chapter 5), issues concerned with both micro- (i.e. face-to-face interaction) and macro-sociology (i.e. how wider social forces such as race or gender affect behaviour) are discussed. Far from isolating the knowledge presented, however, we've tried to take account of its nature by contextualising it within coaching. Hence, as mentioned earlier, an attempt is made to illustrate how the knowledge presented in each chapter informs coaching both generally and uniquely. Each chapter also concludes with a series of discussion points related to the information presented within it, which can also serve to check understanding, and additional web resources from which further knowledge can be gleaned. To close the book, an amended final chapter (Part V: Chapter 14 'Tying it all together') outlines a means through which a more holistic and personal approach to coaching, incorporating all the differing knowledge strands previously discussed, can be considered. The aim here is to illustrate how the various information presented in the earlier chapters can be brought together, analysed and applied at an individual level to address unique, contextually defined coaching problems.

WHO IS THE BOOK FOR?

An Introduction to Sports Coaching is a book true to its title in that it provides an introduction to the sport science knowledge behind coaching for undergraduate students and novice coaches. By design, it is clear and manageable. For some students, it will provide their only formal study of coaching, while for others it will serve as a foundation for further investigation. For all, however, it should enhance their general awareness of the various knowledges that underpin coaching and how each can be applied to practice. A further valuable aspect of the book is that, whilst it consolidates coaching's principal knowledges into coherent sections, it also conveys, to some extent, the complex nature of coaching, thus demonstrating to students a little of what it means to be a coach. Our intention, then, is to introduce the value of considered reflection into the thoughts and practices of those beginning their study of coaching. This is specifically so regarding a heightened appreciation of what kinds of knowledges comprise coaching and how they can be better understood and developed to inform practice.

Robyn L. Jones and Kieran Kingston

PART I

CHAPTER 1

REFLECTIVE PRACTICE IN SPORTS COACHING: THOUGHTS ON PROCESS, PEDAGOGY AND RESEARCH

DAVID GILBOURNE, PHILLIP MARSHALL AND ZOE KNOWLES

INTRODUCTION

For a number of years, all three authors of the present text have commented upon and engaged with reflective practice. We are committed 'users' of all things reflective and, mindful of our histories, we have sought to write this introductory chapter in a critical and cautious way. However, and despite our best efforts, it is inevitable that we comment on the themes and processes of reflective practice in a supportive light and, in doing so, we align with the general pitch and flow of the reflective practice literature (Knowles and Gilbourne, 2010). In our past writings, we have collectively promoted the applied-practice benefits that can be accrued through systematic reflection. Similarly here, with specific reference to coaching, we argue that reflective practice is an ideal way to develop critical self-awareness, and a mechanism through which coaches might monitor, evolve and improve what they do. In this introductory chapter, we explain how the processes of reflection have affected coaching pedagogy, consider how coaches might engage in reflection, and how they can approach the task of writing reflectively derived material. As the chapter progresses, we focus increasingly on how reflection might help you understand your own (coaching) practice.

REFLECTIVE PRACTICE IN SPORT COACHING PEDAGOGY

Over the last few decades, there has been a significant shift in the way the government in the United Kingdom has viewed sport and exercise. Major challenges for the nation's health and well-being have raised the profile of sport as a tool to help address a wide range of issues. This challenge has gone hand-in-hand with the growing profile of performance sport. The award of the 2012 Olympic Games to the UK, bringing an additional need for success at the highest level in sport, has drawn governmental attention to the role of the sports coach. Until recently, the landscape of sports coaching in the UK did not give the impression of a profession that was well equipped to address these major issues (Taylor and Garratt, 2011). The subsequent drive to professionalise sports coaching has centred on the need to deliver an appropriately trained, regulated and sufficiently knowledgeable workforce, and thus to tackle this neglect.

Significant government investment through the work of the UK Coaching Task Force (DCMS, 2002) has been responsible for driving this process of professionalisation. The resulting launch of the UK Coaching Certificate and the UK Coaching Framework aimed to deliver a professionally regulated vocation (sports coach UK, 2008). In an environment of professionalisation, it was perhaps inevitable that the role of reflection and reflective practice would gain the interest of the coaching community. This can be seen in the significance reflective practice has held for researchers in the field of sports coaching over the last decade (see for example Cassidy *et al.*, 2009; Gilbert and Trudel, 1999, 2001, 2004, 2005; Knowles *et al.*, 2001; Knowles *et al.*, 2005; Nelson and Cushion, 2006). In addition, the promotion of reflection in coaching practice has begun to emerge in coach education programmes (Nelson and Cushion, 2006) and in undergraduate university programmes focused on sports coaching (Knowles *et al.*, 2001).

The aforementioned literature, however, has recognised the often *ad hoc* nature of the development of coaching knowledge (Knowles *et al.*, 2001); coaches develop their knowledge not just through attendance at National Governing Body (NGB) coaching awards, but through accessing a range of additional learning resources. These resources can include appropriate literature, internet searches, discussion with peers and knowledgeable others, and involvement in mentoring programmes. Even the formally organised structures of NGB coach education awards are only accessed for very short periods of time, with gaps often amounting to months or years between courses (Knowles *et al.*, 2001). Schön's (1983, 1987) extensive work on the value of reflection suggests that the development of professional knowledge is primarily achieved through experience gained in the field. Similarly, it is acknowledged that sports coaches spend little time in formal educational settings and that their professional learning predominantly takes place in a coaching setting (Gilbert and Trudel, 1999). There is certainly a need in the field of sports coaching for the development of what Schön (1983) described as 'artful competence', or craft skills. These skills and this level of professional competence require a process of reflection to allow their effective development to occur.

While it is accepted that most learning in coaching takes place through experience in the practice environment, learning cannot be assumed as an outcome

4

of this practice. For learning to occur, professionals must actively engage in a process of reflection. As Gilbert and Trudel (2006) suggest, 'ten years of coaching without reflection is simply one year of coaching repeated ten times' (p.114). At the centre of Schön's work is the idea that reflection is stimulated by encountering problematic situations during one's professional practice; on encountering a problem, a practitioner is stimulated to solve it through a systematic process of reflection. Schön describes this type of reflection as 'reflection-in-action'. Schön (1983) argued that reflection-in-action can be seen as a process of reflecting on our activity in the 'action-present'; here, phrases such as 'thinking on your feet' are advanced as descriptors for the act of reflecting while doing (Schön, 1983, p.54).

Gilbert and Trudel (2006) observe that a range of researchers have proposed models of reflection based on Schön's work, in fields such as teaching (Gibbs, 1988), nursing (Johns, 1994) and sports coaching (Gilbert and Trudel, 2001). Gilbert and Trudel's (2001) model suggests a process of reflection which begins with the identification of a 'coaching issue' which can be equated with the kind of problematic situation that instigates reflection, as first outlined by Schön. This identification of a coaching issue is influenced by what Gilbert and Trudel (2006, p.119) describe as a coach's 'role frame'. This is a coach's own approach to coaching, and can be likened to a coaching philosophy (Gilbert and Trudel, 2001, 2004; Nelson and Cushion, 2006). If a 'coaching issue' is deemed to be of significance, a coach may then engage in a four-stage reflective conversation (Gilbert and Trudel, 2006). This reflective conversation is designed to generate a suitable solution to the identified issue. The conversation is a cyclical process, beginning with issue setting and proceeding to the generation of a strategy to deal with the problem. In the experimentation stage, this strategy is tested before being evaluated for effectiveness. If the generated strategy proves to be effective, the reflective conversation can be considered complete. However, if it is ineffective, the process can begin again, with a return to the strategy generation stage.

While the use of reflection is now widely accepted as good practice in the development of effective and professional sports coaches, some researchers have noted that coverage of reflection in coach education courses is insufficient to develop effective practitioners (Knowles *et al.*, 2001; Knowles *et al.*, 2005). They have argued that the development of good reflective skills cannot be assumed by coach educators as a natural outcome of the introduction of reflection in the coaching curriculum. Approaching reflection in this way may mean that sports coaches who do reflect, may do so at a purely superficial level. Indeed, Knowles *et al.* (2005) report that in a range of NGB coaching awards, no discussion took place of coaches' underlying value and belief systems. Such discussions only really took place as part of lower-level coaching qualifications, and even then, in no real depth. This then, brings us back to a closer investigation of

Gilbert and Trudel's (2001) model of reflection in coaching. While the suggested framework offers a useful method for helping coaches structure their own reflective practice, perhaps the starting point for any truly searching level of reflection should be an in-depth consideration of role frame. Nelson and Cushion (2006) link the terms 'role frame' and 'coaching philosophy', while Cassidy *et al.* (2009) make similar connections between the construction of a coaching philosophy and reflecting on coaching practice. They note that 'fundamental issues about one's own personal involvement in coaching' must be answered before 'more detailed reflective questions' can emerge (p.62). Further similarities in terminology exist in the coaching literature. For example, Lyle (2002) discusses the use of 'critical incidents' (p.167) to prompt the analysis and construction of a personal coaching philosophy.

As stated, Gilbert and Trudel's work noted the importance of an awareness of role frame in the process of effective reflection. Here, their investigation identified both boundary and internal elements of coaches' role frames. Of particular importance were the internal elements, which they described as 'tacit' in nature. These internal elements linked most closely with a coach's underlying belief systems and values (other related texts have talked to this issue through the term 'craft' knowledge). The significance of these internal elements led both Gilbert and Trudel (2004) and Nelson and Cushion (2006) to conclude that an in-depth consideration of role frame be included in coach education programmes. Gilbert and Trudel (2004) suggested that this represented a 'critical step in personal and professional development' (p.40).

While it cannot be doubted that any level of reflection will be better than none in making positive changes to coaching practice, for coaching to truly evolve as a profession, these reflections need to progress beyond the consideration of purely tactical and technical issues (a matter developed further in the final phase of our discussion). Rather, a much deeper level of reflection is required for coaching practitioners to develop an increased level of personal and professional awareness. However it is attained, it is hoped a heightened level of awareness will lead to the development of more effective practitioners; practitioners who possess what Schön (1983) described as 'artful competence'.

REFLECTIVE PRACTICE IN APPLIED SPORT SETTINGS

Some time ago, Anderson, Knowles and Gilbourne (2004) suggested that reflective practice was a process that allowed practitioners to explore personal decisions and experiences. Following on from this, Knowles *et al.* (2007) attempted to illustrate these ideas-in-action by presenting ways of helping practitioners to engage in reflective practice; in this instance, within an applied sport psychology

6

training programme. Here, the authors provided examples of *technical* and *practical* levels of reflection by using extracts from an applied psychologist's training diary (Tomlinson's diary). Building on this, in a more recent commentary, Knowles and Gilbourne (2010) developed ideas on how to undertake and disseminate *critical* reflective practice. The intention here was to further engage with the reflective practice debate in a way that allowed all levels of reflection to be considered and evidenced. The following paragraphs provide an illustration of not only the difficulties and benefits associated with 'doing' reflective practice, but also how it has begun to guide the work of sport science and coaching practitioners.

Illustrations of the products of written reflection are commonplace within the sport-based literature, and many of these accounts can be associated with neophyte or new practitioners who have used reflective practice to develop skills and practice-based knowledge (e.g. Jones *et al.*, 2007; Woodcock *et al.*, 2008). More recently, the use of reflective practice with athletes (e.g. Faull and Cropley, 2009; Hanton *et al.*, 2009) has made an important contribution to the overall reflective practice literature which, in the past, had tended to be dominated by the 'educare' based professions such as education or nursing and allied healthcare. Pragmatic 'how to do' processes such as the focus of reflection, diary keeping, supervision, the use of guides and models, levels of reflection and stages of reflection, have now been explored in both sports coaching (e.g. Irwin *et al.*, 2004; Knowles *et al.*, 2001) and sport psychology (e.g. Martindale and Collins, 2005; Anderson *et al.*, 2004; Cropley, *et al.*, 2010a, 2010b; Knowles and Gilbourne, 2010; Tod, 2007).

It is good to see so many sport-based texts connected in one way or another with the reflective practice agenda. That is not to say that such texts are beyond critique. For example, Knowles and Gilbourne (2010) have argued that reflective practice texts, though for the most part interesting and informative, house a generic tendency to provide readers with examples of technical and practical levels of reflection, whilst critical reflection is not readily in evidence. The present introduction hinted at the importance of critical reflection, and in the next section we spend a little time talking over definitions and explanations of what we mean by *levels* of reflective practice.

A coach engaged with a *technical* level of reflection might be expected to focus upon issues such as the organisation and practical running of his or her sessions. *Practical* reflection, in contrast, is centred on a more personal and, sometimes, emotion-focused account of practice. For example, practical reflection can relate to how a coach felt an aspect of their coaching session (warm-up, game situation, etc.) had progressed, and how that had made them *feel*. In contrast to these first two levels of reflection, *critical* reflection moves the process onto a different landscape with an emphasis on an integration of intra, inter and global issues. For instance, a coach might question the efficacy of his or her role in developing elite talent in a world where many children shy away from sports participation. To extend this hypothetical example, the coach may, as a consequence, become drawn more towards participation in community-based coaching, turning away from progression through the elite sporting system and all that it entails.

In philosophical terms, Knowles and Gilbourne (2010) associated critical reflection with the underlying aspirations of critical social science (Carr and Kemmis, 1986). This, in turn, is linked to notions of contesting, challenging and changing practice. Knowles and Gilbourne (2010) position critical social science as an underpinning philosophy or aspiration; a perspective that a reflective practitioner might embrace, work towards or hope to achieve; a point of interest to 'keep in mind' rather than a set of rules that drive everything. That said, the aforemential authors and Gilbourne (2010) argue that, as far as they are concerned, there seems little critical reflection around (not in published form). In addition to this, Knowles and Gilbourne (2010) freely acknowledge that the issues of critical reflection can appear opaque or unclear. Critical reflection is a challenging area, one in need of development, yet it is important for us to outline the topic here. With so little critical reflection in evidence, it is possible to wonder whether the applied sporting community has much appetite for pursuing a critical reflective agenda. We wonder if its members worry over the unrest that a new generation of critical reflective practitioners might unleash on an aspect of professional sports practice that sometimes appears to be rather comfortable. We hope that the scholars and practitioners in sports coaching do not follow the example of some, and become wary of all things critical. Although it is beyond the scope of the present chapter to talk further on issues of critical reflection, we do urge coaches, those established and those just beginning their practical journey, to take time to consider the challenges of critical reflection and how their profession might be invigorated by a generation of reflective thinkers and doers.

DOING REFLECTION

Reflective practitioners are often faced with questions over what to reflect 'on' and how to deduce practical and meaningful insights from a complex and constantly changing environment. It is important to emphasise that confusion and, to an extent, frustration often accompany the early stages of reflective practice. One explanation for what might be deemed 'reflective chaos' is that the immediate stages of reflection will inevitably capture incomplete and messy information. For the newcomer to reflective practice, the sense of messiness may be inflamed or exacerbated by the challenges of trying to deploy a range of

8

reflective techniques such as keeping a diary, jotting down field notes, taking photographs of practice and/or using an audio recorder to record thoughts and feelings.

It might be helpful here to talk a little about the messiness of practice and how that can sometimes contrast with the generally 'tidy' appearance of sport science research, because this might be one reason for reflective practitioners sensing that they are somehow not reflecting correctly. Some may feel, for example, that they should 'see' theory-in-action as they reflect, and it is possible to get frustrated if that does not happen. This might be compounded if what a coach 'sees' is a myriad of complications, such as people not getting along, difficulties with the coaching venue and other such matters. Yet, to us, such messy things, such complicated things, lie at the heart of what practice is actually like.

When trying to consider some of the above ideas, Knowles and Gilbourne (2010) considered the issue of tidiness by talking about the limitations of qualitative research in sport. Their case, put briefly, is that when qualitative research is heavily associated with established theory, it risks being limited by the boundaries of that theory. So, in a piece of research into anxiety in coaching, a researcher might only seek to ask questions about anxiety and to analyse data from the same theoretical perspective. Whilst this is logical enough, the scope of what the researcher seeks to understand might be narrowed by the scope of theory. One outcome from this kind of work is a neat and tidy exploration of a practitioner's world. Gilbourne and Richardson (2006), on the other hand, have argued that the world, rather than being neat and tidy, is more likely to be messy, unpredictable, and emotional. This point was re-emphasised by Knowles and Gilbourne (2010) when stating that if the world of coaching is indeed messy, unpredictable, emotional and so on, then practitioners should be relaxed about reflecting upon all of these untidy things and try to make sense of them. This is not to say that theory is not important, but, first of all, we would say embrace messiness; theory can come later.

In practical terms, and returning to techniques of logging reflections, making sense of what you see, what you hear, and what you feel might be assisted by limiting the ways of recording reflection. Finding time to reflect in a clean and systematic way, when life is busy and things need to be done, is difficult. Once you have decided on the best way to log your reflections (a written diary or a Dictaphone, for example), organising a file system that allows ready access to reflective contributions over a timeline (say, over a playing season) is important. If the material is logged orally (through using an audio recorder), the tape-recorded material can be transcribed at a later date if need be, though it is worth warning that this can be a time consuming and laborious task. The dilemma of 'when to reflect' is also important. Reflecting some time after an event, after a coaching session for example, might allow you to think in a quiet space, away from the noise and interruptions of the practice site. Reflecting on the session at home, maybe later in the evening or in a quiet moment relaxing over a coffee, are simple examples. Quieter reflective moments sometimes allow for a more relaxed reflective experience and, from this, a deeper exploration of the practice experience might unfold.

STAGED REFLECTION

Gibbs' (1988) model states that staged reflection is, first of all, characterised both by an immediate and a delayed phase of reflection. In the immediate phase, the practitioner captures description, thoughts, feelings and evaluation as close in time to the event as possible. This ensures accurate recall of information which may dissipate over time or be influenced by external factors. Such factors include the opinions of others, or, internally, a practitioner might change his or her perspective as they 'think-over' events (referred to as 'reflective episodes' by Knowles *et al.*, 2001). In practical terms, practitioners may capture their immediate reflections by jotting down thoughts in a notebook or by using a Dictaphone and focus generally on the first three stages of the reflective cycle (description, thoughts and feelings, and evaluation). Delayed reflection, on the other hand, encompasses a review of the 'immediate' stages and a purposeful movement around the remaining stages of the process. Delayed reflection requires time and space to be effective and so may occur days after the experience, depending on schedule.

Reflection that takes place over longer periods of time may be assisted by the support of significant others, such as that which might occur in supervision or peer coaching groups. These delayed and shared episodes of reflection may eventually impact on practice, as coaches (learners) engage in a reflective process of 'sense making' and/or action planning. Knowles *et al.* (2007) advocated a process of reflection that allowed for a revisiting of events over an extended period of time. In some professional settings, reflective practice that is longitudinal in nature and structured around supportive others, such as tutors or mentors, may also contribute towards some form of reflective log: a summary record of reflective thinking (see Knowles *et al.*, 2001, 2007).

Conditions that encourage and support staged reflection, as described above, play an important role in establishing systematic engagement with reflection and, consequently, would seem to be important to the efficacy of the reflective process. Establishing appropriate time and space for reflection, together with the need for a good understanding of the process in general, would seem a sensible thing to do. At a practical level, this may mean ensuring time at the end of a

10

coaching session to allow for immediate reflection, alongside time set aside some days later for further delayed reflection. It is logical and, to an extent, common sense, to suggest that an emotionally supportive environment is conducive to the reflective process.

It is useful to forewarn those who seek to engage with reflection, and those who expect to act as reflective mentor, that the process of longitudinal and staged reflection might result in the declaration of personal material; it would not be unusual for emotions and beliefs to be made explicit through these processes of discussing and documenting. On a more cautious note, agendas housed within the coaching context (such as specific traditions or wider social norms, values and prejudices) can sometimes act to restrict and so militate against the openness of the reflective process; a limitation that can be exacerbated where external assessment is involved. Similarly, coaches may be unfamiliar and uneasy with the notion of introspection, and with sharing their thoughts with others either verbally or in print. These structural and personal limitations should be held in mind, and, if possible, overcome and/or supported when reflective practice is being introduced and developed.

FINAL THOUGHTS

We hope this introductory chapter on reflective practice has managed to provide an overview on a literature base that is growing in scope and in conceptual complexity. We also hope that we have signalled a number of different avenues for further reading and thinking. It is clear that reflective practice is a process embraced by professions of practitioners (teachers, nurses, sport psychologists, coaches) who work with, help and care for people. In a short space of words, we have attempted to raise many issues associated with the practice–people interface, and placed emphasis on different facets of 'doing reflection'. We have also hinted at the challenges housed in undertaking different levels of reflection. Brief reviews of reflective practice literature, and even briefer explanations of the contents of series of reflective practice commentaries, also allude to the challenges that have faced practitioners who wish to write and so share their reflective experiences. These writing issues have led many commentators to draw comparisons between reflectively informed texts and themes within qualitative inquiry, such as auto-ethnography and life history. Consequently, readers are encouraged to visit this area of thinking and writing particularly when critical reflection is being considered. Finally, we wish all reflective coaches good fortune as, through reflective practice, they seek to confront what they do and why they do it.

PART II

CHAPTER 2

PEDAGOGY FOR COACHES

KEVIN MORGAN AND JOHN SPROULE

The best coaches are good teachers.

Sir Clive Woodward, England Rugby Union
2003 World Cup winning coach (Cain, 2004: 19)

INTRODUCTION

Traditionally, a divide has existed between perceptions of sports coaching and teaching. Here, coaching has been viewed as 'training' and the attainment of physical skills, whereas teaching has been seen to be about the total development of the individual (Jones, 2006a; Lee, 1988). Pedagogy, then, defined as 'any conscious activity by one person designed to enhance learning in another' (Watkins and Mortimore, 1999: 3) has tended to lie outside the traditional concept of sports coaching (Jones, 2006a). Recent interview data from elite coaches (Jones *et al.*, 2004), however, have demonstrated that such practitioners view their roles not as 'physical trainers' but as educators. For example, British Lions rugby union coach Ian McGeechan talked about establishing a 'learning environment' to 'grow players' and of coaching individuals 'to understand something'. Similarly, Graham Taylor, the former coach of the England football team, suggested that 'coaching really is a form of teaching' as it primarily involves communicating, learning and maintaining positive relationships with those being taught (Jones *et al.*, 2004: 21). Consistent with this perception, other research has found that good coaches act like good teachers, as they care about those over whom they have responsibility and constantly engage in reflection on what they do and how they do it (Gilbert and Trudel, 2001). This suggests that 'athlete learning as opposed to mechanistic performance lies at the heart of coaching' (Jones, 2006a: 8) and that pedagogic theory, therefore, should play a more central role in preparing coaches.

The purpose of this chapter is to identify some of the key pedagogical concepts that could be used to inform coaching practice and consequently enhance athlete learning. The first section deals with learning theories, beginning with the more traditional behaviourist perspective and progressing to constructivist approaches to coaching. Teaching styles are then covered, with particular attention paid to Mosston and Ashworth's (2002) 'Spectrum'. Finally, motivational climate theory (Ames, 1992a, 1992b, 1992c) and associated research (Morgan and Carpenter, 2002; Morgan *et al.*, 2005a; Morgan *et al.*, 2005b) into the teaching behaviours that facilitate an effective learning environment are drawn upon and related to coaching practice.

LEARNING THEORIES

'Learning' has been defined as a change in an individual caused by experience (Mazur, 1990). Two main schools of thought (and their associated theories) have predominated in educational and sport settings since the late nineteenth century, namely, behaviourism and constructivism. Behaviourism focuses on the ways in which the consequences of action, for example, feedback and reward systems, subsequently modify behaviour (Slavin, 2003). Such traditional approaches rest on beliefs that learning is an explicitly linear and measurable process of internalizing knowledge (Light, 2008). Constructivist theories, on the other hand, contend that learners must discover and transform new information themselves to learn effectively. This approach to learning contends that we are not passive learners, but actively construct our own meanings of events based on past experience and knowledge (Vygotsky, 1978). Each will now be examined in more depth.

Behaviourist learning theories

Behaviourist learning theories attempt to discover principles of behaviour that apply to all human beings (Slavin, 2003). Behaviourists, such as Pavlov (1849–1936) in Russia, and Watson (1878–1958) and Thorndike (1874–1949) in the USA, were chiefly concerned with manipulating stimulus (S) and response (R) connections and observing the results. Thorndikes's law of effect states that, if an act is followed by a satisfying change in the environment, then it is more likely to be repeated in similar situations than an act that is followed by an unfavourable effect. Like Thorndike, Skinner (1904–1990) focused on the use of pleasant or unpleasant consequences to control behaviour; this became known as operant conditioning. Pleasant consequences, such as praise, are known as 'reinforcers' and are considered to strengthen behaviour, whereas unpleasant consequences, such as public criticism, are known as 'punishers' and are considered to weaken it (Slavin, 2003).

16

The most frequently used reinforcers in the sporting context include praise, attention from the coach, assessment grades and recognition in the form of trophies, certificates and badges. Although such reinforcers are generally considered to be important motivators, we cannot assume a particular consequence is a reinforcer for everyone, since its value is based on individual perception. For example, some individuals enjoy being chosen to demonstrate a particular sporting skill in front of their peers, whereas others may find it embarrassing and try to avoid being so chosen. Reinforcers that are escapes from unpleasant situations are known as negative reinforcers; for example, not having to do extra practice if the quality of the training session is good. A further principle of reinforcement, known as the Premack Principle (Premack, 1965) concerns promoting less-desired activities by linking them to more-desired ones; for instance, offering a game to athletes at the end of a session if the preceding practice drills are completed successfully.

According to the guidelines on the use of reinforcement to increase desired behaviours (Walker and O'Shea, 1999), one should first decide what behaviours are desired, and then reinforce these behaviours when they occur. Second, the desired behaviours, such as effort, improvement, a positive attitude and fair play, should be clearly communicated to individuals, and an explanation given as to why they are important. Finally, the behaviours should be reinforced as soon as possible after they occur, in order to make the connection between the behaviour and the consequence.

Intrinsic reinforcers are behaviours engaged in for the inherent pleasure without any other tangible reward. Extrinsic reinforcers, on the other hand, are rewards given to motivate individuals to engage in behaviours that they might not otherwise choose to (Slavin, 2003). There is evidence to suggest that reinforcing children's behaviours that they would do anyway can undermine intrinsic motivation, which is considered essential for long-term participation in sport (e.g. Deci *et al.*, 1999). Slavin (2003) suggests that if extrinsic reinforcers are deemed necessary, self-reinforcement or praise should be used before the awarding of any certificates or prizes. Extrinsic reinforcers may, however, be necessary to motivate individuals to do important things that they might otherwise not do.

Punishers are consequences that are intended to weaken behaviour (Slavin, 2003). If an apparently unpleasant consequence does not reduce the behaviour it follows, it is not a punisher. For example, shouting at someone for perceived bad behaviour might give them the attention they desire and enhance their status amongst their peers, thus increasing the likelihood of that behaviour being repeated, rather than reducing it. A frequently and successfully used punishment in PE and junior coaching settings is 'time out', where an individual is required to 'sit out' or is excluded from the activity for a set time (White and Bailey, 1990).

In behaviourism, new skills are taught or shaped through a series of small rein-forcing steps towards the desired final action (Walker and O'Shea, 1999). For example, when teaching a tennis forehand shot to novice players, a coach may first reinforce the correct grip of the racket, then the stance, the contact point and so on, until the complete stroke is performed. Thus, the individual's technique would potentially be improved by reinforcing the individual steps towards the ultimate goal. After a point, reinforcement of the early steps may not be neces-sary to maintain the behaviour because the final outcome of the shot is successful and desirable. Once the technique has been established, reinforcement for correct responses should become less frequent, and also less predictable. This is because, according to behaviourist theory, variable schedules of reinforcement, where reward is given following an unpredictable amount of time and behaviour complexity, are more robust than fixed schedules (Slavin, 2003).

Behaviourist learning theories can explain and justify many coaches' actions but applying the theory is not always straightforward. For example, as already touched upon, what acts as a reinforcer for one person, may be a punisher for another. Some players prefer intrinsic reinforcers, such as the pure challenge and enjoyment of the activity, whereas others respond more positively to extrinsic reinforcers, such as public praise and rewards. Additionally, individual levels of self-esteem and perceived competence may influence perceptions of, and reactions to, different reinforcers and punishers. Furthermore, some partici-pants judge their success through direct comparison with others (i.e. they hold a normative perception of competence), whereas others are more self-referenced in how they define achievement (Nicholls, 1989).

For much of the twentieth century, behaviourism formed the dominant view of learning, and to this day it remains important in underpinning pedagogy (Woollard, 2010). Unsurprisingly then, it has had a strong influence on sports coaching. However, in recent years it has been increasingly criticized for viewing learning as a linear, measureable process of internalizing pre-existing knowl-edge, for separating thought from action, and for viewing recipients as passive beings (Light, 2008). This reductionist, top-down understanding of the process of knowledge transmission (and power) has been highlighted as problematic within PE and coaching settings (Tinning, 1997). For example, it constructs physical educators and coaches as transmitters of expertise, thus not encour-aging continuous critical thinking in learners (Denison and Avner, 2011).

Constructivist learning theories

Constructivist learning theory draws heavily on the work of Piaget (1896–1980) and Vygotsky (1896–1934), both of whom argued that a process of disequilibrium

18

in the light of new information is required in order for effective learning to take place (Slavin, 2003). Based on the work of Piaget, cognitive constructivism views learning as a process through which individuals, when they encounter novel situations (which disturb their learning equilibrium), construct unique knowledge based on personal experience and what they already know (Cobb, 1996). Individual exploration and discovery learning fits well with this type of cognitive or psychological constructivism. Social constructivism (Vygotsky, 1978), on the other hand, views learning as more culturally and socially situated, requiring social interaction and group dialogue (Lave and Wenger, 1991).

Although cognitive and socio-cultural perspectives of constructivism can be seen as contradictory, Fosnot (1996) suggests that a considerable degree of overlap exists between them, and presents four common principles. First, learning is viewed as development, where learners need the freedom to raise their own questions, generate hypotheses, test them for viability and make mistakes along the way. This is important, because it has been shown that an overly prescriptive approach to instruction can negatively impact learning (Ford et al., 2010). Nash et al. (2011) found that expert coaches had the ability to allow practice sessions to develop inductively, placed a considerable emphasis on helping individual performers take responsibility for their own performances, and believed that their role with elite athletes was to be more of a facilitator than a director. However, Partington and Cushion (2011) found that professional top-level youth soccer coaches used high levels of prescriptive instruction although it differed from the stated desires of the said coaches, such as *creating decision makers* and being a *facilitator of knowledge creation*. This is illustrative of cognitive dissonance (Light, 2008), reflecting a gap between declarative and procedural knowledge in coaching practice. Coaches and teachers, therefore, should focus on being facilitators of learning rather than instructors, although instructivist approaches can still be utilized if there is a legitimate demand (Sproule et al., 2011). Second, challenging open-ended investigations in realistic contexts that disturb learners' existing understanding and preconceptions, lead to the construction of new ways of knowing. Conception and interpretation errors are, therefore, a part of learning that need not be avoided or minimized.

The third principle is that reflection 'in' and 'on' action is the driving force of learning. Thus, time for reflection and discussion of experiences is a crucial aspect of learning, and therefore learners should be encouraged to achieve a state of 'mindfulness' during action by paying attention and being engaged in the present moment (Sproule et al., 2011). Finally, learning proceeds towards the development of new ideas or concepts which can be generalized across experiences; examples are streamlining and propulsion in swimming, or principles of play in invasion games.

Focusing more specifically on social constructivism, Fosnot (1996) also stressed that cognition and learning arise from interaction and dialogue within a community. In this sense, understanding emerges from within a community of learners. These learners are often engaged in reflection and conversation, and are required to defend their ideas to the community for such notions to become valid. Interestingly, in their study involving 621 coaches ranging from no formal qualification to the highest level of coaching certification in the UK (level 5), Nash and Sproule (2011) found that the majority of coaches (67 per cent – and especially those with more than ten years of coaching experience – identified working with others (mentors, coaching networks or communities) as extremely beneficial to their development. This finding – that coaches considered informal or less formal networking with other coaches to be essential to their professional progress – is supported by other recent work (Nash and Sproule, 2009).

Social constructivist learning has been strongly influenced by four key principles from the work of Vygotsky (1978). First, he proposed that children learn through social interaction (which could include coaches, teachers and/or peers). Thus, mixed ability groups and cooperative learning situations, where individuals are exposed to the thinking of a range of others, are promoted. An example of this, in the team coaching situation, would be to set a group task involving mixed ability teams working cooperatively to identify the strengths and weaknesses of the opposition, and devise strategies and tactics to outperform them. Such an approach is consistent with the Play Practice model (Thomas *et al.*, 2001) and the Sport Education curriculum model in PE (Siedentop, 1994).

A second key concept was the idea that we learn best when we are in a space known as the 'zone of proximal development'; that is, when engaged in tasks that we cannot do alone but can with the assistance of 'more capable others'. Vygotsky (1978) argued that learning precedes development, and that 'the zone of proximal development' identifies potential. This suggests that skills which the learner can do with assistance today, will be able to be performed without assistance in the future (Vygotsky 1978). An important implication of this principle is that individuals should be challenged at different levels as their 'zone of proximal development' will differ. Differentiation is, therefore, a key aspect of coaching when using a constructivist approach. Such differentiation could take the form of designing tasks at various levels of difficulty or allowing flexible time for their completion.

The third of Vygotsky's concepts, which holds particular relevance here, is known as cognitive apprenticeship. This derives from the first two principles, as it refers to the process by which a learner gradually acquires expertise through interaction with a more knowledgeable other. Within coaching, this could

20

involve a process of mentoring, whereby newly qualified or trainee coaches learn from more experienced practitioners. Similarly, less experienced players can benefit enormously from the guidance of their more experienced team mates.

Finally, Vygotsky's concept of 'scaffolding', or mediated learning, sees the teacher or coach as assisting learning by providing a great deal of support in the early stages and then gradually reducing it as the learners become more able. In practical terms, this might involve the coach initially giving more structure, then allowing the players to take more responsibility and leadership roles as the season progresses. An example of the application of scaffolding in a coaching context could be the use of practical tasks and associated questioning by the coach to enable the players to discover solutions for themselves. This is consistent with a guided discovery teaching style, which will be discussed in the following section.

From a constructivist perspective, questioning should be thought provoking, focusing on 'why', 'how' and 'judgement' issues, rather than just simple recall, thus requiring participants to construct their own conceptions and enhancing their learning. This type of questioning is consistent with the Teaching Games for Understanding perspective (TGfU) (Bunker and Thorpe, 1982), which is a good example of a constructivist approach to the teaching of PE (Light, 2008). Similarly, Game Sense (den Duyn, 1997), which is a variant of TGfU, is a game based approach to coaching which employs questioning to stimulate thinking, rather than telling players what to do. Play practice (Thomas *et al.*, 2001) strategies are also consistent with constructivist perspectives on learning, based on consideration of the learners' needs, and making connections with previous experiences to scaffold and anchor learning (Perkins, 1999).

From an individual sport perspective, Light and Wallian (2008) presented a constructivist approach to teaching swimming, which could be adapted and applied to other such sports. One example they give in their paper is based on how to achieve streamlining in swimming. Starting with a discussion of the techniques the learners already know, they suggest asking swimmers to propose strategies for meeting the demands of the task linked to the core concepts of propulsion and resistance. This is followed by having the swimmers try out different body positions, including efficient and inefficient positions, whilst striving to gain maximum drive and glide off the wall following a turn. Morgan (2011) used similar constructivist ideas in the teaching of track and field athletics. Focusing on developing understanding of athletics techniques, the purpose here was to allow learners to work out the correct principles of running, jumping and throwing events through a series of progressive practices and follow up questions. Such pedagogical approaches are consistent with the student-centred production end of Mosston and Ashworth's (2002) Spectrum of teaching styles, to which we now turn.

THE SPECTRUM OF TEACHING STYLES (MOSSTON AND ASHWORTH, 2002)

The 'Spectrum' of teaching styles is a continuum based on the level of decision making by the teacher and/or learner in the planning (pre-impact), teaching (impact) and evaluation (post-impact) phases of a lesson (Mosston, 1966). At one end of the Spectrum is the 'Command' style in which the teacher makes all the decisions across the three phases. At the other end is the 'Self Teaching' style in which the learner makes all the decisions. Between these two, Mosston and Ashworth (2002) systematically identify a series of other styles, each with its own decision-making anatomy (see Table 2.1).

The Spectrum can be further categorized into two distinct clusters, one associated with 'reproduction' and the other with 'production' of knowledge and skills. In the reproduction cluster (styles A–E), the central learning outcome is for pupils to reproduce or recall motor skills and known information. Alternatively, in the Production cluster (styles F–K), the central learning outcome is for pupils to discover new information or unique solutions to problems. The Reproduction and Production clusters are, therefore, consistent with

Table 2.1 Teaching styles adapted from Mosston and Ashworth (2002)

Style	Essential characteristics	Focus
A. Command	Teacher makes all decisions	Motor development
B. Practice	Pupils practice teacher prescribed tasks	Motor development and autonomy
C. Reciprocal	Pupils work in pairs, one as the teacher and one as the learner	Social, motor and cognitive
D. Self check	Pupils evaluate their own performance against set criteria	Motor, cognitive, independence
E. Inclusion	Teacher provides alternative levels of difficulty for pupils	Differentiation, motor, cognitive
F. Guided discovery	Teacher plans a target and leads the pupils to discover it	Cognitive and motor development
G. Convergent discovery	Teacher presents a problem and pupils find the correct solution	Cognitive, motor, social and affective development
H. Divergent discovery	Teacher presents a problem and pupils find their own solution	Cognitive, motor, social and affective development
I. Individual programme	Teacher decides content and pupils plan and design the programme	Cognitive, personal (autonomy) and motor development
K. Self teaching	Pupils take full responsibility for the teaching and learning process	Personal (autonomy), cognitive, affective and motor development

behaviourist and constructivist learning theories respectively, as reviewed earlier in the chapter.

According to Metzler (2000), the selection of a particular teaching style is dependent on a number of factors including the intended learning outcomes, the teaching context and environment, and the learner's developmental stage. For example, the same football coach may have different learning outcomes for two separate sessions. In session A, he/she may want to focus on developing the players' decision making in games, whereas in session B, he/she may want to concentrate on improving the players' techniques. Based purely on these learning outcomes, a more Production style, such as Guided Discovery (see Table 2.1) would be most appropriate for session A, as the aim is to develop players' ability to understand the game and make appropriate decisions in different situations. In order to achieve this, consistent with a constructivist TGfU approach (Bunker and Thorpe, 1982), the coach could set up different game situations and guide players through a series of practical tasks whilst asking searching questions. Effective divergent/open questioning requires players to use different thought processes, thus allowing them to work out the most appropriate responses for themselves (Chambers and Vickers, 2006), which has been argued by some to increase the quality of the learning experience (Pearson and Webb, 2006). In session B, on the other hand, the coach would be better off selecting from the Reproduction cluster (e.g. the Practice style), in order to maximize the opportunity for players to improve their techniques through repetition and practice. This is consistent with a 'non-versus' perspective (Mosston and Ashworth, 2002), which states that each style has its own place in reaching a plethora of learning outcomes, and that no one style is better than any other.

As stated earlier, the learner's developmental stage and the teaching environment could also be considered when selecting a style to teach (Metzler, 2000). If, for example, the learners in session B are more experienced players, a reciprocal style may work better for the technique practices, as they are already likely to have a foundational technical knowledge to pass on to others. However, in poor weather conditions, for example, or where the coach is dealing with large numbers of inexperienced players, the more direct Command or Practice styles may be better employed to keep the session 'active' and to demonstrate appropriate techniques. Metzler (2000) also suggests that when safety is a key consideration, as in situations such as javelin throwing and swimming, the direct instruction or Command style of delivery may be the best one to adopt. However, if developing understanding is more important, the Reciprocal or Discovery styles could be better choices.

The differing learning preferences or 'intelligences' of the participants are a further consideration in selecting the most appropriate teaching styles (Gardner,

1993). Gardner identified several intelligences in this context (see Table 2.2) and suggested that, to maximize the learning environment, practitioners should use a range of styles to engage them all. Individuals can be high or low in each type of intelligence, with some intelligences being more prominent than others.

A coaching session is likely to include several different Spectrum styles depending on the intended learning outcomes of each phase of that session. In fact, according to Mawer (1995), the best practitioners can change their style to suit the situation and have the flexibility to use several different styles in one session. Therefore, returning to the football example in the previous paragraphs, a Reproduction style, such as the Practice method, may be the most appropriate for the delivery within a physical conditioning phase, whereas a tactical phase may be best delivered using a Discovery style.

In discussing the teaching and learning relationship, Tinning *et al.* (1993) suggested that teaching styles should not simply be viewed as strategies to be implemented by the teacher, but more as a set of beliefs about the way certain types of learning can be achieved. In which case, they are 'as much statements about valued forms of knowledge as they are about procedures for action' (Tinning *et al.*, 1993: 123). This view challenges the 'non-versus' perspective referred to earlier, and is a firm reminder that coaching or teaching is a social practice which involves the values and philosophy of the individual coach and athletes, the objectives of the activity and the social context. Sicilia-Camacho

Table 2.2 Multiple intelligences adapted from Gardner (1993)

Intelligence	Learner characteristics
Verbal/Linguistic	Capable of using words effectively. Learn most effectively by reading, writing, listening and discussing
Visual/Spatial	Perceive spatial relationships and think in pictures or mental images. Learn most effectively through visual input such as demonstrations, video or viewing diagrams
Kinesthetic	Can manipulate objects and use a variety of gross and fine motor skills. Learn most effectively through practical participation and interacting with the space around them
Musical/Rhythmic	Able to communicate or gain meaning through music. Learn most effectively by listening to and creating music or rhythms
Mathematical	Think in, with and about numbers. Learn most effectively through activities that promote logical thinking or using numbers
Interpersonal	Interact successfully with others. Learn most effectively in cooperative group situations
Intrapersonal	Are introspective and focus on internal stimuli. Learn most effectively when given time to process information individually, formulate their own ideas and reflect on these

and Brown (2008) have also criticized the 'non-versus' perspective on the basis of a de-personification of the individual teacher and pupil, and have consequently suggested revisiting it.

In Mosston's original (1966) version of the Spectrum, a 'versus' (opposing) perspective of teaching was advocated, with the more pupil-centred end of the Spectrum deemed more desirable for the development of independent-learner decision making. The paradigm shift occurred in the second edition of the Spectrum (Mosston, 1981), where it moved to a 'non-versus' perspective. This altered the central aim of the Spectrum away from facilitating independent learning towards a position where each style had its own place in achieving a plethora of learning outcomes, and where no style was considered better or best (Mosston, 1981). This raises some interesting questions about coaching philosophy, which should not be overlooked in the choice of coaching styles adopted. Carless and Douglas (2011) have suggested that coaches who have not developed an explicit coaching philosophy are less likely to be aware of the reasons *why* they do what they do, and this might hinder their effectiveness when faced with new contexts, scenarios or challenges. They ask coaches to consider how and why one course of action is taken over another.

In a study that combined the Spectrum with the teaching behaviours that influence pupils' motivation in PE, Morgan *et al.* (2005b) found that Reciprocal and Guided Discovery teaching styles resulted in more positive athlete motivation, in comparison to more direct teacher-centered styles of delivery, such as Command and Practice. The motivational climate created by coaches through their coaching styles and behaviours would, therefore, appear to be an essential aspect of all coaching situations. The final section of this chapter deals specifically with how a positive and effective learning climate can be created in coaching situations.

MOTIVATIONAL CLIMATE

Motivational climate is defined as a situationally induced psychological environment influencing the goals that individuals adopt in achievement situations (Ames, 1992a), such as sport coaching. According to Ames (1992a), two types of motivational climate, predominate in such situations: a comparative (performance/ego) climate, which focuses on normative ability comparisons, and a self-referenced (mastery/learning) climate, which focuses on personal effort and improvement. Research in sport and PE (Carpenter and Morgan, 1999; Ebbeck and Becker, 1994; Kavussanu and Roberts, 1996; Ntoumanis and Biddle, 1998; Ommundsen *et al.*, 1998; Papaioannou, 1997; Spray, 2002; Walling *et al.*, 1993) has revealed that perceptions of a mastery climate are associated with positive motivational responses. These include perceived competence, enjoyment, effort, learning, intrinsic motivation, a preference for challenging tasks, a belief that success is due to effort, and the development of lifetime skills. In contrast, perceptions of a performance/ego climate are linked with potentially negative responses such as high levels of worry, a focus on comparative ability and a preoccupation with enhancing one's social status.

Based on Epstein's (1989) work, Ames (1992b, 1992c) suggested that the task, authority, recognition, grouping, evaluation and time structures (TARGET) of the learning environment can be manipulated by a teacher to promote a mastery motivational climate (see Table 2.3). In accordance with Ames' suggestion, in order to develop a mastery climate, the tasks within coaching sessions should be designed to emphasize self-referenced improvement goals, variety, novelty and differentiation. Challenging learners at different levels of ability is difficult to achieve, but coaches should endeavour to differentiate the tasks as much as possible, in order to get the best out of their charges.

Consistent with a constructivist perspective and the concepts of empowerment (Kidman, 2001) and shared leadership (Jones and Standage, 2006), the authority structure (within the TARGET concept) should involve participants in the learning process by providing them with choices and opportunities to make decisions within the sessions wherever possible. The grouping structure should focus on co-operative group learning and the use of mixed ability and varied grouping arrangements. However, according to recent research (Hassan, 2011), ability groups may not be desirable in certain coaching situations (e.g. where the confidence of the less able athletes could be adversely affected by working with better performers, or where the quality of the sessions would be negatively

Table 2.3 TARGET behaviours that influence motivational climate (Epstein, 1989; Ames, 1992b)

TARGET Behaviour	Mastery	Performance
Task	Self-referenced goals, multi-dimensional, varied and differentiated	Comparative goals, uni-dimensional and undifferentiated
Authority	Students given leadership roles and involved in decision making	Teacher makes all the decisions
Recognition	Private recognition of improvement and effort	Public recognition of ability and comparative performances
Grouping	Mixed ability and cooperative groups	Ability groups/Large groups
Evaluation	Self-referenced. Private diaries and consultations with teacher based on improvement and effort scores	Normative and public
Time	Flexible time for task completion	Inflexible time for task completion

26

affected by mixing ability levels). Furthermore, if ability groups are to be arranged, an attempt should be made to do this without making it obvious or affecting the self-confidence of the lower ability participants. Consistent with the mastery task and authority structures and an Inclusion teaching style (Mosston and Ashworth, 2002), differentiating the tasks and allowing an element of choice can be used to provide equal opportunity for learning to all groups or individuals, regardless of ability.

The recognition and evaluation structures should be focused on individual effort and improvement, and be given privately whenever possible, thus providing all participants with equal opportunity for success. The logistics of the coaching setting often make this a difficult and sometimes impossible task (Hassan, 2011); nevertheless, comparative feedback should still be avoided when trying to foster a mastery learning climate. Finally, activity and learning time in sessions should be maximized, with individuals being allowed flexible time to complete tasks. This also presents real difficulties for coaches who are often restricted by the set time they have to complete sessions (Hassan, 2011). However, allowing learners to have flexibility in the time to complete tasks is a form of differentiation that helps to maximize learning when the participants are fully engaged.

Several researchers (e.g. Morgan and Carpenter, 2002; Solmon, 1996; Treasure, 1993) have found that a mastery focused TARGET intervention programme enhances participants' motivation in PE and sport settings. In contrast, a perform-ance climate emphasizes uni-dimensional (i.e. the same task for all) competitive tasks, teacher authority, normatively based public recognition and evaluation, similar ability groups and inflexible time to practice (see Table 2.3).

Recently, Morgan *et al.* (2005a) used the Behavioral Evaluation Strategies and Taxonomies (BEST; Sharpe and Koperwas, 1999) software to develop a computer-based observational measure of the TARGET behaviours (Ames, 1992b). This measure allows researchers to film coaching sessions and to systematically code and analyse the coaching behaviours that affect athletes' perceptions of the motivational climate. In a subsequent study, Morgan and Kingston (2008) developed a mastery intervention programme for PE practitioners and assessed its effect on TARGET behaviours and pupils' motivation. This intervention was found to improve teachers' reflective abilities in developing their own contextual strategies in relation to utilizing mastery focused TARGET behaviours, whilst enhancing the motivation of the more disaffected pupils in the class. Finally, Morgan and Kingston (2010) also evaluated the effects of an intervention programme to promote a mastery motivational climate on coaching behaviours and student learning experiences in a higher education undergraduate football unit. Observational analysis of subsequent coach behav-iours revealed increases in student-set mastery goals, greater differentiation of tasks, increased individual coach feedback on effort and progress, and more flexible time to learn. Group interviews with students revealed that the mastery programme had a positive impact on their motivation and learning experiences.

CONCLUSION

The purpose of this chapter was to establish that, conceptually, coaching has much to do with 'teaching and learning', and to identify some of the key pedagogical theories and research that could be applied to coaching. It does not claim to cover all the pedagogical concepts that could be applied to coaching, or that the examples chosen are necessarily the most important ones. It does, however, contribute to the re-conceptualization of coaching as teaching, with the purpose of further informing coach education and practice. It is acknowledged that many 'successful' and experienced coaches may not be consciously familiar with the teaching and learning theories presented in the different sections. However, we believe that an awareness and knowledge of the key concepts discussed will result in a deeper level of coach reflection and assist coaches in developing a greater understanding of how individuals learn, and of the impact of their coaching on the learning and motivation of athletes.

It is suggested within this chapter that individuals learn most effectively in a constructivist way. However, it is important to acknowledge that good coaching practice also draws on many aspects of behaviourist theory, particularly in the feedback and evaluation processes. Similarly, the best coaches draw from a whole range of learning theories, and from both Reproduction and Production teaching styles, to achieve their learning outcomes. The key message of this chapter, therefore, is that coaches should continually evaluate their sessions within a broad pedagogical framework, which will allow them to become more reflective and better coaches.

COACHING SCENARIOS/QUESTIONS

The coaching scenarios presented below are designed to promote discussion of how teaching and learning theories can be applied to guide key decisions in coaching situations. They are purposely problematic, thus not providing a 'right' or 'wrong' answer, as a whole multitude of individual and social factors could affect a coach's decision making. The aim, therefore, is to discuss these scenarios with others and, by doing so, gain a broader perspective on a range of typical coaching problems.

▼

28

1   You are the newly appointed assistant coach of a youth team. The head coach has a very traditional behaviourist approach to coaching. You prefer using more constructivist coaching methods to develop players' understanding. The head coach has asked you to prepare a session and you would like to show him/her some of your preferred methods. Give some examples of the sorts of practices and coaching methods you would use.

2   Your preferred method of correcting mistakes in training is to publicly highlight player errors in front of the whole group, so that everyone learns from the mistakes made. Some players are fine with this, whereas others seem to get very defensive and their confidence seems to suffer. How does your understanding of behaviourist learning and motivational climate theory allow you to explain the different players' responses? With this knowledge, would you change your approach?

3   The primary learning outcome that you have planned for an invasion game is to improve tactical decision making in attacking play. Your preferred teaching styles are Command and Practice and these are the ones you predominantly use with your team. You are aware of the 'production' cluster of teaching styles and have used them with the team in the past, with varying degrees of success. Some players respond well to the extra responsibility, whereas others prefer to be told what to do. You have a whiteboard and video playback facility available. You have a good supply of equipment and a suitable training surface to work on. The weather conditions are good. How will you plan, deliver and evaluate the session?

4   You are aware of the benefits of fostering a mastery motivational climate, but there is also a great deal of pressure on you as a coach to produce winning performances. Furthermore, you are also aware that researchers have recently suggested that, in competitive sport, high ego involvement, in addition to high mastery involvement, is essential for long-term achievement. What are the implications of this for your coaching?

5   Explain Vygotsky's principle of the 'zone of proximal development' and give some practical examples of how you would apply it in your coaching sessions.

6   Give an example of how you have 'scaffolded' the learning of others in your coaching sessions, or how previous coaches of yours have 'scaffolded' your learning.

7   What range of Spectrum teaching styles have you experienced as a participant and what different styles have you used in your own coaching?

1   Discuss Vygotsky's key principles of social constructivist learning in relation to the strategies that you adopt in your own coaching.

2   How would you describe your coaching philosophy? Discuss how this philosophy might influence the range of teaching styles that you adopt.

3   Discuss the range of learning objectives in your coaching sessions and reflect on their breadth. Examine the range of teaching styles you currently adopt to achieve these objectives. Identify other methods that could be used to achieve a broader range of objectives.

4   Discuss the use of the TARGET structures in your coaching sessions and the successes and challenges of applying motivational climate theory to your practice.

Web Resources

http://www.tgfu.org/

http://www.spectrumofteachingstyles.org/colleagues

These are the official websites for Teaching Games for Understanding and the Spectrum of Teaching Styles. Each website has a range of information, research, further links and related resources.

30

CHAPTER 3

SKILL ACQUISITION FOR COACHES

GAVIN LAWRENCE, KIERAN KINGSTON AND VICTORIA GOTTWALD

Appropriate organisation of practice and the ways in which you provide feedback are pivotal to improving skills.
                    Dave Pearson, former Head Coach, England Squash

INTRODUCTION

As active human beings, we hardly ever stop moving. Most of these everyday movements are acquired with the help of parents or teachers, while others we develop through trial and error. In sporting situations, many of these basic movements act as foundational skills for more complex actions that may take years to master. The effectiveness of the coach in facilitating the learning of skilled movements can be enhanced through a more detailed understanding of how athletes learn, and how best to structure the environment to support this learning.

How people learn to execute skills effectively poses an interesting set of questions: questions that researchers continue to wrestle with in an attempt to illuminate the sometimes misty world of effective coaching. The aim of this chapter is to discuss some of these questions and to illustrate the value to coaches of knowledge about the acquisition of skills. Further, it seeks to provide a framework for understanding and applying that knowledge, which will, it is hoped, have a positive impact on the coaching and learning experience.

Schmidt and Wrisberg (2000) developed an academic road-map for providing instructional assistance. The upper layer of their model guides readers to a number of open-ended questions relevant to addressing skill acquisition and subsequent performance issues. These include: Who is the learner? What are the characteristics of the task to be performed? and, What are the conditions under which the performer wants to be able to perform? Although this information is critical, most coaches seldom ask such questions as they appear to implicitly understand athletes, the sport and their requirements. Consequently, our objective hero is not to examine individual differences between participants and across tasks, but to concern ourselves with the second layer of Schmidt and Wrisberg's model – the learning experience. Specifically, we will examine three aspects of this experience to illustrate how coaching professionals can (a) structure the practice environment, (b) provide effective feedback, and (c) identify an appropriate attentional focus (i.e. on what one should concentrate) for performers while executing motor skills. For each of these areas we will present the main principles and contemporary research findings and discuss the application of this knowledge. We conclude with a brief summary that brings together the main points raised.

STRUCTURING THE PRACTICE ENVIRONMENT

Often, the time constraints placed upon coaches require them to teach more than a single skill in a training session. Thus, most sessions demand that the learner practises a number of activities. In football (soccer), for example, a training session may well include dribbling, passing and shooting, in addition to practising the many variations of these skills. Therefore, it is important that coaches understand how to schedule different activities within a training session so that learning is maximised. Two types of practice scheduling that have been widely referenced within the skill acquisition or motor learning literature are blocked and random practice (see Schmidt and Lee, 2011).

Blocked versus random practice

Blocked practice can be defined as a practice schedule in which the performer repeatedly rehearses one task before moving on to another. It is typically observed in repetitive 'drills', and is often adopted by coaches as it is seen as allowing the learner to refine and, if necessary, correct a skill before attempting the learning and practice of another. For example, a squash coach wanting to teach the forehand, the backhand and the serve in one session, would choose do devote a fixed block of time to repeatedly practise each, on the premise that uninterrupted time on one task will cement the movement skill into the learner's memory. Alternatively, in a random practice schedule, the session is structured so that the learner practises a variety of skills in no particular sequence. Here, the coach organises the practice session to include a large variation in skill rehearsal; the learner alternates amongst the skills to be learned in an assorted or intermingled fashion and, in extreme cases, never practises the same skill consecutively.

32

An important misconception between these two practice schedules is that because blocked practice often leads to more proficient performance during training, it also leads to greater learning (i.e. the retention and transfer of skills over time). However, research investigating practice scheduling challenges this, and actually reports greater learning when practice occurs in a random, rather than a blocked, sequence (Battig, 1966, 1979; Lee and Magill, 1983; Perez *et al.*, 2005). This counter-intuitive pattern of results, where conditions of practice that lead to poor performance lead to better learning, has been termed 'the contextual interference effect' (Shea and Morgan, 1979; Magill, 2010). This phenomenon has been explained using a variety of theories, but the two most commonly cited are the action plan reconstruction hypothesis (Lee and Magill, 1985) and the elaboration hypothesis (Shea and Zimny, 1983).

According to the action plan reconstruction hypothesis, continually reconstructing a plan for new movement, as occurs in random practice, undermines performance. However, since the learner has devoted more cognitive effort to developing a memory representation for each skill (i.e. remembering how to do it), learning is enhanced. In essence, the extra cognitive effort required for random practice enables the performer to create a library of action plans in memory, and retrieve the appropriate one to meet specific task demands at a later date (e.g. during a game situation). Conversely, in blocked practice, a given action plan need only be constructed on the first attempt of a movement skill and simply applied to subsequent attempts over the entire block of trials. This uninterrupted repetition of the same action plan leads to good performance during practice, but the minimal experience learners have in reconstructing action plans means that applying that learning in a variety of contexts is less effective.

The principal idea behind the elaboration hypothesis is that random practice forces the learner to engage in a variety of cognitive processing activities, the result of which means information about each to-be-learned skill is more distinctive. That is, when the learner switches from practising one skill to another during random practice, they compare and contrast the separate tasks. This results in the establishment of more meaningful or distinctive memories, thus making for easier retrieval at a later time. In contrast, the continued repetition of a single skill in blocked practice, does not provide the learner with the opportunity to engage in such cognitive activity. Therefore, learners develop less distinctive memory representations of each practised skill.

Factors influencing the contextual interference effect

Although there is a large body of research supporting the contextual interference effect, it is not a completely robust phenomenon and does not apply to all learning situations. Thus, the degree to which the contextual interference mediates skill learning may depend on a number of individual and task related factors (Magill and Hall, 1990). The two most probable factors here appear to be age and skill level. Experiments utilising children as participants are rather limited, but those that have been conducted have failed to fully support the view that there is greater skill retention under conditions of random practice (Del Rey *et al.*, 1983; Pigott and Shapiro, 1984). Similarly, in a recent review of the literature, it was concluded that practice schedules of lower contextual interference (i.e. blocked practice) lead to greater skill learning in children (Brady, 2004). With regard to the skill level of the learner, it has been observed that individuals with very low skill levels perform better on a retention test when subjected to blocked practice (Herbert *et al.*, 1996). Experienced performers, however, learn better when subjected to conditions of random practice (Hall *et al.*, 1994). Although these findings are at odds with the contextual interference effect, they can be explained by the interactive effects of the performers' stage of learning and the practice schedule adopted (Guadagnoli *et al.*, 1999). For example, in the early stages of learning, athletes often struggle to understand the movement to be learned (Gentile, 1972, 2000). In attempting to do so, they simplify the required task's demands by reducing the number of potential moving body parts involved in the skill (Bernstein, 1967). Thus, constructing the learning environment to include high levels of contextual interference at this stage of learning may be over-whelming, and actually interfere with the development of a stable action plan for movement (Wulf and Schmidt, 1994). Before progressing to random practice, then, children and beginners alike may need time to explore and develop the basic required coordinated pattern of movement (Gentile, 1972, 2000).

In relation to task factors, Magill and Hall (1990) hypothesised that the beneficial learning effects associated with practice schedules, inclusive of high levels of contextual interference, are more consistent when the skills practised are controlled by different generalised motor programmes (GMPs) (Schmidt, 1975, 1991). A GMP is essentially a memory-based mechanism that the learner uses to control particular classes of actions, such as throwing, kicking, catching and jumping, that have common (i.e. the rhythm of the movement, in terms of timing, force, and the order of the components) yet unique features (i.e. the particular timing and force of the movement). Therefore, according to Magill and Hall (1990), when the learner practises a number of movement skills that require different patterns of coordination, adopting a high (as opposed to low) level of contextual interference within the practice schedule will result in better learning. In contrast, if the practised skills are generally similar or from the same GMP (e.g. swinging the same golf club to hit the ball different distances), then a practice schedule with a high level of contextual interference will not necessarily benefit learning over a low contextual interference schedule.

Constant versus variable practice

If random practice benefits the learning of skills that are from different GMPs, how would a coach structure the practice environment to enhance the learning of a variety of movements from the same class of actions or GMP? One option is to ensure that only one variation of the skill is practised in any one session (e.g. throwing a ball to a single unchanged target that is always positioned the same distance away). This type of practice schedule is not dissimilar to blocked practice and is often referred to as constant practice. However, if the learning goal is essentially to produce a number of versions of the same skill, then it is important to have learners practise different versions of the action in each practice session; something referred to in the literature as variable practice. Indeed, research has demonstrated the learning benefits of variable over constant practice both in laboratory tasks (Shea and Kohl, 1990, 1991) and experiments involving sports skills (Shoenfelt *et al.*, 2002).

It appears from the previously discussed practice schedules that learning is greater under situations which are cognitively challenging (i.e. random and variable practice) providing the learner can both understand the task and can deal with the increased challenge. This suggests that the practice environment should change as the learner's capabilities evolve. Consequently, an important question facing coaches is 'when, during the learning continuum, are performers able to benefit from increased contextual interference?' A possible solution to this question can be found in the findings of recent research by Porter and Magill (2010), who examined the effects of a practice schedule offering gradual increases in levels of contextual interference. Specifically, participants were required to learn three separate skills or three variations of the same skill under a blocked, random or gradual practice schedule. In the gradual schedule, the first third of practice was delivered in a blocked fashion, the middle third was practised in a serial fashion (e.g. skill 1 was followed by skill 2, skill 2 by skill 3, and skill 3 by skill 1, etc.) and the last third was practised in a random schedule. The results revealed that the gradual practice schedule resulted in greater learning than either the blocked or random practice schedules. This suggests that schedules that offer systematic increases in contextual interference facilitate skill learning to a greater extent than fixed practice schedules of a blocked or random nature.

Specificity of practice and learning

Henry's (1968) specificity of practice principle suggests that practice conditions closely matching the movements of the target skill and the conditions of the target context, result in optimal learning. This may also explain why random and variable practice conditions often lead to greater learning (i.e. they more closely match the random and variable conditions often experienced in game situations). Research findings have consistently demonstrated that when learning conditions vary from acquisition to transfer (e.g. through changes in sensory conditions or the emotional state of the learner), then performance can suffer (Proteau and Marteniuk, 1993; Tremblay and Proteau, 1998, 2001; Lawrence *et al.*, 2011). Researchers have accounted for this by suggesting that learners plan their movements according to the information available during acquisition (Khan and Franks, 2000; Mackrous and Proteau, 2007). This movement plan is then adopted throughout practice, unless sensory or emotional conditions change, in which case the movement plan may no longer be suitable for optimal performance.

While research has observed these specificity effects in physiological training and motor skill learning, there is a body of literature that suggests memory recall is also optimised when there is congruence between emotions experienced during learning and those of the subsequent recall. This notion of mood-state-dependent memory (Bower *et al.*, 1978; Gilligan and Bower, 1983) has been examined to explain the positive effects of practising under conditions of anxiety (Lawrence *et al.*, in press) – and specifically, that learning a skill in these situations prevents the reduction in performance typically observed in the stressful competitive environment (Oudejans, 2008; Oudejans *et al.*, 2009, 2010). This finding is not actually surprising, since the anxiety experienced during training replicates the anxiety-invoking competition context. While this research suggests that training with anxiety can have positive implications (for subsequent performance in anxiety-invoking conditions), additional research is required to determine the exact mechanisms to account for these findings.

To summarise this section, whatever the skill to be learned, coaches should be aware that it is important to introduce practice variability, and also to organise the practice environment according to the principles of contextual interference and to match conditions of practice to those of competition. Although practising under conditions of high contextual interference (i.e. random practice) does not always lead to immediate good performance, research suggests that it often leads to better long-term skill learning. The level of contextual interference that is likely to lead to optimal learning, however, depends on a number of task and individual factors; namely, whether the to-be-learned tasks are from the same or different GMPs, and the age and skill level of the learner. Finally, while there is no agreement as to how the structure of the practice environment influences skill learning, both the action plan reconstruction and the elaboration hypotheses concur that making practice more cognitively demanding (i.e. making individuals work problems out for themselves) forces the learner to

36

process skill-related information in a more active and independent manner that, ultimately, facilitates learning.

NATURE AND ADMINISTRATION OF FEEDBACK

Augmented feedback is information provided to the learner from an external source. It is the general term used to describe information given about the performance of a skill that enhances (or adds to) the intrinsic feedback that is naturally available from the performer's senses (i.e. his or her auditory, proprioceptive and visual systems). Augmented feedback can be provided verbally or non-verbally, during (concurrent feedback), immediately following (terminal feedback), or within some period after the completed skill (delayed feedback). It can provide information about the movement outcome (knowledge of results [KR]) and/or the movement pattern (knowledge of performance [KP]).

From the coach's perspective, the most important question when considering the use of augmented feedback is: can it help in the acquisition of the to-be-learned skill? Unfortunately, the answer to this question is not simple, as (similar to the previous section on structuring the practice environment) it is dependent on both individual and task factors. First, there may be situations where augmented feedback is not required, as the task intrinsic feedback alone provides sufficient information for skill learning to occur. In these situations, athletes can make future adjustments to their movements based on their own sensory feedback from either their individual performances or by observing the performances of others of the same (Herbert and Landin, 1994), or higher, skill level (Magill and Schoenfelder-Zohdi, 1996). However, if the athlete cannot utilise the available task intrinsic feedback to enhance their performance (e.g. when injury has damaged essential mechanisms for the detection and/or utilisation of such feedback, or where the constraints of the task mean that critical intrinsic feedback is not readily available), then augmented feedback is essential for skill acquisition. In addition, there may be situations where task intrinsic feedback is readily available, yet is not immediately useful to the learner, due to his or her limited experience in perceiving its meaning; these situations often occur during the early stages of learning. In such cases, augmented feedback can help the novice learner better understand the meaning of the task intrinsic feedback. However, this process can sometimes be problematic. For example, if the task intrinsic feedback is minimal, or is perceived as overly difficult to understand, the augmented feedback may actually reduce learning. This occurs if the learner substitutes the intrinsic feedback with the offered augmented feedback, subsequently becoming reliant on the latter for accurate performance. Consequently, where augmented feedback is not available, such as in competition, a decrease

in performance is likely to occur. This is referred to in the motor learning literature as the guidance hypothesis (Salmoni *et al.*, 1984), and will be further
discussed later in this chapter.

Types of augmented feedback

Verbal feedback provided by the practitioner is perhaps the most commonly
used form of augmented feedback in the practice environment. However, there
are a number of other ways of providing augmented feedback. An increasingly
utilised form is through video. However, for videotape feedback to be effective,
at least two important factors need to be considered: the learner's skill level
(Kernodle and Carlton, 1992), and the period of time for which this type of feedback is utilised (Rothstein and Arnold, 1976). Here, research suggests that skilled
performers benefit from unaided video replays of their performance, whereas
novices tend to be overwhelmed by the information available in the video and
require the addition of specific verbal cues to point out critical information
(Kernodle and Carlton, 1992; Newell and Walter, 1981; Rothstein and Arnold,
1976). Research has also suggested that learners need sufficient time to familiarise themselves with video replays as a form of augmented feedback so that
they can understand what information is important to extract and act upon.
While it may be possible to reduce this time period by providing the addition of
attention focusing cues as described above, it has been recommended that video
replays should be utilised for a period of at least five weeks in order to become
an effective teaching/learning tool (Rothstein and Arnold, 1976).

Another useful form of augmented feedback is biofeedback. Here, information is
presented to the athlete about internal physiological actions such as heart rate,
muscle activity and/or joint movement. This form of augmented feedback is
generally used in the clinical setting for the purpose of rehabilitation (Brucker
and Bulaeva, 1996; Intiso *et al.*, 1994; Shumway-Cook *et al.*, 1998). However, it
has also been used in the sporting environment to enhance the learning and
performance of skilled swimmers, by providing information about their optimal
stroke rate (Chollet *et al.*, 1988), and elite rifle shooters, by supplying audio
signals enabling them to shoot between potentially disruptive heartbeats (Daniels
and Landers, 1981).

The frequency and timing of augmented feedback

While it is important to consider both the skill level of the performer and the
characteristics of the task when deciding if and what type of augmented

feedback is required for learning, it is also crucial to take into account the amount and frequency of such feedback as well as its timing (i.e. when it should be given). Early views regarding the presentation of augmented feedback suggested that 'the greater the amount, the better the learning' and that it should, therefore, be presented after every practice attempt. However, this view is no longer tenable following the emergence of the guidance hypothesis (Salmoni et al., 1984). According to this hypothesis, augmented feedback essentially directs the performer to the correct movement pattern and increases skill acquisition. However, if the learner receives augmented feedback after every trial, he or she may develop a dependency on it, thus undermining the benefits of important intrinsic sensory feedback required for error detection and correction (Bjork, 1988; Schmidt, 1991). Consequently, when augmented feedback is not available, performance suffers as the learner has come to rely upon it to produce the required skill effectively. A number of studies have been conducted to examine augmented feedback using a variety of techniques (e.g. Janelle et al.,1995; Lawrence et al., 2011; Lee et al., 1990; Young and Schmidt, 1992; Winstein and Schmidt, 1990), the results of which appear to support the guidance hypothesis. Specifically, the research indicates that low-frequency schedules or delayed feedback are advantageous to skill learning because they promote problem solving and encourage the learner to explore the dynamics of a skill while utilising task intrinsic feedback.

A common misconception with regards to the timing of augmented feedback is that it should be provided as soon as possible after completion of the practice trial, to negate the learner forgetting the skill. Research, however, does not support this. Rather, it has demonstrated that that there must be a minimum time period given to the learner before augmented feedback is presented (Lawrence et al., 2011; Swinnen et al., 1990). This is in accordance with the principles of the guidance hypothesis, which suggests that, if the KR delay is too short, the learner is unable to fully engage in important intrinsic error detection and correction mechanisms, thus compromising learning. Simply delaying the feedback, however, may be insufficient to prevent dependency. For example, recent research (Lawrence et al., 2011) has revealed that providing either immediate or delayed augmented feedback leads to similar guidance and dependency issues when the delayed feedback provides particularly detailed information. A second important timing issue relates to the interval between the presentation of augmented feedback and the beginning of the next practice trial (the post KR delay). While there is no evidence indicating either an optimal period for this interval or an upper limit, the general conclusion is that this period can be too short (Gallagher and Thomas, 1980; Rogers, 1974; Weinberg et al., 1964). This is because the learner requires sufficient time to process both the augmented feedback and the task intrinsic feedback from the previous trial to produce an action plan for the subsequent response. Thus, for optimal learning, the post-KR delay should be long enough to permit these important learning processes to occur.

To conclude, primary considerations when using augmented feedback include an assessment of both the characteristics of the learner (i.e. skill level) and the nature of the to-be-learned skill (i.e. the amount of available task intrinsic feedback). These will determine what role additional feedback could play in learning (e.g. is it necessary for learning to occur?). If augmented feedback is deemed necessary for skill learning, a number of different types of presentation techniques are available to the coach. These include verbal information, video replays and biofeedback, the merits of which again depend on individual and task factors. For example, video replays are particularly useful to skilled performers (Rothstein and Arnold, 1976); however, to be effective for beginners, videos should be supplemented with cues designed to focus the learners' attention on critical aspects of the skill. Finally, in line with the guidance hypothesis (Salmoni *et al.*, 1984), the frequency and timing of presenting augmented feedback should be considered in order to facilitate optimal learning.

ATTENTIONAL FOCUS

The previous two sections of this chapter have looked at ways in which the environment can be manipulated to facilitate learning. The third will focus specifically on the instructions given to learners regarding their focus of attention, the objective of which is to help them produce the appropriate action to realise the desired movement goal. The question of what learners should concentrate on when executing motor skills has received a good deal of recent attention. Traditionally, learners have been given instructions to direct attention towards aspects of the required movement and the coordination of their body to achieve it. It has long been assumed that making learners aware of what they are doing is a requisite for successful performance (Baumeister, 1984). Indeed, underpinned by research in the field of sport psychology (e.g. Kingston and Hardy, 1997), performers are frequently encouraged to adopt a process or task focus, in order to pay explicit attention to technical aspects of the skill. This, it is argued, will enable them to successfully complete the skill. The specific nature of such instructions, however, have been questioned in the context of learning and coaching (Baumeister, 1984; Hardy *et al.*,1996b; Jackson *et al.*, 2006; Masters, 1992; Mullen and Hardy, 2000). Indeed, there is mounting evidence suggesting that instructing performers to be consciously aware of their body movements during skill execution is not a very effective learning strategy, and can actually undermine performance. Wulf and her colleagues (see Wulf, 2007, for a review), for example, demonstrated that directing learners to focus on their body

40

movements (as a way to control technique) – that is, to induce an 'internal' focus of attention – resulted in no learning benefits or even in learning decrements, relative to not giving learners instructions at all (McNevin *et al.*, 2003). Others, however, continue to espouse the merits of giving athletes the 'what' and 'how' of a particular skill to be performed (Masters, 2000). The obvious question arising, therefore, is what should athletes be directed to focus upon in order to facilitate learning and the execution of complex sport skills?

Support for an external focus of attention

One reasonable objective for a coach is to help athletes execute skills in an auto-mated fashion, because this is the most efficient manner to perform (and charac-terises many expert performers). As mentioned above, current research suggests that 'instructing learners to focus on the details of their movements during performance can be detrimental to the performance and learning' (Wulf *et al.*, 2000: 230) as it has the potential to reduce the automaticity of action. In expanding and refining this line of research, Wulf and colleagues found that directing learners' attention to the effects of movements (i.e. the result of kicking a ball) was more effective than focusing on the movements themselves (i.e. the action of the leg during the kicking action). Indeed, the learning benefits of focusing on the effects of movement action, as opposed to the action itself, have been observed in basketball (Al-Abood *et al.*, 2002; Zachry *et al.*, 2005), jumping (Wulf *et al.*, 2007), golf (Wulf *et al.*, 1999), balance (Wulf *et al.*, 2001), and leg cycling tasks (Totsika and Wulf, 2003).

To promote engagement by coaches into the use of an external focus of attention, it is important to justify why the proposed benefits of doing so may occur. According to the action–effect principle (Prinz, 1997), there is a compatible rela-tionship between movement planning and outcome, with 'actions planned and controlled in terms of their effects' (Prinz, 1997: 152). Thus, if movements are planned in relation to their outcome, then focusing externally (i.e. on movement effects) should increase performance by enhancing the effectiveness of action plans (i.e. GMPs) (Wulf *et al.*, 1998). Wulf *et al.* (2001) combined the notion of the action–effect principle with research involving focus of attention, and proposed the constrained action hypothesis (CAH). Consistent with Prinz's (1997) action–effect principle, the CAH maintains that adopting an external focus of attention enhances the efficiency of motor programming and promotes automatic processing which leads to increased performance. Conversely, if performers focus on their movements, the link between movement programming and movement outcome diminishes. This, in turn, interferes with normally auto-matic control processes and, ultimately, reduces both performance and learning.

The negative self-focused attention effect is not exclusive to beginners. Masters (1992) suggests that under certain conditions (e.g. elevated levels of stress/anxiety) the automatic control processes utilised by expert performers are over-ridden by the desire to ensure task success. He coined the phrase 'conscious processing' to describe this behaviour. In such cases, individuals adopt a mode of control primarily associated with the early stages of learning (Fitts and Posner, 1967), resulting in less effective performance. However, it appears that adopting an external focus of attention is beneficial in preventing this stress/anxiety induced performance decrement (also known as choking). Supporting such a belief, Bell and Hardy (2009) recently revealed that expert performance of golf chipping was enhanced through the use of external focus under both low and high stress/anxiety situations.

While the learning and performance benefits of an external focus of attention appear robust, there is a body of literature (Beilock *et al.*, 2002; Ford *et al.*, 2005; Perkins-Ceccato *et al.*, 2003) which suggests that novice performance is enhanced if learners are encouraged to adopt an internal (or technique-based) focus. These findings have been explained by the de-automisation of skills hypothesis (Beilock *et al.*, 2002). This proposes that, since novice performance is not yet automatic, it cannot be disrupted through conscious control and is, in fact, facilitated by allowing performers to attend to step-by-step processes of the skill. Complete novices who have yet to grasp the fundamentals of complex tasks may, therefore, benefit from some form of self-monitoring of the action, such as focusing on details of their movements.

Wulf and Su (2007) recently re-examined the different effects of internal and external foci of attention on expert and novice performance. Results revealed that both experts and novices performed better when directed to adopt an external focus of attention. Since these findings are inconsistent with the de-automisation of skills hypothesis, and the work of Beilock *et al.* (2002) and Ford *et al.* (2005), it is important to justify why these differences may have occurred. One possible explanation could be due to the method by which the focus was manipulated. For example, Wulf and colleagues encouraged an external focus of attention by using direct *verbal* instructions (i.e. 'focus on the movement of the golf club'), whereas Beilock *et al.* (2002) and Ford *et al.* (2005) encouraged an external focus by using indirect distracting tasks such as asking learners to listen out for specific sounds during performance (the rationale here was that if learners were focusing on detecting the sound, their attention would be directed away from the movements of their body). However, using verbal instructions to focus attention could be considered more consistent with Prinz's (1997) action–effect principle than using the indirect dual task manipulations of Beilock *et al.* (2002) and Ford *et al.* (2005).

42

Outcome tasks versus form sports

The majority of previous research concerning skill acquisition has been conducted within sports such as golf, football, tennis or basketball. Here, movement outcome has been selected as the primary measure of performance (e.g. speed, or accuracy). Consequently, Lawrence *et al.* (2010) elected to examine a 'form' sport (gymnastics), where performance is measured by the production of movement technique as opposed to movement outcome. Here, movement effects are not so obvious with regard to how an individual's action might result in a change to the environment (there is no club, ball or target to attend to). Contrary to research into sport skills which involve a tangible movement outcome, in the case of 'form' based sports, the benefits of an external focus of attention appear to be negated. This can be accounted for by Prinz's (1997) action–effect principle, which suggests that actions are planned in terms of their movement effects. Adopting an external focus of attention enhances automaticity between movements and their effects and, as a result, improves performance. In the absence of an obvious movement outcome (i.e. in a form sport such as gymnastics, high diving or karate kata), the benefits of an external focus of attention appear reduced.

Practical implications

So what does all this mean for coaches? We will now summarise the implications of the preceding discussion, and provide some guidance for coaches in relation to attentional focus, while considering the broad skill level of those being coached and the complexity of the task itself. The weight of evidence currently suggests that there are benefits to learning motor skills in the absence of internal or self-focused attention on the desired body movements. This is because an internal focus leads to a perception of explicit rules about task performance that has the potential to hinder learning (Hardy *et al.*, 1996b; Poolton *et al.*, 2006). Furthermore, Liao and Masters (2002) provided evidence that learning under self-focused attention appears to lead to more vulnerable (i.e. weaker) performance under stress/anxiety. Therefore, it is necessary to identify coaching means and methods that minimise the tendency of athletes to engage in self-focused attention.

An unconscious learning strategy, by definition, encourages the development of implicit (non-verbalisable) knowledge that is unavailable to consciousness. Learning under such conditions negates the potential for poor performance due to self-focused attention, because there are no explicit rules for self-focused attention to access. One strategy to promote implicit learning is to coach by analogy. The objective of analogous coaching is to encourage athletes to perform the skill being learned using a general analogical rule that acts as a movement metaphor and that, by default, incorporates the technical rules necessary for successful execution of the skill (Masters, 2000). For example, the top-spin forehand in tennis can be taught by using the right-angled triangle as an analogy. The learner is asked to imagine following the outline of the triangle using their racket from the preparation of the racket head at the highest (acute) point of the triangle, to dropping the racket to the ninety-degree angle, before drawing back along the base of the triangle in order to strike the ball as the racket head returns squarely to the hypotenuse. Embedded within the analogy are many of the rules often associated with teaching this stroke to beginners. Similarly, learner golfers might be asked to replicate the grip used on a hand-axe (in carrying out a chopping action) when being taught the position of the lower hand (right hand for right-handed golfers) of the golf grip. The key with analogies is for the coach to be creative while ensuring the metaphor itself is clearly understood by the athlete, thus promoting an external rather than an internal focus of attention.

While analogies give learners the general idea of the movement without the use of explicit rules, they may not enable the learner to garner sufficient information to evaluate effectively and then alter an unsuccessful performance (Bennett, 2000). Consequently, for more complex skills, it may be important that learners have knowledge of the fundamentals of the skill to be performed in order that they can monitor and evaluate their performance effectively, should problems arise. For example, Bennett illustrated (in golf) the value of some fundamental knowledge associated with the stance that would enable a slicing golfer to make adjustments to remedy that problem. Such fundamentals can be taught by coaches through facilitating appreciation in athletes of the desired technique with recourse to explicit rules, providing these rules are located as an external focus of attention. For example, recent research (Gottwald et al., 2010) suggests that learning explicit fundamental knowledge of skill execution is efficacious or effective if this knowledge centres on rules that are linked to movement effects (e.g. moving the feet to create a wider stance and placing the club head further towards the front foot when performing a golf drive). The reasoning here is that, while this coaching technique leads to the learning and development of explicit rules, the nature of these rules (i.e. external) prevent access to the self-focused knowledge often deemed responsible for performance decrements both under normal (see Wulf, 2007, for a review) and stressful (see Maxwell and Masters, 2008, for a review) conditions.

For more capable/skilled performers, coaches can be left in a tricky situation. With too much explicit knowledge, players are likely to be susceptible to negative stress effects caused by conscious processing (Masters, 1992). However, without such knowledge, it is unlikely that players would achieve high levels of

44

performance. A solution is to ensure that players have strategies in place to negate the tendency (under stressful conditions) to use explicit rules inappropriately when attempting to ensure task success (as these undermine rather than support successful task execution). One coping strategy that has received widespread support in this respect is the use of pre-performance routines (Jackson *et al.*, 2006). These are most relevant in sports that have closed-skill elements (i.e. where the environment is stable, as in golf). Here, absorbing one's self in a given set of behaviours designed to support task performance may provide a means of resisting the effects of self-focused attention.

While there is widespread support for focusing on a set of processes that are chunked together to form a pre-performance routine (see, for example, Boutcher, 1990), an alternative strategy is to focus on an isolated aspect of the skill that, if executed effectively, will permit successful performance. This describes what has been coined in the sport psychology literature as a 'process goal' (Kingston and Hardy, 1997). However, despite supportive evidence that focusing on isolated aspects of technique might facilitate performance (e.g. Filby *et al.*, 1999; Kingston and Hardy, 1997; Zimmerman and Kitsantas, 1996), such a process focus has been questioned. Primarily it has been challenged on the premise that promoting step-by-step monitoring and control of complex procedural knowledge, which typically operates automatically, results in performance impairment (e.g. Jackson *et al.*, 2006; Masters, 1992). Furthermore, and more specifically, Jackson *et al.* (2006) provided strong evidence that movement related process goals were detrimental to performance regardless of individual tendencies for self-focused attention and situational pressure. However, in line with Kingston and Hardy (1997), Jackson went on to suggest that subtly different process goals might have different attentional functions. For example, process goals that take attention away from the physical movements being performed (e.g. functioning as holistic cues for the desired action) do not encourage explicit monitoring (Jackson *et al.*, 2006). To illustrate, 'holistic-process goals' (as distinct from isolated [or part] process goals), which are less rule-based representations of the to-be-performed skill, may encourage performers to use more automatic control structures (Jackson *et al.*, 2006). This rationale is similar to that discussed previously in this section to account for the positive effects of developing explicit rules that are external in nature (Gottwald *et al.*, 2010). Similarly, research by Bell and Hardy (2009) suggested that simply asking expert performers to focus attention on movement effects prevented the performance decrements typically associated with performing under pressure. Finally, more global strategies to reduce the tendency for performers to engage in self-focused attention during potentially stress-inducing situations might be to promote trust (Moore and Stevenson, 1994) and self-confidence, and to incorporate anxious situations into practice sessions (Oudejans, 2008; Oudejans and Pijpers, 2009, 2010) (both self-confidence and stress and anxiety in sport are examined in greater depth in Chapter 4: 'Psychology for coaches').

In closing this section on attentional focus, it is important to reinforce our intention to critically appraise traditional notions of coaching where athletes are instructed to focus on their movements while executing skills. It is clear that subtle differences in athletes' foci of attention can have significant effects on both learning and performance. Furthermore, these effects vary (and in some cases will produce the opposite effect to that desired) according to both the skill level of those to whom the instructions are given, and how these instructions are delivered.

CONCLUSION

The aim of this chapter was to identify the current state of play regarding three of the central issues (i.e. the practice environment, feedback and attentional foci) pertinent to the acquisition of skills as specifically related to what Schmidt and Wrisberg (2000) coined the 'learning experience'. For each, a contemporary review of the literature was presented, accompanied by illustrations of how this knowledge can be applied by coaches. Broadly speaking, we have attempted to demonstrate how learning may be facilitated through a variety of easily manipulated, but often overlooked, factors. These include: practice schedules that promote cognitive (mental) activity; the appropriate use of certain types of feedback, with particular consideration given to frequency and timing; and the utility of an appropriate (external) focus of attention that encourages learners to allow natural (automatic) control processes to run free; and a movement strategy that often results in performance robustness under pressure. Although these suggestions provide lines of good practice in relation to skill learning, it is important to remember that coaches still need to consider carefully both the individual performer and the task to be performed in structuring optimal learning environments.

DISCUSSION TOPICS AND REVIEW QUESTIONS

1   Why are random and variable practice schedules important for developing skill learning? What are the reasons for their positive effects and how are they most effectively applied?
2   Why does practising under conditions of anxiety lead to increased performance in competitive or stress-inducing situations?
3   The use of augmented feedback should be tailored according to a number of factors; what are these and how should the delivery of feedback be adjusted to effectively deal with them (discuss in terms of frequency and timing)?

46

4 What is the most efficacious focus of attention? How can you explain its effects?
5 Why should coaches consider focus of attention when attempting to reduce performance decrements under pressure?

Other Resources

Although our intention (in line with others) was to provide accompanying informative web resources here, this has not been possible for the topics considered within this chapter. While this inconsistency may prove frustrating, we felt it far more appropriate (given the commercial leanings of websites which looked at feedback and practice scheduling in particular) to recommend texts, and urge interested readers to review these (and others) instead. Key phrases here, if using electronic search techniques, could include 'external focus of attention in sport', 'practice scheduling in sport' and 'feedback in sport'. The recommended texts alluded to include:

Wulf, G. (2007). *Attention and motor skill learning.* Champaign, IL: Human Kinetics.
Schmidt, R.A. and Lee, T.D. (2011). *Motor control and learning: A behavioural emphasis (5th edn).* Champaign IL: Human Kinetics.
Magill, R.A. (2010). *Motor learning and control: Concepts and applications* (9th edn). London: McGraw-Hill.

CHAPTER 4

PSYCHOLOGY FOR COACHES

KIERAN KINGSTON, OWEN THOMAS AND RICHARD NEIL

Competitive sports are played mainly on a five-and-a-half inch court: the space between your ears.

> Bobby Jones (the only person to complete golf's
> Grand Slam of all four major championships in one year)

INTRODUCTION

The formal application of psychological principles to sport has increased tremendously over the past 20 years. This has been evidenced by the number of athletes and coaches now looking to sport psychology to gain an edge over their competitors (Williams and Straub, 2005). Despite this recognition, coaches' application of sport psychology has been, and often remains, *ad hoc* and unstructured in nature. The aim of this chapter is to further illuminate the value of sport psychology to coaches and, rather than simply providing a 'paint-by-numbers' of techniques, to illustrate how appropriate theoretical principles can be systematically applied to maximise athletic performances. We start by defining the discipline of sport psychology before focusing on the areas of motivation, self-confidence, and stress and anxiety. Each of these is then examined in terms of pertinent theories and their potential application by coaches, taking into account certain mediating factors. Finally, we conclude with a summary that highlights the value of the constructs discussed for sports coaches.

WHAT IS SPORT PSYCHOLOGY?

One would imagine that defining what has become a recognised field of academic pursuit would be a simple enough exercise: this is not, however, the case. Indeed,

Dishman (1983) has suggested that sport psychology sometimes suffers from an identity crisis. The reason for this is the many and varied perspectives that exist within the field. Nevertheless, a summary definition (based on a number given by Feltz and Kontos, 2002) describes sport psychology as the study of people's behaviour and thoughts in sporting contexts. Furthermore, the general goal of applied sport psychology is to provide athletes and coaches with the necessary mental skills to manage the demands of training and competition, thus helping each realise their potential.

Under the broad umbrella of sport psychology, we have identified three principal areas for attention; namely, motivation, self-confidence, and stress and anxiety. A reasonable question might be, why these and not others? In response, we believe that, as applied practitioners (i.e. sport psychology consultants), a high proportion of the issues we come across either fall within or are under-pinned by these aspects. That is, much of the work we do focuses on developing and sustaining athletes' confidence and motivation, while providing them with tools to regulate anxiety and arousal. In identifying the areas most pertinent to cover, we have been led by the needs of athletes and coaches. Furthermore, while one might reasonably expect a section on team issues, we determined that when working in such environments, most of the psychological issues that arise do so at an individual level. Readers interested in the psychology of teams, therefore, are guided to other, more specific texts (for example, Carron *et al.*, 2005).

MOTIVATION

Understanding the dynamic and complex psychological processes of motivation is critical to comprehending human behaviour, especially in sport (Roberts, 2001). Motivation refers to the personality factors, social variables and cognitions which act in situations where one is evaluated, competes against others, or attempts to attain a standard of excellence (Roberts, 2001). In an applied context, it can be thought of as 'the personal drive that leads individuals to initiate, direct, and sustain human behaviour' (Kingston *et al.*, 2006: 2). Motivation lies at the core of biological, cognitive and social regulation, and is, therefore, a pre-eminent concern to those whose roles involve mobilising others to act, such as coaches (Ryan and Deci, 2000).

Currently, one of the most popular theoretical areas from both research and applied standpoints is self-determination theory (SDT; Deci and Ryan, 1985). SDT adopts a social-cognitive perspective, and has proved effective in illuminating our understanding of motivational processes in physical activity and sport (Sarrazin, *et al.*, 2007), and the associated cognitive, affective (i.e. emotional)

50

and behavioural outcomes. For these reasons, it is especially relevant for tho: concerned with promoting motivation in the sports domain.

Promoting motivation in athletes: A self-determination approach

Self-determination theory (SDT) is based on the premise that individuals have innate tendencies toward psychological growth and development, to master ongoing challenges and, through their experiences, to develop a coherent sense of self (i.e. who they are as individuals) (Deci and Ryan, 2000). Central to this theory lies the concept of intrinsic motivation. Intrinsic motivation describes an inclination towards assimilation, mastery, spontaneous interest and exploration (Ryan and Deci, 2000). It involves people engaging in activities voluntarily in the absence of material rewards or external pressures or constraints (Deci and Ryan, 1985, 2000). Athletes who practise because they find it interesting and for the pleasure associated with striving to overcome challenges, are considered to be highly intrinsically motivated (Vallerand, 1997). Not surprisingly, therefore, the promotion of high levels of intrinsic motivation should be a primary objective for anyone interested in the development and maintenance of sport participation and skills (i.e. coaches).

Within SDT, Deci and Ryan (1985) present a number of sub-theories. One such component aspect, basic needs theory, proposes three universal psychological needs: the need for competence, autonomy and relatedness. These needs are considered fundamental to promoting motivation and psychological well-being. The need for competence encompasses people's strivings to interact effectively with their environment (Harter, 1978), to seek control over outcomes and to experience mastery (Kingston *et al.*, 2006). The need for autonomy refers to the desire to be self-initiating in determining one's actions (Vallerand and Losier, 1999). Finally, the need for relatedness concerns the wish to feel connected and to have a sense of mutual respect and reliance in relation to others (Baumeister and Leary, 1995). For all individuals, regardless of age, gender or culture, these needs represent psychological nutrients that are essential for psychological growth, integrity and well-being (Ng *et al.*, 2011).

The extent to which psychological needs are supported by the social context (e.g. the sporting environment) influences the degree to which an individual's motivation is self-determined (Deci and Ryan, 2000). More self-determined forms of motivation are associated with positive consequences, for example, performance increases (Vallerand, 1997). Furthermore, within sport settings, research has supported the importance of need satisfaction upon intrinsic motivation (Kowal and Fortier, 2000; Standage *et al.*, 2003; Hollembeak and Amorose, 2005), well-being (Reinboth and Duda, 2006), and other indicators of adaptive functioning, such as flow (Kowal and Fortier, 2000). Similarly, basic need satisfaction has a negative association with less adaptive outcomes, such as burnout (Hodge *et al.*, 2008; Ng *et al.*, 2011).

The recognition of the importance of need satisfaction has led to greater attention to how basic needs can be fulfilled within the sporting context. Cognitive evaluation theory, a further sub-theory of SDT, explains variability in intrinsic motivation through the extent to which social-contextual factors facilitate or forestall satisfaction of the innate needs of autonomy and competence. Consequently, it has served as a useful theoretical framework through which to consider basic needs and their consequential effects on intrinsic motivation. For example, threats, deadlines, directives, pressured evaluation and imposed goals have been shown to undermine intrinsic motivation, whereas choice, acknowledgment of feelings, and opportunities for self-direction have been associated with increases in intrinsic motivation (for a fuller review, see Ryan and Deci, 2000).

The extent and diversity of factors that can affect basic psychological needs are numerous. Unsurprisingly, however, the behaviours and general styles of leadership displayed by the coach are some of the most important influences on athlete motivation (Mageau and Vallerand, 2003; Iachini *et al.*, 2010). The general consensus amongst sport scientists is that coaches who are more 'autonomy-supportive', that is, they support rather than undermine perceptions of autonomy, competence and relatedness, are more effective in terms of supporting athlete motivation (Iachini *et al.*, 2010).

Largely based on the predictions of SDT and their review of the coach–athlete literature, Mageau and Vallerand (2003) produced a framework through which, it was argued, coaches could positively affect athletes' basic psychological needs. Accordingly, autonomy-supportive coaches acknowledge athletes' feelings and perspectives, allow them to be involved in the decision making process within specific constraints, provide non-controlling informative feedback, avoid controlling behaviours, and minimise the use of pressure and the promotion of ego-involvement within athletes (Deci and Ryan, 1987; Mageau and Vallerand, 2003). In a more recent study, which involved interviews with eleven high-school coaches, Iachini *et al.* (2003) explored the coaches' views on strategies to support basic needs. To support competence perceptions, content analysis suggested that positive verbal communication (encouragement/reinforcement), the use of self-set goals, an emphasis on individual opportunities to be successful while ignoring mistakes, and a personal style that was relaxed, positive and constructive, were critical. For relatedness support, the coaches described strategies associated with effective management of social interactions, creating unity through team-building activities (both in and away from the sport), an emphasis on the concept of 'team', and peer mentoring. Finally, while the coaches seemed to have more difficulty in describing strategies to promote autonomy, providing choice and opportunities for team input into decisions (regarding management and organisation, games and training), and giving a degree of control to the athletes, were viewed as effective means to facilitate autonomy perceptions.

While promotion of athletes' basic needs appears increasingly important, implementing strategies to support this is not always simplistic. A number of factors potentially influence the coach's ability to be effective in promoting the needs of athletes. For example, a coach's implicit views of motivation may not incorporate all three basic needs, in particular relatedness and autonomy (Iachini *et al.*, 2010). Additionally, many coaches perceive that controlling motivational strategies, characterised by the use of rewards and punishments, are the most effective motivational strategies (Mageau and Vallerand, 2003). Similarly, coaches' perceptions of barriers associated with, for example, time, facilities, skill level and participant behavioural and demographic characteristics, all have the potential to limit their ability to implement desired motivational strategies. Furthermore, in the context of elite sport, full-time professional athletes may be subject to many external pressures (financial rewards, public and corporate image issues, public expectations and increasingly difficult competition), many of which are not conducive to developing and satisfying autonomy, competence and relatedness (Deci and Ryan, 2000). Consequently, in addition to providing coaches with education, and encouraging a reflective approach to their practice, it is incumbent upon coaches across all levels to work hard and be creative in searching for ways to provide an environment that continues to support the innate needs of competence, autonomy and relatedness, if optimal athletic performance is to be obtained.

SELF-CONFIDENCE IN SPORT

The importance of confidence in sport is well documented; this is evidenced by numerous anecdotal accounts both in the media and within the sport psychology literature. Indeed, confidence has been noted as the most critical psychological attribute associated with mental toughness (Bull *et al.*, 2005; Jones *et al.*, 2002), and has consistently been identified as a key characteristic of successful elite performers (Gould *et al.*, 2002a, 2002b).

One constant feature of definitions related to self-confidence is the reference to an individual's belief about personal abilities and/or expectancy of success. Within the sport psychology literature, two main approaches to examining self-confidence have predominated; Bandura's self-efficacy theory (Bandura, 1977, 1997), and Vealey and colleagues' model(s) of sport-confidence (Vealey, 1986, 2001; Vealey and Chase, 2008).

Embedded within social-cognitive thinking, Bandura's self-efficacy theory has remained prominent within the sport psychology literature. According to Bandura (1997), efficacy expectations (i.e. one's belief that a certain level of performance can be attained) are predicted from four hierarchical sources of information: (1) *Performance accomplishments* provide the most influence over self-efficacy due to the fact they are based upon an athlete's previous successes and performance of sports skills; (2) *Vicarious (i.e. vivid) experiences* relate to a performer gaining self-efficacy through watching others perform sporting skills; (3) *Verbal persuasion* refers to information conveyed to the performer by the self (i.e. through self-talk) or significant others (i.e. the coach) that helps manipulate behaviour; and (4) *Physiological and emotional arousal control*, the least powerful predictor of self-efficacy, relates to levels of control the performer believes they hold over their physiological and emotional states (e.g. anxiety). The major implication coaches should derive from Bandura's approach is to expose athletes to sources of information that relate directly to these four source domains with a focus towards the top of the hierarchy. Although, for many, self-efficacy theory has obvious application for competitive sport, Vealey and associates have raised concerns about whether the sources of efficacy within Bandura's framework were the most salient within a sporting context. Rather, they suggest that athletes' beliefs are influenced by the unique social, organisational and demographic factors within sport. As such, over the last 30 years, Vealey's work has pioneered and evolved several models of sport-confidence (see Vealey, 1986, 2001; Vealey and Chase, 2008).

The more recent derivatives of the Vealey models show some obvious similarities to Bandura's work through the inclusion of sources of sport-confidence. A critical step in this process was Vealey *et al.*'s (1998) proposition of nine sport-specific sources of information that athletes use to gain confidence. These nine sources were subsequently adopted within Vealey and Chase's (2008) most recent model of sport-confidence, and are listed and contextualised within Table 4.1. In an attempt to provide information on the importance of each of the nine sources, Vealey *et al.* noted that physical/mental preparation, mastery and social support were consistently rated amongst the top five sources of sport-confidence by high-school and collegiate athletes. More recent research, however, has indicated that elite performers use additional sources of information from which to derive their beliefs (Hays *et al.*, 2007). The sources of sport-confidence that emerged from Hays *et al.*'s sample of top-level athletes are also described within Table 4.1. Key differences identified by Hays *et al.* include that holistic preparation (e.g. gaining confidence from preparation activities such as video analysis, vision training, nutritional advice, access to physiotherapy treatment and sport massage), innate factors (e.g. gaining confidence from being born with certain abilities such as an analytical personality, natural competitiveness, natural ability, and natural speed/skill) and trust (e.g. gaining confidence from trusting those around you in the support team and trusting your team mates), were additional sources that elite athletes used to gain belief in their ability to succeed. In line with Vealey et al.'s earlier work, the world-class performers within this latter study also placed emphasis on accomplishment

Table 4.1 Summary and comparison of sport-confidence sources

Vealey and Chase (2008) sources	Athletes gain confidence from . . .	Hays et al. (2007) sources	Athletes gain confidence from . . .
Mastery	mastering or improving personal skills	Performance accomplishments (competition/ training)	accomplishments in competition/ accomplishments in training
Demonstration of ability	showing off skills to others or demonstrating more ability than one's opponent	Preparation (mental/physical/ holistic)	effective physical, mental and holistic preparation
Physical/Mental preparation	feeling physically and mentally prepared with an optimal focus for performance	Coaching	believing in the abilities of their coach to set the right training programme and handle their performance preparation
Physical self-presentation	perceptions of one's physical self (how one perceives one looks to others)	Social support	a supportive environment from players, coaches, family, partners and/or friends during competition and preparatory training
Social support	perceiving support and encouragement from significant others in sport, such as coaches, family and team mates	Innate factors	believing they were born with certain abilities (e.g. an analytical personality, natural competitiveness, natural ability, natural speed/skill)
Vicarious experience	watching others, such as team mates or friends, perform successfully	Experience	familiarity with competing on the elite stage and overcoming career lows
Coaches' leadership	believing the coach is skilled in decision-making and leadership	Competitive advantage	seeing the opposition crack or perform poorly under pressure
Environmental comfort	feeling comfortable in a competitive environment	Trust	trusting those around you (e.g. team mates and support team)
Situational favourableness	feeling that the breaks of the situation are in one's favour	Self-awareness	understanding and being secure of where they are in their sport career

(i.e. mastery), preparation (physical/mental/holistic) and social support as critically important sources used to build their belief.

In relation to the multidimensional nature of sport-confidence, Vealey and Knight (2002) classified three broad 'types' of sport confidence. Hays *et al.* (2007) added to these by suggesting six discrete types of sport-confidence (see Table 4.2 for both). Sport-confidence 'types' refer to the aspects of the sport that athletes are confident about; for example, to achieve certain outcomes, to cope with the psychological demands of the situation, and the ability to bounce back following setbacks. Although further research is required to fully conceptualise the multidimensional nature of sport-confidence, the emergence of these sport-confidence types has helped create a clear distinction between 'where' athletes derive their confidence from (i.e. sport-confidence sources) and 'what' athletes are confident about (i.e. sport-confidence types).

Only one study has systematically examined the mediating effects of sport-confidence through affect, behaviours and cognitions (the ABCs) with

Table 4.2 Summary and comparison of sport-confidence types

Vealey and Knight (2002) types	Athletes are confident about . . .	Hays *et al.* (2007) types	Athletes are confident about . . .
Sport-confidence: Physical skills and training	their ability to execute the physical skills required to perform successfully	Skill execution	their ability to execute sport-specific skills with correct technique and fulfil the requirements of their sport or position
Sport-confidence: Cognitive efficiency	their ability to mentally focus, maintain concentration, and make the effective decisions required to perform successfully	Achievement	their ability to achieve certain outcomes or (performance) targets
Sport-confidence: Resilience	their ability to regain focus and bounce back after performing poorly and/or overcome doubts, problems, and setbacks to be able to perform successfully	Physical factors	their physical attributes (e.g. strength, speed)
		Psychological factors	their psychological attributes (e.g. ability to deal with nerves and pressure)
		Superiority to opposition	their superiority over opposition
		Tactical awareness	their ability to be tactically more astute than their opponents

performance. Again, with world-class performers, Hays *et al.* (2009) indicated that high sport-confidence was associated with positive affective responses (e.g. enjoyment, happiness), adaptive behaviours (e.g. confident body language, increased effort) and effective cognitions (e.g. focus on the task or outcome) which realised successful sports performance. Conversely, low sport-confidence was synonymous with maladaptive thoughts, feelings and behaviours, which resulted in lower levels of athletic performance. Clearly, although these early findings are encouraging, further research is required to fully explore the mediating effects of confidence-related affect, cognition and behaviour on performance.

One further line of enquiry within the sport-confidence domain relates to attempts to systematically study confidence stability, and the more enduring nature of athletes' beliefs. Linked to the proposal of 'sport-confidence resiliency' as a type of sport-confidence within Vealey and Chase's (2008) model, and the consistent suggestion within the mental toughness literature that an 'unshakable' and 'resilient' confidence is a fundamental aspect of a mentally tough performer (Bull *et al.*, 2005; Jones *et al.*, 2002, 2007), recent research has investigated confidence stability and the notion of 'robust' sport-confidence (Kingston *et al.*, 2010; Thomas *et al.*, 2011). Here, Kingston *et al.* (2010) assessed the stability of sport-confidence sources during a six week pre-competition period with male and female elite performers. Overall, their findings suggested that mastery, demonstration of ability, physical/mental preparation and social support were the most important sources used by athletes during this period, with the importance of demonstration of ability and physical/mental preparation increasing as the event moved closer. These early findings suggest that focusing upon such sources of sport-confidence during the time leading up to performance, may help to foster stable and more enduring sport-confidence beliefs.

The previous sections have described the major developments and recent research interests within the sport-confidence domain. Although reference to self-efficacy theory remains integral, the work of Vealey and colleagues surrounding the conceptualisation of sport-confidence, and the subsequent research studies that have been conducted under that umbrella, have helped create a sport-specific knowledge base, particularly in terms of understanding where athletes glean confidence.

Promoting confidence in athletes

The provision of specific models and research within sport-confidence, coupled with the implications that emerge from self-efficacy, provide us with considerable insight into how confidence can be developed. Unsurprisingly, the coach has a significant role to play here in creating a sense of achievement in both the training and competitive environments, and in nurturing a perception of (social) support. Vealey (2001) identified three broad domains oriented around the sport-confidence sources within her model: (1) A*chievement* (i.e. mastery and demonstration of ability); (2) *Self-regulation* (i.e. physical/mental preparation and physical self-presentation); and (3) *Social climate* (i.e. social support, vicarious experience, coach leadership, environmental comfort and situational favourableness). Essentially, Vealey indicated that these three domains could act as a framework to guide coaches' attempts to target and develop athletes' confidence. Lines of accepted practice in this regard include: acknowledging the athlete's perception of prior competitive success, introducing game scenarios within training sessions (e.g. performance-related scenarios), encouraging athletes to use reflective log-books detailing past competitive success, considering the use of highlighted DVD footage that demonstrates skill execution, in addition to engaging in effective goal-setting programmes that alter the perceived difficulty of performances (Vealey, 2001). In relation to goals, it is important for the coach and performer to set goals that are controllable for the performer in both competition and training, and to evaluate these in terms of personal performance rather than social comparison (Kingston and Hardy, 1997). Further, it is apparent from research across several areas that performers should attempt to draw their beliefs from the more controllable sources of sport-confidence (e.g. mastery, performance accomplishments, physical preparation, mental preparation and holistic preparation). Thus, coaches should seek to prioritise a focus towards these sources when preparing their athletes (Hays *et al.*, 2007; Kingston *et al.*, 2010; Vealey *et al.*, 1998).

Self-regulation (i.e. the management of one's behaviours, thoughts and feelings) provides a further domain through which the coach and psychologist can strive to foster performers' confidence (Vealey, 2001). This links to mental skill training through the (self-regulatory) strategies of goal mapping, imagery and self-talk. Coaches could promote the use of goal mapping through the creation of a goal plan that incorporates systematic and ongoing assessment of progress towards achieving these goals (Burton *et al.*, 2001). Effective monitoring of programmes allows athletes to gain confidence through self-regulation, while imagery, or visualisation, of successful performance provides them with confidence gains through vicarious information. Imagery can either be used within a self-regulatory capacity (i.e. imaging control of the self, emotions and behaviour within the competitive environment) or within an achievement context through imaging successful performance and accomplishments of specific sports skills (Vealey, 2001). The effective management of self-talk by athletes can also foster confidence through verbal persuasion. Here, coaches and sport psychologists can assist athletes through self-talk programmes that provide control over negative thought processes while promoting the use of positive self-affirmation (Zinsser *et al.*, 2001). It should also be noted that successful implementation of these skills may impact confidence through the achievement domain. These factors, in addition to the emphasis placed on athlete-centred physical, psychological and holistic support, as noted in Hays *et al.*'s (2007) work, provide coaches with a solid framework to provide effective, confidence-orientated preparation for competitive athletes.

Confidence can also be enhanced through the leadership style the coach adopts and the consequent social climate created. In particular, coaches need to be flexible in order to influence an athlete's perception of control. For example, the adoption of a collaborative style, if used appropriately, could facilitate confidence to achieve shared goals and allow the coach to provide contingent reinforcement and informative feedback. Ensuring effective social support to the athlete also serves as an important source of confidence, in terms of that athlete's perception of the resources available to cope with the various demands of competitive sport. These issues can be targeted through team-building activities and the education of significant others (e.g. spouse, parents, peers). A coach can also facilitate this process through an awareness of the social context and the individual situations of athletes. Given the findings of Hays *et al.* (2007) with respect to the important role of the coach as a critical source of sport-confidence for elite performers, the social support provided by the coach to these performers, and the verbally persuasive techniques used, appear of considerable importance.

The source based sport-confidence frameworks provided both by Vealey and colleagues (Vealey *et al.*, 1998; Vealey, 2001; Vealey and Chase, 2008) and Hays *et al.* (2007), coupled with the implications that emerge from self-efficacy theory, provide guidance on the effective construction of confidence related interventions. It is important to note that the bias towards certain sources by certain groups within the sport-confidence research (e.g. elite versus non-elite, male versus female) may directly affect the content of interventions. Further, although work has begun to systematically assess the more enduring, stable aspects of 'robust' sport-confidence, further detailed research is required to provide an evidence base for how such beliefs are developed and maintained.

STRESS AND ANXIETY IN SPORT

Perhaps the first major development within competitive anxiety was the distinction made between trait and state anxiety (Spielberger, 1966). That is, anxiety symptoms were considered both as responses to situation-specific stressors or stimuli (i.e. state-like) as well as a dispositional response that exists across all settings (i.e. trait-like). A further advance was the development of multidimensional anxiety theory (MAT: Martens *et al.* 1990), within which state anxiety responses were separated into cognitive and somatic components. Cognitive anxiety was defined as the cognitive elements of the anxiety response, characterised by thoughts of worry, concern and negative self-evaluation (Martens *et al.*, 1990). Somatic anxiety was, in contrast, described as individuals' perceptions of their physiological arousal (state) in response to the stressful situation they find themselves in (e.g. butterflies, sweaty palms), manifested through experiencing feelings such as nervousness and tension (Martens *et al.*, 1990). Through MAT, Martens *et al.* (1990) also predicted how each component of anxiety would separately influence performance. Cognitive anxiety was proposed to demonstrate a negative linear relationship with performance, with increases in such anxiety leading to poorer performance. In comparison, somatic anxiety was predicted to exhibit an inverted-U relationship, where performance is seen to increase up to an optimum level of symptom intensity, beyond which, performance decrements will occur.

Given the negative predictive effects of anxiety on performance, interventions have been designed to match the anxiety component to the required treatment (Morris *et al.*, 1981; Maynard and Cotton, 1993). For example, techniques such as progressive-muscular relaxation (PMR) programmes (Ost, 1988) have been used to target somatic anxiety symptoms, while thought stopping and positive thought control (Suinn, 1987) have been employed to target cognitive anxiety. The primary function of these techniques is to reduce the level (i.e. the intensity) of anxiety symptoms experienced by athletes.

PMR, thought stopping, and positive thought control are strategies aimed at dealing with the symptoms of competitive anxiety. Continuing with the focus on helping athletes, researchers have also considered the antecedents (i.e. the precursors and/or causes) of competitive anxiety and the changes in anxiety's intensity and frequency over time. The principle here was to identify what influenced anxiety, so that interventions could be designed to prevent it occurring. A number of factors have been shown to be associated with cognitive and/or somatic anxiety including perceived ability, years of experience, perceptions of readiness for peak performance, the performer's attitude toward previous performances, perceptions of environmental conditions, and goals directed towards 'race position' (i.e. I want to get into the top three to qualify for a major championship) (see e.g. Hanton and Jones, 1997). Such findings suggest that athletes need to: (1) be within a training environment that fully prepares them for competition; (2) learn to focus on previous successes and identify how to overcome perceived failures; and (3) have goals that allow them to focus on their own specific roles.

A further conceptual development within the anxiety literature, was provided through Hardy's (1990) catastrophe model (see Woodman and Hardy, 2001a, for a complete review). In comparison to MAT, this model sought to describe the interactive influence of cognitive anxiety and actual physiological arousal on performance. Some of the key implications from the model were that cognitive anxiety does not always have a negative influence on competitive performance and that, under conditions of high cognitive anxiety, it is the performer's ability to deal with increases in physiological arousal (e.g. through relaxation techniques) that determines whether their performance levels remain high (Hardy, 1990).

The notion that anxiety is not always detrimental to performance links to recent developments where, in addition to the intensity (i.e. level or amount) of anxiety experienced, interpretations of anxiety symptoms have been considered (Jones, 1991). These interpretations are described as directional perceptions, and relate to the extent to which performers interpret the intensity of their anxiety symptoms as positive (facilitative) or negative (debilitative) towards upcoming performance (Jones, 1995). Research in this area has indicated that, generally, elite athletes interpret their anxiety symptoms as more facilitative than their non-elite counterparts, and report greater levels of self-confidence (Hanton and Jones, 1997). Findings from qualitative investigations have suggested that elite performers maintain facilitative interpretations of anxiety through being high in self-confidence, underpinned by the rationalisation of thoughts and feelings before competing via the combined use of psychological skills such as self-talk and imagery. These developments have led to a shift in approaches towards adopting techniques that foster facilitative interpretations of anxiety symptoms (i.e. reinterpreting anxiety symptoms as positive rather than negative), as opposed to techniques that are designed to solely reduce the intensity of anxiety (Hanton and Jones, 1999a, 1999b). From a coaching perspective, the implication here is that it is not the amount of anxiety but rather the way in which the athlete interprets that anxiety which is critical for performance. This point becomes more important when considering the demands of certain sports. For example, some sports (e.g. contact sports) may require higher levels of anxiety (or activation, as it is labelled when describing the cognitive and physiological activity that is geared towards a planned response [Pribram and McGuinness, 1975]) to achieve the desired performance. Consequently, it may be illogical in this context to reduce the anxiety symptoms via traditional stress management techniques. Rather, coaches should recognise the need for a restructuring approach through, for example, encouraging athletes to view their symptoms as reflective of an optimal level of preparedness, as opposed to ones that may debilitate performance (Mellalieu et al., 2006).

An important implication when considering anxiety symptoms is that they have the potential to change during the time leading up to competition (Mellalieu et al., 2006); both the intensity and the frequency of anxiety symptoms tend to increase as competition moves closer. Within this context, it has become apparent that, in comparison to intensity, frequency is more sensitive to fluctuations during the seven days directly preceding competition (Swain and Jones, 1993; Hanton *et al.*, 2004). Consequently, those athletes with more facilitative interpretations of anxiety report lower frequencies of anxiety symptoms and higher frequencies of confidence symptoms during the time preceding competition. For the coach, these findings suggest that athletes can alter the way they view their mental states during the time leading up to performance (Hanton *et al.*, 2004; Thomas *et al.*, 2004). Coaches and athletes should then seek to integrate psychological skills (e.g. imagery, goal-setting, cognitive-restructuring) into their preparation within seven days prior to competition, specifically focusing on the final 48 and 24 hours before the competitive event (see Thomas *et al.*, 2007). This could potentially offset increases in the intensity and frequency of experienced cognitive and somatic anxiety and, with an appropriate restructuring strategy, lead to a more facilitative interpretation of cognitive and somatic symptoms during the time leading up to performance (Hanton *et al.*, 2004).

Competitive stress

Anxiety is just one part of a broader holistic stress-related process which may offer a more complete explanation of the experiences of individuals and thus provide practitioners (be they coaches or psychologists) with more options when intervening. While competitive anxiety is described as a specific negative emotional response to competitive stressors, stress itself is considered as an ongoing transaction between environmental demands and a person's resources. Negative emotions, such as anxiety, result from an imbalance between these demands and resources (Hanton *et al.*, 2008). Grounded within Lazarus' (1999; Lazarus and Folkman, 1984) transactional perspective of stress and the more contemporary cognitive-motivational-relational (CMR) theory of emotions, an individual's appraisal of environmental stressors is considered fundamental to the stress process. According to CMR theory, these appraisals (classified as threat, harm, challenge or benefit) are influenced both by the environment and personal characteristics and result in the experience of emotions that could, in turn, influence behaviour (e.g. athletic performance). To illustrate, let us consider the case of a male soccer player. The player perceives that the coach has overloaded him with information regarding what he is required to do in a game (this acts as a stressor). Consequently, the player perceives that he will not be able to carry out all of the coach's instructions and worries that failure to do so will result in him performing poorly (threat appraisal). This threat appraisal could cause the player to experience anxiety (an emotion) and, consequently, negatively affect his attention and subsequent performance.

62

Informed by the more holistic perspectives put forward by Lazarus, research has begun to move away from investigating just the emotional response (e.g. anxiety) to focus on the whole process of stressors, appraisals, emotions, coping and resultant performance behaviour. Nicholls *et al.* (2012), for example, showed that negatively toned appraisals, such as threat, result in unpleasant emotions, distraction or disengagement, and performance dissatisfaction. Conversely, more positively toned appraisals, such as challenge, resulted in the experience of pleasant emotions, task orientated coping, and performance satisfaction.

Adopting a qualitative approach to their research, Neil *et al.* (2011) provided a more in-depth account of the stress and emotion process and showed that performance (and organisational) stressors can influence athletes' appraisals during competition. These appraisals elicited a range of emotional responses, with the impact on performance behaviour dictated by individual interpretation of this emotional response. To elaborate, when the appraisals and the negative emotions experienced (e.g. anger, anxiety) were interpreted as debilitative, the athletes' behaviour was affected due to a lack of control over these thoughts and symptoms. In comparison, when stressors gave rise to appraisals and negative emotions which were interpreted as facilitative, an associated increase in focus and/or effort was reported.

The work described in the previous paragraph, reinforces the view that stressors are not only associated with the demands of competitive performance, but also with the organisational structure to which the athlete belongs (Fletcher *et al.*, 2006). According to Fletcher *et al.*, organisational stressors are defined as 'environmental demands (i.e. stimuli) associated directly and primarily with the organisation within which an individual is operating' (Fletcher *et al.*, 2006: 329). In this context, four major stress-related domains have been identified: namely, environmental, personal, leadership and team issues (Woodman and Hardy, 2001b). Fletcher and Hanton (2003) provided support for these categories of stressors, while additionally identifying several other related issues. These included accommodation, travel, competition environment and safety. Taken collectively, these findings suggest that it is important not only to consider performers' anxiety responses in relation to competitive demands, but also to take into account organisational and environmental pressures when preparing athletes for competition.

Managing the stress process

In terms of intervening and helping athletes to manage the stress process, adopting Lazarus' (1999) CMR theory of emotions (that synthesises the concepts of stress and emotion in a more holistic manner) affords an opportunity to intervene at three specific levels (Fletcher *et al.*, 2006). Primary-level interventions involve eliminating or reducing the stressors encountered by athletes within their performance environments (i.e. training and competition). If we consider the example of the soccer player earlier, the stressor encountered by the performer was too much information from the coach. Helping the coach understand the consequences of his or her instructions would represent a primary intervention. If the coach was educated to become more aware of the amount of information given to the athlete, and the negative implications of such overload, then the stressor could be eliminated. Secondary-level interventions focus on stress management training, which is designed to modify the cognitive and emotional responses to stressors. For example, specific cognitive-behavioural interventions could be used to manipulate these responses so that functional behaviour is the result of stressful encounters. In addition, interventions may include team members generating 'what if?' scenarios, where coping with relevant situations are discussed together with contingency plans to deal with them (Fletcher and Hanton, 2003). Such strategies are intended to result in more positive appraisals due to the situations having already been encountered and dealt with in practice. Finally, tertiary-level interventions involve the treatment of problems once they have occurred. In these cases, practitioners (i.e. coaches and/or sport psychologists) could promote educational coping programmes and athlete-centred strategies such as clinical counselling and reflective practice training (Fletcher *et al.*, 2006; Hanton *et al.*, 2007) designed to ensure that athletes are better able to deal with future stressors.

CONCLUSION

The objective of this chapter was to illustrate the value of psychological knowledge to coaches by providing a theoretical context for its application. While this opportunity precludes us from covering as wide a range of topics as might be considered in a sport psychology text, in focusing on the three areas of motivation – confidence, stress and anxiety – we have tried to consider the types of knowledge that coaches might most readily draw upon in their dealings with athletes. Although the three areas we have considered use different literature bases, a number of common messages are evident that can assist coaches in their attempts to create a more adaptive psychological environment for their athletes. In terms of motivation, helping athletes to satisfy the fundamental psychological needs of autonomy, competence and relatedness can be achieved through, for example, giving athletes control over decisions, allowing them to experience success in both training and competition (perhaps through effective self-referenced goals), and promoting a sense of 'teamness' or support from those they train with. Similarly, for developing confidence, strategies might include providing opportunities for achievement through setting and achieving personal goals, focusing on controllable 'sources' of confidence, and the adoption of a collaborative leadership style, where athletes perceive some flexibility and control, and a belief that resources are available to facilitate their achievement. Further, for coaches seeking to support athletes suffering from negative emotions (such as anxiety), it is important for coaches to appreciate the broader stress process, and help athletes appraise the stressors that exist in both competition performance and the organisational culture in a more positive light. This can be achieved by recognising previous success, making a stronger link between training and competition, and through the use of self-referenced goals that promote a focus on individual performer's roles and responsibilities. Finally, a pervasive message to coaches seeking to create an environment supportive of optimal athlete performance is that, whatever the issues that arise, consideration must to be given to athletes' (often) changing perceptions of task demands and their individual differences in psychological make-up.

DISCUSSION TOPICS AND REVIEW QUESTIONS

1   What is intrinsic motivation and why is it important for coaches to promote this within athletes?
2   Describe a number of strategies for both team and individual performers to promote the fundamental psychological needs of autonomy, competence and relatedness.
3   Describe the key differences identified between the sources of sport-confidence in Vealey and Chase's (2008) model and the work of Hays *et al.* (2007). Consider how these differences impact on the strategies coaches can use to build the confidence of non-elite and elite performers.
4   With illustrative examples, describe how sport-confidence has become conceptualised as a multidimensional phenomenon.
5   Why is it important to consider more than just the intensity of anxiety symptoms when working with an athlete?
6   What is CMR theory, and how can an understanding of this help the coach to support an athlete suffering from performance anxiety?
7   Identify and justify three basic psychological strategies that can help, (a) support athlete motivation, (b) facilitate athlete confidence, and (c) manage competitive anxiety.

Web Resources

www.appliedsportpsych.org/

The Association of Applied Sport Psychology is an organisation whose objective is to extend theory and research into the field, and to educate coaches, athletes, parents, exercisers, fitness professionals and athletic trainers about the psychological aspects of their sport or activity. This website is a useful resource to help readers understand the profession of sport psychology, in addition to accessing valuable resource materials.

www.athleticinsight.com

Athletic insight is an online journal that contains valuable resources which include research articles on sport psychology, links to recommended texts, conference information and other services.

www.sportpsychology.com

This website provides a portal to the field of sport psychology designed to help both athletes and practitioners (coaches) achieve peak performance.

PART III

CHAPTER 5

SOCIOLOGY FOR COACHES

NIC MATTHEWS, SCOTT FLEMING AND ROBYN L. JONES

We work in an environment which involves us continually managing interactions with people. In this respect social knowledge is absolutely essential.

Chris Davey, Wales Rugby Union U21 coach (1997–2006);
Grand Slam winner (1999, 2003, 2005)

INTRODUCTION

Over 20 years ago Jarvie (1990a) argued for the application of sociology to the experiences of the sport practitioner. It was proposed that any critical examination of participants in sport should acknowledge the impact that an array of social factors might have on those experiences. If we interpret 'participants' in an inclusive way, this suggests that any exploration of the experiences of the athletes, officials, administrators, spectators, volunteers or other stake-holders should be framed by an understanding of the social settings in which those sporting endeavours take place. Subsequently, Potrac and Jones (1999), and later Jones (2000), argued explicitly for the salience of sociology to the education and continued professional development of coaches. The case set out was one which located sport practices within their wider societal contexts.

A good coach must recognise how individual differences such as gender, ethnicity, socio-economic status, sexuality, (dis)ability and age (amongst others) can shape the athlete as a person and as a performer[1]. More recently, the case for sociology being a useful part of a coach's education and professional 'armoury' has developed to include a more refined theoretical position (e.g. Jones *et al.*, 2002) whilst also being supported directly by empirical studies (Cushion and Jones, 2006; Jones *et al.*, 2004). Furthermore, Purdy (2006) examined the power-laden coach–athlete relationship while others have offered insight into the 'micro-politics' of coaches operating within club structures (Potrac and Jones, 2009a, 2009b). From these (and other) investigations, it is clear that coaching practice has come to be increasingly recognised as a 'complex and dynamic social endeavour' (Potrac *et al.*, 2007: p. 35). This growing body of literature suggests that the many interactions between coaches, players, club committee members and other interested parties, all combine to shape the climate within which individual athletes train and perform. A coach must, therefore, recognise that his or her practice is influenced by social processes as much as by their own skills, competences and personal coaching philosophies (Cushion, 2007).

Despite this volume of work in which the case for a sociological perspective to critique coaching practice has been asserted, it is evident that more can still be done to promote its role in coach education. Potrac *et al.* (2007) highlighted the case of English football (soccer) and the absence of literature examining the practices of professional coaches working within it. They argued that the subculture of this community has discouraged 'scientific research, innovation and scrutiny' (p. 34), despite its governing body, the Football Association, acknowledging that coach education needs to be improved through a more scholarly *modus operandi*. It is true, of course, that coach education programmes across many sports do increasingly provide coaches with an awareness of how social issues manifest within sports environments (child protection being a case in point). However, recognition of how coaches might understand, and then navigate their way through, some of the more intangible aspects of their work environments (e.g. social networks and organisational cultures) remain conspicuous by their absence. It is precisely in these situations, when coaches have to deal with structural constraints and institutional dynamics, that *some* appreciation of sociology and social processes is valuable. Equally, understanding how individual differences might influence athletes' experiences of sporting environments and contests might support a coach's dealings with those individuals.

The aim of this chapter is to further clarify the relevance of sociology and the related notion of sociological competence to coaches, whilst also suggesting ways in which coaches can better develop such competence. Following a brief definition of sociology, and in particular the ongoing debate surrounding the influence of agency (i.e. a person's free will) and social structures (i.e. education, family, etc.) on behaviour, a general case for how sociological knowledge can help coaches is presented. This, in turn, is followed by a discussion of both macro- and micro-sociological perspectives with, again, their particular relevance for coaches being outlined. Finally, a conclusion will look to the future place of sociology in coach education.

70

WHAT IS SOCIOLOGY?

Coach education programmes are intended to raise standards in coaching practice. Many have attempted to do so through reliance on the traditional sport science disciplines of physiology, psychology and biomechanics. What has been harder to 'sell' in this respect has been the case for the incorporation of sociology into such programmes. We begin this section by establishing what sociology is about, as only then can a persuasive case be made for its inclusion in the coach's 'armoury'.

Charles Lemert (1997) proposed that individuals have no good reason to think about such an abstract concept as society. Indeed, most of us already have enough common sense of what goes on in the social world; otherwise we could never survive within it. Such sense refers to our personal sociologies; that is, our knowledge of how to manage our lives in terms of our interactions with others. Sociology then, refers to our understanding of how we live with others, thus comprising a society. Similarly, social life works because most people exercise their sociological competence – the practical, seemingly ever-present capacity to sustain social relations. For Lemert (1997), everyday tasks such as greeting strangers, or even asking for a Big Mac without fries, all entail exercising one's sociological competence. Such situations require social rules be adhered to in order that we achieve the desired outcome. Most people, however, take such knowledge for granted (i.e. they utilise their common sense). Hence, they are unwilling or unable to understand and articulate the complex social relations and interactions that affect them. The challenge for sociologists, then, is to make explicit the link between personal (individual) and public (social) issues. The ability to do this was referred to by C. Wright Mills (1959) as the 'sociological imagination' – a theme to which we will return later. The value of sociological knowledge, therefore, is to increase social competence, that is, to better understand why we behave in the ways we do. This involves developing an understanding of the social structures through which power and influence are exercised (Jones, 2000). Indeed, an explanation of power and the ways it is manifest is central to the sociological enterprise, which seeks to examine the tensions between an individual's free will (agency) and the social forces which affect that will (structure).

Within sociology, there exists ongoing debate between different schools of thought. There are those who consider that a person's behaviour is shaped principally through the influence of social forces, such as ethnicity, gender, sexuality, (dis)ability, the family, social class, and so on. Such theorists favour a structural explanation of action. Alternatively, other scholars prefer to emphasise the importance of an individual's agency in determining behaviour. However, many, of course, acknowledge individuals are who they are partly because of what they do with what they have, *and* partly because of the challenges and opportunities which the wider social context presents (Lemert, 1997). These differing approaches offer coaches contrasting perspectives on their work environment and their relations with those around them.

SO HOW CAN SOCIOLOGY HELP COACHES?

Defining sociology and illustrating the notion of sociological competence is one thing, demonstrating their application to coaching practice is quite a different challenge. In proposing a framework for a social analysis of coaching, Jones *et al.* (2002) suggested that the concepts of role, interaction and power might be useful starting points. These, they argued, hold the particular benefits of locating coaching practice within cultural contexts and help to recognise the influence that individual experiences and personal philosophies might have on the coaching process. The argument for a social analysis is further underpinned by what coaches themselves say (and have said) about the nature of their job.

Contemporary literature suggests many elite coaches consider their work to have a social dimension (Jones *et al.*, 2004; Potrac *et al.*, 2002). Central to these discussions are coach–athlete and coach–coach relationships – that is, the establishing and maintaining of the respect of athletes and peers, and ensuring individuals 'buy into' the coaching regime. Given the potential complexity of relationships in general, it is a tall order to identify and evidence the myriad of social factors which might influence the rapport between coaches and performers. Nevertheless, sociology offers a lens through which to assess these interactions. Such characterisations of the coach–athlete relationship reflect the micro-politics set out by Potrac and Jones (2009a), and bring into focus the need for coaches to develop their sociological competence. They must find ways to manage the 'inexact science' of dealing with social beings, who are also seeking to achieve their own personal and professional goals. A social tightrope, then, often needs to be walked by coaches as they navigate through some very choppy social waters. Within this contextualisation, the value of sociology and of developing coaches' sociological competence becomes increasingly clear. Coaching practice involves managing relationships and fostering appropriate social environments to achieve the desired ends – which are often getting others to do what you want them to when maybe they don't want to do it. The following section makes this case for sociology in greater detail through the exploration of both macro- and micro-sociological approaches, each of which has merits as part of a coach's education.

MACRO-SOCIOLOGY: HELPING COACHES UNDERSTAND THEIR SOCIAL CONTEXT

Macro-sociology is concerned with the systematic study of societies through an examination of human behaviour and interactions within the contexts and social institutions in which they occur. Typically, macro-sociologists focus on particular aspects or institutions of society, for example, government, education, media, religion and work. Sporting practices are also subject to scrutiny as social constructions. Sociologists challenge us to critique the organisation and structure of sport, and the implications for the experiences of participants. Consideration is given to the deployment of resources and power within sports and the impact on relations between administrators, coaches, parents, athletes and others (Coakley and Pike, 2009).

Macro-sociologists are interested in the social structures that mould the experiences of individuals and, as alluded to in the introduction, there are contrasting explanations for how such structures shape these life-chances. For example, some consider structure to create consensus in society, thus adopting a functional approach (i.e. they seek to understand how different groups and organisations contribute to the smooth operation of society). Meanwhile, there are others who are concerned with conflict, and see the social order as characterised by hierarchy and inequality (i.e. they seek to demonstrate how power is used to retain divisions between social groups). Whilst these interpretations suggest a polarised set of opinions, there are, inevitably, further sub-divisions of social theory (for a further discussion of these and their application to sport, see Giulianotti, 2004; Jarvie, 2006; Jarvie and Maguire, 1994). Given the potentially bewildering array of ways to view the social world, there is a danger that the merits of conducting a sociological analysis are lost, as practitioners attempt to get to grips with the language that accompanies each theoretical perspective. In order to counter this, it is important to illustrate what macro-sociology can contribute to the coach's understanding of sporting practices, and how social issues manifest themselves in sporting contexts.

Almost fifty years ago, Peter Berger (1963)[2] wrote about what he called the sociological perspective. Subsequently, John Macionis (2007) identified three main features of this perspective: (i) seeing the general in the particular; (ii) seeing the strange in the familiar; and (iii) seeing personal choice in social context. We now consider each of these in turn.

First, it is generally acknowledged that sociologists often attempt to see the general in the particular. That is to say, they seek to establish patterns in human behaviour based on an understanding of particular people. In a study of South Asian youth, one of our authors (Fleming, 1995) spent time in an inner-city secondary school in London, and as an assistant coach in some neighbouring sports clubs. The purpose of the study was to gain a better understanding of one group's experiences of sport. It was not claimed that this understanding would apply to all South Asian youth, not even to all South Asian youth in London. Rather, the context and circumstances of the school were described and, based on this evidence, inferences and implications were drawn about similar schools in similar kinds of places.

Indeed, the exploration of race and ethnicity in British sport plainly illustrates this more general approach. From Cashmore's (1982) work based on elite sportsmen, through a series of edited collections by Jarvie (1991), Carrington and McDonald (2001) and Long and Spracklen (2011), the effects of ethnicity and racism on sportspersons are clearly highlighted. These examples all illustrate, to some extent at least, the ways in which macro-sociological analyses are derived from empirical research, and how an understanding of particular instances or evidence is generalised more widely.

Second, macro-sociologists often look for the strange in the familiar. Rather than accepting experiences that are routine in our lives and the lives of others, such sociologists question those things that are sometimes taken for granted. They often start from the understanding that things are not always what they seem. Recent sociological enquiry into some of the abusive practices that exist in sport illustrates this. Whilst many of us are advocates of the benefits of participation in sport, this is not the experience of all. There is now a body of literature that has examined the attitude of voluntary-sector clubs to child protection (Brackenridge, 2002), the media representation of sexual abuse in sport (Brackenridge et al., 2008), the development of child protection in England in the wake of high profile cases of abuse in swimming and equestrian sports (Brackenridge, 2004), and coaches' responses to increased scrutiny of their practices in light of concerns over sexual exploitation in sport (Bringer et al., 2006). Fasting and Brackenridge (2009) make the case explicitly that training on issues associated with sexual harassment are often, 'either missing from coach education programmes altogether or subsumed within broader themes such as (gender) equity and diversity management' (pp. 30–31). This is the less familiar face of sport; the 'strange' face of sport, and some coaches (albeit a small number) are implicated. Some have even been prosecuted and convicted of criminal offences.

As familiar as sport itself, is the broadcast media coverage of sport. This might seem to be merely a matter of presenting the sports action and offering punditry. However, as Garry Whannel (1992, 2008) has demonstrated, it is much more complicated than that, and involves particular representations of institutions, ideologies and social roles. For example, the way women's sport and sports-women are treated by the print, broadcast and electronic media often betrays a marginalised and trivialised status for female athletes, not to mention their objectification and sexualisation (Hargreaves, 1994). This has done little to challenge the social construction of sport as a (predominately) masculine domain, or broader notions of gendered identities within society. Equally, this means that prospective male athletes are confronted with particular images of masculinity. This can present challenges for young elite athletes in an era characterised by an interest in celebrity and conspicuous consumption (Whannel, 2002). Furthermore, some observers have reflected how a handful of celebrity 'metrosexual' athletes are transforming the image of the male athlete, notwithstanding a continuing concern over 'jock culture' and some of its more destructive behaviours (Coad, 2008).

Farooq and Parker (2009) examined alternative constructions of masculinities in their discussion of the role that sport, physical activity and Islam played in the lives of young, male Muslims in an independent school. Such examples illustrate the way that macro-sociologists look beyond the obvious, seek alternative (often critical) perspectives, and deploy their own sociological imagination by examining afresh those everyday features (of sport) that are often taken for granted. One can only speculate what sociologists thought of the all-male shortlist for the 2011 BBC *Sports Personality of the Year*. With the shortlist voting rights in the hands of a select group of sports editors, some will undoubtedly want to examine the gender balance of these editors, in addition to coverage of both men's and women's sport in their respective publications.

Third, macro-sociologists see personal choice in social context. They are interested in how society and societal factors shape the choices individuals make. For example, Ken Roberts' (2004) analysis of General Household Survey data shows the ways in which social class within British society continues to shape participation levels. The higher socio-economic strata participate more, and the reasons for the skew are straightforward: 'the better-off are the most likely to possess the transport, equipment, interest, skills and social networks that allow them to take advantage [of the opportunities available]' (p. 50). These observations reflect Sport England figures from the late 1990s, as discussed by Collins (2008b) in his overview of social exclusion from sport. Here, it was found that 40 per cent of adults from a professional background visited sport and leisure centres (double the proportion that did in the 1960s). In contrast, visits by unskilled adults only rose from 7 to 8 per cent over the same period. These differential participation rates are subject to scrutiny through annual monitoring by the *Active People Survey*, while those charged with increasing participation (including coaches) should consider their response to such figures carefully.

The challenge remains, however, to show how this sociological knowledge might inform coaching practice. In *The sociological imagination*, Wright Mills (1959) noted the importance of history and biography and the relations between the two. As Knuttila (1996) elaborates, each of us has an individual life story being situated in, and shaped by, a particular socio-historical context. In short, humankind displays astonishing social diversity, and it is important (even essential) for coaches to recognise this diversity in their interactions with athletes. Hence, although it is common practice to acknowledge that children are not merely mini-adults, and are not treated as such by coaches, other aspects of social diversity need to be similarly identified and accommodated with the same understanding.

In addition, Wright Mills (1959: 14) noted the connection between personal troubles and public issues, 'an essential tool of the sociological imagination and a feature of all classic work in social science'. Thus, when *one* aspiring young athlete living in a rural area is unable to access high quality coaching because of geographical remoteness, that is a regrettable personal trouble. If however, *many* (perhaps even *all*) aspiring young athletes living in rural areas encounter the same difficulty, that is then a public issue of social structure, and needs to be tackled on a societal level (see Jarvie, 1990b).

MICRO-SOCIOLOGY: HOW MIGHT IT HELP COACHES?

Micro-sociology is concerned with face-to-face interaction (Powers, 2004). Consequently, rather than emphasising the influence of social structures on the experiences, behaviours and life-chances of people, such a perspective focuses on the behaviour of individuals usually in response to the behaviour of others (Marsh *et al.*, 1996). It is often associated with theories such as social and symbolic interactionism, which examine how people understand one another, 'interpret what is going on around them and choose to behave in particular ways' (Marsh *et al.*, 1996: p. 71).

Recent work utilising this approach has recently been carried out into the coaching context (e.g. Cushion and Jones, 2006; Potrac *et al.*, 2002). This has been done from both the perspective of coaches (Jones *et al.*, 2003; Purdy, 2006) and athletes (Jones *et al.*, 2005; Purdy, 2006). A common theme that has developed throughout this work relates to the social complexity of coaching; that there is no 'one-size-fits-all' magic formula of how to coach. Rather, both coaches and athletes have to work hard at establishing respectful relationships where each party is aware of what the other requires and is willing to fulfil that need. Naturally, each relationship requires different levels of investment and 'return', often highlighting the exchange nature of the interaction.

This knowledge can help coaches in a number of ways. The findings from one particular piece of research are drawn upon to illustrate them. Here, a study by

Jones *et al.* (2005) focused on the experiences of a former elite swimmer, Anne (a pseudonym), whose career was interrupted and finally terminated by an eating disorder. The aim was to explore how the interaction Anne had with her coach not only led her to develop a strong but brittle swimming identity, but also how that identity was broken, leading to the onset of *bulimia nervosa*. The story begins in earnest when a new coach arrived at Anne's swimming club. In her own words:

> My new coach promised exciting things and had a lot of new ideas and philosophies. He showed a lot of enthusiasm about my potential, so I took a lot of effort to please him. I was constantly encouraged by him as he seemed to have big plans for me. I wanted to do so well for him.

Through their initial interaction, a strong bond was soon established between Anne and her coach as she 'bought in' to his ideas, knowledge and methods without question. Her self-identity and self-esteem became increasingly centred, not on the social person she was, but on how well she swam. Consequently, her times and perhaps more importantly, what the coach thought and said regarding them, really mattered.

Then came what Anne termed 'the meeting', which was intended to bring swimmer, coach and parents together to discuss progress, future goals and ways of achieving them.

> He [the coach] told me that I was doing well, that I was showing progress with my swimming . . . but then he said 'it would probably be more beneficial if you were lighter and slimmer and could lose a bit of weight'. It just shot me down completely. And I remember feeling so embarrassed, in front of my parents and all. I came away feeling really down. My body was [now] the problem. I was judged by my body shape not just how well I could do in the pool. It [my body] became the focus and I became very conscious of it.

The comment sparked a downward spiral for Anne, as she became increasingly obsessed by her body image. Consequently, what she ate and the amount of exercise she took became fixations for her. Eventually, she was diagnosed with *bulimia nervosa*, a condition with which she continued to struggle.

Although it would be a gross oversimplification to attribute Anne's eating disorder to a single utterance by her coach, neither should we ignore the coach's comment as unimportant either. This is because, in many ways, it was (and remains) reflective of a general coaching culture driven by measurable times, appearance and weight. Undoubtedly, Anne was vulnerable to such criticism, a vulnerability created in large part by the heavy reliance on her identity as a swimmer, and upon her coach as an important person in creating that identity. What the coach said and did, then, had come to matter so much to Anne that it left her exposed and defenceless to the negativity expressed by him about her weight and appearance. Having sacrificed other aspects of the person she was, she had nothing to resist it with. This position is supported by previous research on disordered eating in female athletes which concluded that pressure from coaches was an influential factor in the onset of such illnesses (Griffin and Harris, 1996; Patel *et al.*, 2003).

What can be learned from Anne's story? Principally, that coaches exercise a great deal of power over their athletes. Fed by the dominant language of measurable and observable performance, many coaches, albeit subconsciously, tend to treat athletes like machines to be trained and monitored. In turn, athletes, viewing coaches as knowledgeable experts, often 'buy in' to the latter's wishes and demands without question. This is not to say that a hierarchical relationship between coach and athlete is always a problem; rather, it means that coaches should take great care when interacting with athletes, thus better respecting the elevated position they hold. Given that human relationships lie at the heart of sociology, a micro-sociological analysis can help in accurately describing and explaining such and similar situations, making both coaches and athletes question why they act in the ways they do. It can do so both by highlighting the external factors that influence behaviour (in this instance, the dominant role occupied by the coach in influencing athletes' self-perceptions) and the decisions coaches are able to take within such malleable boundaries. In considering the consequences of his or her words and actions, the development of a coach's sociological competence, then, would appear to be vital.

As touched upon earlier, this was further emphasised in recent work (e.g. Potrac and Jones, 2009a, 2009b) on the micro-politics of coaching. Here, coaches' actions were posited as socially strategic, in that they were constantly forging and re-forging alliances with relevant contextual stakeholders (e.g. athletes, assistant coaches, managers) to secure their objectives. In the words of the authors, the value of such work not only 'relates to uncovering the contextual social rules that underpin action', but also 'the norms that bound such actions and how they can be overcome' (2009a: 233). This latter point is most important within the realm of micro-sociology; that is, although acknowledging the power of social structures to influence behaviour, it gives room for individuals to obey, transgress and/or resist such rules in the quest for personal objectives. People, then, are not judged simply as cultural dupes, but more emphasis is given to agency, albeit within certain social boundaries. In this respect, it builds on earlier work which used the writings of the sociologist Erving Goffman to explain coaches' actions. Here, coaches were considered to put on

78

a certain 'front', related to being expert, authoritative and somewhat caring, all in order to generate athletes' respect (e.g. Jones, 2006b; Jones *et al.*, 2004; Potrac *et al.*, 2002). The focus here was on coaches' face-to-face micro-interactions, as they tried to manipulate relationships and contexts to secure desired ends.

CONCLUSION

The chapter started by asserting that as social phenomena, sporting experiences should be examined with reference to their societal context. Turner and Nelson (2009) concur, arguing that coach education should recognise that a coach is an 'educator,' and that coaching is 'an intellectual endeavour requiring practitioners who are capable of engaging in complex socio-cultural processes' (p. 5). Sociology can offer coaches a different lens through which to reflect critically on their work with athletes and others. The sociological perspective, then, can encourage engagement with challenging questions that will make coaches more considered and insightful practitioners. Indeed, by adopting Berger's (1963) sociological perspective and seeking to see the general in the particular, the strange in the familiar, and personal choice in social context, coaches can engage actively in understanding the social processes involved in coaching, the athletes they coach and the organisations (i.e. clubs and governing bodies) they work within. Similarly, by drawing the distinction between personal troubles and public issues, as Wright Mills (1959) encourages us to do, matters of social structure can be questioned in a meaningful way, and ways of acting individually in the quest for coaching excellence can be better explored.

Coaches and athletes both produce, and are products of, their own history and biographies (Wright Mills, 1959). In this respect, they are creations of their experiences. There are factors that characterise the socio-historical context in which coaching occurs – age, socio-economic status, (dis)ability, ethnicity, gender and sexuality amongst them. The importance of these individual differences varies; whilst one person may have her or his experiences affected most by disability, for another, sexuality might be the key factor. Furthermore, these variables do not operate in isolation, rather they intersect in ways that account for social difference in much more nuanced ways. Yet, by acknowledging and embracing the importance of personal histories and biographies (including their own), coaches can understand athletes better, and interact with them more effectively. Such engagement enables coaches to think about each athlete, even in team sports, as an individual with different wants and needs. This is not to say that each athlete should be treated so individualistically that no coherent pattern of behaviour emerges from coaches, as this leaves the door open to accusations of inconsistency, or worse, favouritism. Rather, it can make coaches better aware of the consequences of their behaviour, encouraging them to reflect on the best course of action. Finally, embracing sociological concepts also allows coaches to develop a deeper appreciation of the power they hold in relation to athletes and how it can be best utilised to the benefit of all.

DISCUSSION TOPICS AND REVIEW QUESTIONS

1 How can the study of micro- and macro-sociology help coaches in their practice?
2 Sociology is the 'invisible ingredient' in coaches' knowledge (Potrac and Jones, 1999). Discuss.
3 How can a 'sociological imagination' (Wright Mills, 1959) and taking a 'sociological perspective' (Berger, 1963) help sports coaches?
4 How important is it for coaches to understand social context in order to have productive interactions with athletes (and other stakeholders)? What are some of the factors that need to be considered here?

Web Resources

http://physed.otago.ac.nz/sosol/v2i1/v2i1.htm

This website contains an archived special edition of the journal *Sociology of Sport Online* dedicated to the sociology of coaching.

http://www.nasss.org/

This is the website for the North American Society for the Sociology of Sport (NASSS). Although rarely does it specifically address coaching, NASSS exists to promote, stimulate and encourage the sociological study of play, games, sport and contemporary physical culture.

http://www.britsoc.co.uk/

This is the website for the British Sociological Association, an organisation that promotes sociology, 'supports sociologists, and is the public face of sociology in Britain'.

NOTES

1 Indeed, in an attempt to move towards equal opportunities in the workplace and in wider society, the recent Equality Act in the UK (Home Office, 2010) makes unlawful

the unfair treatment of persons on the grounds of age, disability, gender reassignment, marriage and civil partnership, pregnancy and maternity, 'race', religion or belief, sex, and sexual orientation.

2 As with Wright Mills' (1959) *The sociological imagination*, Berger's (1963) *Invitation to sociology* may seem rather dated, especially when contrasted with the rapid and recent theoretical advances made in other coaching sciences disciplines (e.g. psychology). However, the works by Mills and Berger are examples of 'classic' theoretical contributions to sociology that have not lost their 'currency', even with the passing of time.

CHAPTER 6

HISTORY FOR COACHES

MALCOLM MACLEAN AND IAN PRITCHARD

Knowing the historical and cultural baggage a sport carries with it is vital if you are to succeed as a coach. You have to know where your athletes are 'coming from' in addition to the boundaries you're working within and what's expected of you.

Lyn Davies, former Olympic Gold medallist and
current President of UK Athletics

INTRODUCTION

In the middle of the afternoon of Saturday 25 July 1981, Rob Louw joined other Springboks in the stand at Hamilton's Rugby Park for the second match of his team's tumultuous tour of New Zealand. The team did not play that day – several hundred anti-apartheid protestors broke through the park's fences and occupied the centre of the field. After over an hour of negotiation, when several thousand angry rugby fans surrounded a few hundred protestors, with a police force not sufficient for an orderly clearance of the occupying group, the match was cancelled: some of the protestors seemed lucky to survive the day and many were badly injured by the fans. Louw later noted that he

> could see the different faces among the demonstrators. At one stage I noticed a communist banner and a religious banner side by side. Amongst the demonstrators were anarchist trouble makers who knew and cared very little about South Africa. There were also highly principled people who believed that it was right to stop the tour at any cost. Together they made a highly formidable force.
>
> (Louw, 1987: 90)

Louw's response to the protest found a different voice in South Africa, which had only had television since 1976. The images on South Africa's televisions that morning were at odds with the received views of the white minority there, that the protests were led, initiated and peopled by *skollies* (hoodlums).

The shock experienced in South Africa was partly due to the debunking of such propaganda myths, but a more significant factor was rooted in events 25 years earlier, when Waikato had humiliated the visiting 1956 Springboks by beating them 14–10. Despite a victory over a weak Waikato team in the lacklustre 1965 tour of New Zealand, the 1981 tour was the Springboks' chance for revenge, as Waikato had regained its former standing. Instead of an emotionally vital match in a key rugby tour, an anti-apartheid message was broadcast directly into a vast number of South African homes and clubs from the most important rugby nation still hosting South African teams. Understanding the history of sport, the history of rugby and its place in the white colonies of settlement, the history of New Zealand–South Africa sporting relations, and the history of the international campaign against apartheid, are all vital in making sense of this one moment. This was an event of sporting history that requires a hard-nosed grasp of the past. Such a sense of history is more challenging and demanding than an all-too-common view of sport's past often determined by present concern rather than previous realities; a perception shaped by nostalgia and dominated by middle-class, imperialist views of a positive sports ethic.

This chapter has two aims. The first is to explore the historical processes that underpin the status of the sports coach and, with it, the identities so often linked to sport and its performances. The second is to sketch the meaning and type of history that coaches must grasp to deal effectively with identity-related sport performances, while also outlining some of the key gaps in historical scholarship. This chapter, therefore, draws together the fluctuating status of the sports coach and the emergence of sport-related identities to consider the effects such identities may have on coaches, particularly those involved in 'national' sports. In doing so, the role of the sports coach in history is first examined. This is followed by a discussion of history and national identity and, in particular, the role of the sports coach within it. The penultimate section is a brief examination of how 'doing history' can have an effect on our understandings of both the past and the present. Finally, a conclusion draws together the principal points highlighted. The value of the chapter lies in making explicit the impacts of the past on the social expectations to which coaches are subject. Such knowledge is important as it can make coaches aware of the boundaries within which they work and the pressures they face, so that they can manage them better.

THE SPORTS COACH IN HISTORY

The recent professionalisation of coaching is part of a long set of changes in coaching's status. However, it is not the logical or only possible outcome of those changes, and was certainly not the goal when those we now label as coaches first appeared in sport. In historians' terminology, this professionalisation is contingent on, but not necessarily intended by, what went before. The earliest sports to be codified – that is, for their agreed rules to be formally recorded (for example, horseracing, cricket, boxing and golf) – were technically complex enough to require formalised skill learning procedures. However, although aristocratic patronage and the prospective financial gains resulting from gambling meant that individuals organising these sporting activities were willing to pay for expert tuition, those involved as instructors were of a lower social status than their wealthy patrons. These conditions resulted in a public perception of the coach as little more than a semi-skilled artisan, who, in this sense, was little different from any others who earned their livings from sport.

The first half of the nineteenth century saw a prolonged cultural struggle in Britain between this commercialised sporting culture and the emerging middle class, with its code of moral respectability and adherence to the amateur ethos, resulting in further cultural belittling of the sports coach. The rapid industrialisation that began in Britain in the mid-eighteenth century, had created a growing and increasingly affluent socially-ambitious middle class. Parts of this new class educated their sons within the public school system, where its masculinist and elitist code served the interests of the aristocracy and its upper-class allies to secure their social status as part of an enlarged ruling elite. At this time, there also emerged a new group of public school headmasters who shared an outlook that better management of all aspects of school life would improve the moral, spiritual and academic development of their charges. These headmasters and the demands and concerns of the fee-paying middle-class, produced a revived English public school system where many of its value-laden moral and ethical imperatives were embodied in games.

As various groups of public school old boys sought to continue competition, there emerged another wave of sports codification during the second half of the nineteenth century (Chandler, 1991). This development propagated a value system within public school sports that demanded both a strict adherence to an amateur ethos and, despite the seriousness with which these activities were taken, a relaxed 'devil-may-care' attitude of not being seen to try too hard, which excluded both practice and training. This fusion of moral earnestness, feigned physical laziness and class-based superiority, all characteristics of the 'Cult of Athleticism', stigmatised sports coaches and undermined organised coaching structures in Britain for the best part of a century. The result was that coaching was seen as an undesirable combination of professionalism and working-class earnestness, both of which were concerned primarily with winning.

Many working-class athletes were still willing, or needed, to earn 'a spare bob or two' from activities outside work. In sport, this clashed with the middle-class amateurist ideal. Despite the social class divide in British sport, the middle-class cultural hangover concerning sports' values and morals lingered through the twentieth century. This was evident even in those activities that attracted the greatest level of working-class involvement and interest, such as association football, which resisted organised skill learning and tactical applications until well after the Second World War. In most cases, association football clubs maintained a management and coaching structure based upon and rooted in amateurist ideals: they employed an administrator-secretary, but formalised skill learning was *ad hoc*, unorganised, and remained the responsibility of the senior players. This restricted opportunities to coach, even for those with the inclination to do so. Although in the 1930s, Herbert Chapman (initially at Huddersfield FC and then more prominently at Arsenal FC) and others like him began to change this situation, recognised manager-coaches did not appear until after the Second World War. Even then, Walter Winterbottom, who became English football's first national coach in 1946, was both team manger and FA director of coaching for 16 years without ever selecting any of the players in his teams! In sports dominated either by a middle-class value system or by middle-class administrators, resistance to any form of team management, coaching or tactical development, outside of that provided by the team captain and senior players, remained embedded until much later. For example, the Welsh Rugby Union only appointed David Nash as its first national coach in 1967 (Morgan and Fleming, 2003); even then, the Welsh RFU was criticised by the other 'home' unions until into the 1970s. In the home of contemporary codified sport – the UK – the period that saw its rapid emergence and establishment as a major cultural institution was marked by the marginalisation and often vilification of tactical development and formalised skill learning (that is, coaching) because of class-based myths associated with the idea of a British 'national character'.

These contradictions within modern formalised coaching were not the same worldwide. Whereas in Britain, training and coaching during the later nineteenth and early twentieth century was associated with working-class sports, in North America, a more complex relationship emerged. In both the United States and Canada, there was a class-based amateurist rejection of coaching similar to that seen in Britain. There were, however, significant differences. The financial benefits of college sport and the commercial basis of sports leagues increased the need for a team to have some comparative advantage over its rivals; hence, the cult of the 'self-made man' contributed to the respectability of the professional athlete in these consumer-based spectator sports. In the case of college sport, this

86

advantage became an important element in boosting an institution's profile, attracting students, increasing income and enhancing alumni (former students') contributions.

Despite the class differences between college and professional league sports, the imperative for advantage was similar: financial security. In North America, leagues tended to be centrally organised by sporting bureaucrats whose primary interest was the economic security or profitability of the league rather than any moral imperative. Such leagues (more than often) had closed membership, thus making members dependent on one another for financial security. For the most part, there was no promotion and relegation, with leagues governed by commercial considerations where a club owner or franchise holder ensured their own security and that of their respective league. In Britain, however, sports leagues tended to be more amateurist in outlook and practice. For example, the (English) Football League continued until the middle of the twentieth century to be governed by the ethos of a class-linked national character, with commercial considerations being less important (Taylor, 2005). The more complex circumstances of North American leagues meant that as soon as one team sought comparative advantage through, for instance, professional staff to enhance skill development and tactics, others quickly followed. This form of commercial demand where a 'level playing field' was arguably more important for financial than ethical reasons, meant that the development and history of coaching followed a very different path and trajectory from that in Britain, at least for significant components of popular and commercial sport.

After a century of effort to drive out its perceived corrupting influence, the final third of the twentieth century saw British sport institutionalise formal provision for coaching. Four changes in and beyond sport contributed to this shift. First, organisations in Britain recognised not only that sport had become more complex, but that increases in skill levels meant that specialist knowledge was needed beyond that which could be provided by senior players. Second, changes in the commercial structure, particularly of mass spectator professional sports, since the 1960s, meant that individual sports organisations were carrying greater financial risks. Consequently, greater skill development was required to minimise that risk. Third, the structure of British education and vocational training, reflecting a broader cultural shift, changed markedly during this period, with extensive development of, and demand for, more specialist awards, staged qualifications and recognised credentials. Finally, since the early 1990s, there had been a growing concern about issues such as child protection and the abuse (physical, mental and sexual) of athletes by coaches at all levels. Formal systems of coach education and credentialisation became widely seen as one mechanism by which sports organisations could exercise their duty of care to sports participants.

The contemporary coach, then, in a world of centrally regulated, credentialed, stratified and rationalised sport can be seen as working within the limits and logic of contemporary capitalism and a view of sport as entertainment. In many ways, these roots continue to influence how coaches and others view their job. They are, however, not the only limits, as there is an additional set of cultural and social factors that can be seen broadly as identity related. One of the most far-reaching of these is based on assumed national traits and characteristics.

HISTORY AND NATIONAL IDENTITY

The way in which social worlds were organised altered markedly during the nineteenth century. Two factors were crucial in this change: the spread of capitalist economic and social relations, and the development of nation states. The identities related to these emerging nation states were not the same as older local identities, although it is important to remember that identities, be they based in localities, socio-economic relations, gender, ethnicity or any other factor, are social rather than essential. The most important difference between most other forms of social identity and national identities is that 'nation' is much more abstract than locality or most other forms of social identification. There is no chance of an individual knowing or even having met many of the people with whom he or she shares a national identity. Indeed, it is becoming increasingly common for analysts of national identity to accept Benedict Anderson's (2005) case that nations are best understood as 'imagined communities', the members of which assume that there are shared characteristics that give them a common basis for membership.

National identity is one of those things that many people know they have, but have little idea about what it might be in real terms. Definition is even more complex because the English language does not clearly distinguish between a state and a nation. For example, Wales, Catalonia and Chechnya, despite having most of the characteristics of nations and having clearly identifiable national identities, are not states. What is more, these three nations (Wales, Catalonia and Chechnya) are parts of bigger states (United Kingdom, Spain and the Russian Federation) one of which (Russian Federation) is fighting a war to prevent its member nation (Chechnya) becoming a state, while the other two recognise degrees of political autonomy. This means that there is not a simple relationship between states and nations. Consequently, to begin to talk about and explore national identity, we need to have a different way of understanding the two: enter history.

Nationality and national identity can combine with sport to become a powerful social force and a way of defining ourselves and the groups to which we belong

88

(Cronin, 1999). Association football in England is a case in point. Although the Football Association had agreed the rules of football in 1863, by 1871 the FA had barely a dozen members, while the rules it had agreed were still not the only ones by which football was played. For example, the members of the Sheffield Football Association played by slightly different rules, and it was still the case that there were often negotiations over which rules to follow before a game started. Yet, by the end of the 1880s, football had acquired an identifiable set of 'institutional and ritual characteristics' (Hobsbawm, 1983b: 288). The FA Cup competition had been launched, professionalism had been accepted, and the Football League had been formed. Alongside these institutional developments had come a set of primarily masculine working-class rituals – regular attendance at Saturday afternoon matches; the formation of groups of supporters; an annual outing for many to watch the FA Cup Final – while club rivalries were intensifying. Football, then, became distinctive in England because, unlike other sports such as rugby union, it had rapidly acquired a national organisation. Indeed, after 1895, rugby was even less national because of the regional and class division associated with the Northern Union's separation from the Rugby Football Union. As Hobsbawm has noted, sport came to embody national identity because of

the ease with which even the least political or public individuals can identify with the nation as symbolised by young persons excelling at what practically every man wants, or at one time in life has wanted, to be good at. The imagined community of millions seems more real as a team of eleven named people. The individual, even the one who only cheers, becomes a symbol of his nation himself.

(Hobsbawm, 1992: 143)

The effect was that not only was football seen by the English as an English game, it was (and continues to be) seen as such by many others as well. In Denmark, for instance, it is not uncommon to hear football discussed as the English game, even though it has acquired what are held to be Danish characteristics.

These commemorative rituals and similar events that 'flag the homeland' (Billig, 1995) are often seen as traditional. Many of these traditions, however, have been 'invented', in that they can be seen to have emerged at a particular time under specific circumstances. Once again, Hobsbawm allows us a better understanding of this issue. In his analysis, these invented traditions are

taken to mean a set of practices, normally governed by overtly or tacitly accepted rules which seek to inculcate certain values and norms of behaviour by repetition, which automatically implies continuity with the past. In fact, where possible, they normally attempt to establish continuity with a suitable historic past.

(1983a: 1)

Sport is full of invented traditions. Leaving aside the Olympics with its cornucopia or wealth of fabricated truths, one of the most powerful is the notion that in 1823, at Rugby School, William Webb Ellis picked up the ball and ran, thereby inventing rugby football. The claim first appeared in a Rugby School magazine in the 1890s, citing as its source the recollections of a former schoolboy; no earlier source has been located and no evidence provided that it ever happened. The timing is significant: during the 1890s, there was a struggle for control of rugby football between the middle- and upper-class clubs of the South, and the working-class clubs in the North. The clash led to a split in the Rugby Football Union in 1895, and the subsequent creation of the Northern Union that eventually became the Rugby League. To be able to link the formation of the game to an event at a public school allowed the middle- and upper-class clubs to claim to be the authentic representatives of the game's traditions (Collins, 1998, 2009). The reality is very different. Most public schools played their own version of football, only some allowed handling. During November and December 1863, there was a series of meetings organised by what became the Football Association which agreed the rules of football. For several of those meetings, it looked as if handling would be allowed. Subsequently, a number of clubs left the FA to eventually agree, in 1871, rules of a form of football that became known as Rugby Football that allowed handling (Harvey, 2005). This history is well known, yet in the mid 1990s, when launching a World Cup for men's rugby, the International Rugby Board called the trophy the Webb Ellis Trophy and, in doing so, continued to grant legitimacy to the myth of the game's origins.

SPORTS COACHING AND NATIONAL IDENTITY

National identity is a double-edged sword in the context of coaching. An appeal to national identity can enhance access to the best athletes. Paradoxically, this can often be difficult to ensure in the most popular and commercialised sports, which are also the clearest markers or carriers of an ideal of national identity. In the UK, for instance, players and clubs in both football and rugby union are caught between several sets of demands. Playing seasons in recent years have been around ten months long. As the number of national and international club-based competitions has increased, so have international matches. Additionally, clubs have more financial investment in players. The honour of representative sport in some cases, therefore, has come to clash with the commercial demands of professional sport. As a result, there have been a number of intense disputes between national bodies and clubs during the 1990s and 2000s over the availability of, and threat of injury to, international players. A reasonable case can be made in this instance that the bigger the club and the smaller the nation, the more likely it is that the club will come out 'on top', as may be seen in the case of Ryan Giggs balancing the demands of Manchester United and Wales, or many sub-Saharan African footballers in European leagues.

Although these sorts of commercial considerations can, and often do, weaken the positive influence of national identity on coaches in general, there are more beneficial impacts. For instance, when issues related to national identity are clear, and when the sport in question is seen as a marker of national identity, athletes and coaches may find themselves in positions that are culturally central and highly visible. However, this can also result in greater pressure for success that may not be at all positive or beneficial. It is something coaches should be aware of and, accordingly, plan for.

It is often the case that less immediately obvious or direct support is developed in association with national identity markers and alongside certain sports as nationally distinctive. For example, the development in the last quarter of the twentieth century of mass formalised coach education systems is linked to the demands of high performance sport to be internationally competitive. It is increasingly common for coaches to take the blame for team failures, and the complexity of contemporary commercialised elite sport often means that there is more than one team coach. These systems of coach education, linked to a broader sense of the need for specific credentials in a range of occupations, have intensified rapidly. Consequently, in many sports there are now strict limits on who may do what, in that an aspiring coach will require certification by the relevant governing body to work at a specific level. Although there is a debate about whether these formal coach education systems are necessarily a good thing, there is little doubt that their development is, in part, the result of concerns about elite sports performance and comparative competitive standings.

A less obvious effect of the link between national identities and sports is related to popularity and participation rates. Sports that carry with them the weight of national identity tend also to be the most popular with the highest participation rates. In this respect, well supported and popular sports tend to provide more opportunity for full-time employment (for coaches and others), although this is more so for sports traditionally seen as 'men's' than 'women's'. For example, netball, the most widely played 'women's' sport in the UK, has proportionally far fewer opportunities for full-time or paid coaching work than 'men's' sports. Gender disrupts a sense that sport and national identity are linked in an obvious or standard manner (Williams, 2003). Even allowing for this gendered differential, when combined with a system of formal coach education and qualifications, the sport, popularity and national identity dynamic clarifies the mechanisms for coaches upward mobility, and contributes to the growing potential for full-time employment.

As coaches and athletes have discovered over the years, a close association between their sport and national identity is not always a good thing. Indeed, in many cases, this association can have significant negative consequences. As many coaches have found to their cost, in sports heavily invested with a sense of national identity, there is a great and often over-emphasis on success at all levels. Closely related to this heightened emphasis is an exaggerated media focus not only on coaching decisions and skills, but often on all aspects of the coach's life. Consider, for example, the attention paid to Nancy Del'Olio during Sven-Goran Eriksson's time as the coach of the English men's national football team. This media focus can become intrusive to the extent that coaches lose credibility, while their abilities may be affected by the intensive and distracting focus as measured by the team's performance. Coaches may, therefore, suffer as a result of heightened expectations – as can be seen in the cases of successive English national men's rugby coaches after Clive Woodward, and of Graham Henry as coach of the Welsh national men's rugby team. Similarly, 'foreign' coaches often seem to struggle between their own national identity and the one they seem required to adopt or assume.

Some sports (and by implication, coaches) may, therefore, benefit from a close association with a national identity in terms of enhanced support, a greater allocation of resources from the state and other sources, and more secure career structures. These benefits have disadvantages for other sports not so central to national identity. In a context where financial and other resources are limited, such sports can be marginalised not only by the media but also by central and local government, as well as other financial agencies. Sometimes, this is a direct product of the normally close fit between gender and national identity, as seen in the previously cited netball example. More often than not, however, most of us remain unaware of this marginalisation. For example, it is common for migrants to recognise the extent to which the English sports media is dominated by men's football (soccer). This domination often extends to coverage of the semi-professional 'fifth division' Blue Square Conference League at the expense of national and international success in other less popular sports such as gymnastics, hockey, netball and women's football (both association and rugby). In these cases, and many others, the close association between the dominant sports and English national identity means that financial resources are directed elsewhere, undermining professional, commercial and career structures of such sports.

A further, less obvious problem, although one that is becoming more real, is the over formalisation of learning processes leading to an exclusion and/or alienation of both potential and lower level coaches, which may be exacerbated by a perceived dominance of 'foreign' coaches within elite level sport. Many national governing bodies now have a system of coaching awards that apply at all levels of a sport, meaning that a parent who has skills in a specific sport and who may want to coach their child's team (and in doing so, become a sport volunteer and the backbone of mass sport globally) may find themselves obliged or under pressure to study for a coaching qualification. There is, therefore, a risk that high-profile sports success and popularity leading to a formal career structure may end up placing obligations beyond those that such parents consider necessary or possible to undertake. It would be reasonable to assume that this alienates those people willing, happy or wanting to be part of a mass sport experience. Investment in national identity-related factors, then, can actually drive people away from the sport.

The final issue to be discussed here relates to the cultural centrality of a sport and how it can lead to constant over-expectations of success and rapid recrimination upon failure. In recent years, a number of national team coaches have lost their jobs in the wake of perceived failure, which is often a failure to meet expectations. John Hart resigned as All Black coach on the day the team lost to France in the play-off for third place in the 1999 men's Rugby World Cup. This was the lowest placing the team had ever achieved in the competition, a competition they were expected to win. Similarly, late in 2006, Andy Robinson resigned as the England men's rugby coach after a series of losses that matched their worst run ever. This could also be seen as a failure to meet expectations following the World Cup success in 2003, although it could equally be argued that English rugby had merely returned to a level of performance seen through most of the last quarter of the twentieth century.

MAKING SENSE OF THE PAST

A focus on the nation is, however, limiting – very few coaches ever find themselves working at a nationally representative level. Consequently, the issues outlined above need to be considered in a more nuanced manner as being shaped by two sets of issues. The first is the limitations posed by the state of sport-related historical scholarship, and the second by the character of history-the-discipline. Socio-cultural studies in sport, including history, make clear that identities of the kind sketched previously are unstable and shifting. Alongside this problem of keeping up with the shifting terrain of identity, is the issue of the integrity of the nation as a source of identity: in short, there is little that is 'pure' about sport-related national identities. Take, for instance, identities linked to cricket. Mike Marqusee (2005) has shown in his analyses of English cricket that the sport is just as much a sign of national ailment as it is of power, of uncertainty as it is of mission, of crisis as it is a secure sense of nationhood, while for many the game remains a Home Counties vision of village greens and arcadia. In a similar manner, C.L.R. James (1994) paints a picture of West Indies cricket as a complex amalgam of imperial, colonial and anti-colonial forces. James's analysis of West Indies cricket then takes it well beyond straightforward nationalism and a simple sense of a national identity (Ferrall, 2011; MacLean, 2010). These instabilities are intensified by the local conditions that for many coaches may be as, or more, relevant than national ideals and myths.

Local and club identities are likely to be as uneven and contingent as national identities. Making sense of those local identities, therefore, requires close analysis of the local conditions. Take, for example, the different sporting experiences of Cheltenham and Gloucester – neighbouring urban areas. Rugby union has traditionally been seen as a middle-class game centred on South East England. Yet Gloucester, a predominantly working-class city in South West England, has long supported a nationally significant rugby club. Its neighbouring borough, with a town centre fewer than 15km from Gloucester, is Cheltenham, with a more middle-class image although declining comparative wealth since the early twentieth century. It has a rugby club that barely registers at a national level, but a moderately successful lower league professional football club. The sporting profiles of these two areas belie stereotypical understandings. For the most part, British historians have not made much sense of these local identities, unlike their North American counterparts who have produced a number of important urban and other local sporting histories (Hardy, 2003; Reiss, 1991). Still, British urban and local studies have focused on the North of England (for instance, Hill and Williams, 1996; Budd, 2011), while the *Played in Britain* series included a number of essential local investigations, as well as important thematic national studies (notably in this context, Polley, 2011). The key thing that all these studies show is that, despite national images and myths, local historical circumstances and conditions continue to have a vital effect on sports cultures. Without this local historical awareness, coaches are unlikely to be able draw on the subtle factors of identities that may be important in building involvement, loyalty and attachments.

These gaps in historical analysis present practitioners with the significant problem of knowing how to understand the past to help make sense of the present. This can be seen within club histories in particular. Professional and academic sports historians have not paid much attention to either individual sports clubs or clubs in general (Szymanski *et al.*, 2008). This is not to say that a large number of club histories do not exist, but that readers need to be careful about making sense of them. Importantly, many club histories are written as a record of the club – they are what would once have been seen as a chronicle; a

94

record of events rather than a critical interpretation of those events. The distinction is important, because historians would argue that history (the subject) is not the same as the past. This is because history is both more than the past (because we know what happened) and less than the past (because we cannot know everything that happened) (Lowenthal, 1985).

The way historians interpret and make sense of the past is important to consider – and there is a crucial difference between using history to explain how things are now, and to make sense of how things were in the past, which may or may not explain how things are now. For instance, a taken-for-granted assumption in rugby league history is that the split in the Rugby Football Union in 1895, which eventually led to the formation of the rugby league, was primarily over the question of professional players. It was more subtle than that. Rather, the key issue at hand was whether players could be reimbursed for wages lost because of their playing obligations, which is arguably different from paying professionals to play. However, as Collins (1998, 2009) has shown, there was a deeper issue of control of the game at stake, where the Northern clubs, although being the strongest and possessing the most vibrant supporter base, felt excluded from the RFU London-centred political elite. This question of political influence and control gives the split a different meaning. Player payments became a key difference between the two forms of rugby, and the schism which gave birth to the professional form was reconstructed to explain that basic difference. Historical analysis, however, shows that it was not the underlying cause. In the 'taken-for-granted view', the contemporary legacy of the game had become the thing that determined the historical explanation (Hobsbawm, 1983a). Meanwhile, in other cases, that legacy shaping has been influenced by commercial factors, as in the early advertising campaigns after the New Zealand All Blacks rugby union team signed with *adidas* (see, for instance, the *Captains* advertisement at http://www.youtube.com/watch?v=kfKoz0l8ifo&feature=endscreen&NR=1). Sport has a powerful sense of its past, and there is a strong popular attachment to its history. Alongside this, there is also a sense of nostalgia for a golden age and a sense that sport is in a state of decline (MacLean, 2011). As 'users' of the past, it is important that coaches retain a critical sense of how concerns of the present influence our understanding of the past.

CONCLUSION

Coaches work in a world where they need to balance demands as diverse as the nutritional needs of their athletes and the expectations of supporters. A significant factor shaping supporter expectations is the role that the sport in question plays in the particular national identity and its relationship to the myths and traditions of nationhood. This is in addition to the class, gender and ethnic associations of the sport in the context of the nation. A sport central to a sense of national identity will present as many issues to be managed and problems to be controlled as a sport marginal to that sense of national identity, while the significance of that sport may vary according to local social, cultural and historical factors. To make sense of these, coaches need a critical understanding of how the past is understood and invoked in contemporary circumstances. These identity related factors do not only have an impact on the context of sporting action, but on the day-to-day business of team selection, systems of coach education, funding, social and political support, and facilities and sporting infrastructure. In none of these cases is the relationship with national, local or sporting identities (central or marginal) entirely positive or negative; in all cases, however, it is extremely influential, and ignored by coaches at their peril.

DISCUSSION TOPICS AND REVIEW QUESTIONS

1 To what extent do you agree with the argument that the differences in the development of coaching can be linked to the commercial organisation of sport in Britain and North America? Justify your answer.

2 Using scholarly sources and examples, explore whether there is a popular or official sense of a 'golden age' in sport, and if so whether the current era is seen as being in decline. Why is this nostalgia important for coaches to understand, and how might it be used in coaching practice?

3 Analyse the positive and/or negative impact that employing an overseas national coach may have on all levels of any given sport in a country of your choice.

4 Consider how national identity affects a sport you are involved in, in terms of (a) resources available to the sport, (b) that sport's local and national profile, and (c) the experience of your sport in relation to others with a similar number of participants but with a different relation to national identity?

5 What impact has the past had on the relationship between national identity and women's sport in a country of your choice?

Web Resources

LA84 (www.LA84foundation.org) includes in its digital archive and library an extensive set of historical resources including Olympic histories and scholarly journals.

Played in Britain (http://www.playedinbritain.co.uk/) includes a number of important local sports histories, including images of historic sport sites.

Most scholarly sports history societies have their own websites, many of which provide access to important historical material, including:

- The British Society of Sports History (http://www.sportinhistory.org)
- The North American Society for Sports History (www.nassh.org)
- The Australian Society for Sports History (www.sporthistory.org)
- The International Society for the History of Physical Education and Sport (http://www.ishpes.org/home/)
- European Committee for Sports History (http://www.cesh-site.eu/)

CHAPTER 7

PHILOSOPHY FOR COACHES

ALUN HARDMAN AND CARWYN JONES

A coach's practice is founded on his or her philosophy; it will affect their choices of what is right and wrong. This is extremely important in top-level sport, because there are many temptations to make short cuts.
Atle Kvålsvoll, Coach of Thor Hushovd, winner of the
Green Shirt (sprint) in the Tour de France, 2005

INTRODUCTION: WHAT IS PHILOSOPHY AND HOW CAN IT HELP US UNDERSTAND COACHING?

The term 'philosophy' is generally used both in coaching and everyday life to refer to a world view or approach, or even a kind of personal ideology. Indeed, often one hears a coach being asked 'What's your coaching philosophy?' The word philosophy as used here, however, could be replaced by 'style' or 'approach' without much loss of meaning. Conversely, in the context of this chapter and this book, a far more precise and formal use of the term will be discussed. Philosophy is considered the original or first academic discipline, with roots going back to 3000BC and beyond. The early philosophers tried to address fundamental issues about the world, society, human nature and religion. Similarly, current philosophy continues to seek answers to important questions such as: what is good? Or, what is a person? Or, what does it mean to be happy? In order to answer such questions, philosophers (often to other people's frustration) seek clarity, draw distinctions, and generally insist on precision in the use of language. The chapter is divided into three parts. The first provides a detailed understanding of philosophy as a discipline and its relevance to coaching. The second identifies and explains three philosophical concepts that we consider to be particularly appropriate to coaching, before a final section demonstrates the application of philosophical ideas in a practical coaching scenario.

As mentioned, philosophy – literally, the love of wisdom – has a long and distinguished history. It includes famous names like Plato, Socrates, Hobbes, Descartes (to whom the phrase 'I think, therefore I am' is attributable), Mill, Kant, Nietzsche and Wittgenstein. Philosophical questions can be crudely divided into four types: those to do with values (axiology), morality (ethics), meaning (ontology) and experience (phenomenology). So, for example, a philosopher of sport might ask: what is the value of youth sport? How should children conduct themselves when playing sport? and How might sport contribute to a meaningful and happy life?

We begin by drawing a distinction between philosophy as an activity and philosophy as a topic, before analysing the value of both to coaching (Best, 1978). The term 'philosophy as an activity' describes a process or method. One can philosophise (do philosophy) as well as study philosophy, in the same way that one can coach as well as study coaching. The philosophical process can be encapsulated with reference to two crucial and important questions: What do you mean? and How do you know? (Best, 1978). Both these questions encourage reflection about all sorts of claims and statements. These questions also demand critical thinking, an important skill in general and for a good philosopher in particular (Ryall, 2010).

Let us examine the difference between these questions in relation to a claim commonly made about sport, that is, sport is good for your health. The first question (What do you mean?) is essentially related to clarification and in asking for more detail. At this stage, one is not disagreeing with the statement, just requesting more clearness and lucidity; perhaps an explanation of what is meant by health (physical or psycho-social), and which activities in particular the claimant includes in the category 'sport' (e.g. swimming, darts, rally driving, American football). In response, it is incumbent on the claimant to explain in as much detail as possible what is meant by health and sport. If he or she claims that darts and snooker are not sports, a philosopher may legitimately probe further and ask the claimant to explain their definition of sport. This takes us to the second type of question (How do you know?). This is a justificatory question, where the questioner is looking for evidence to support the statement made. In this case, they might ask: How do you know that darts is not a sport? In reply, one might expect a philosophical, sociological or historical account of sport which supports the assertion that darts is not a sport. Or, it might be that the questioner is seeking evidence to verify the implied claim that, for example, rugby is a health promoting activity. What might be required to justify this claim is relevant and appropriate evidence that is both valid (true) and reliable (dependable). The evidence for the health promoting benefits of rugby is likely to be empirical in the shape of facts and figures, trends, health indices and so forth. But this will not always be the case. Indeed, where empirical facts provide evidence, there may be different interpretations or weight given to such information. For example, what should we make of the fact that a significant number of injuries and even deaths occur in sport (including rugby) each year, events which nearly always further strain the National Health Service? The questioner might not be looking for empirical data here, but rather a justification for using the given terms in a certain way. Consequently, the need to precisely outline what we mean by the term 'health' and what form of sport is compatible with such a belief or account (i.e. that rugby is good for one's health) becomes obvious (McNamee and Parry, 1990). One can immediately see how asking these questions opens up a whole host of other questions which demand further clarification and justification. The discussion can get messy and complicated, but carefully developed philosophical analysis and skills can be very useful in making sense of the complexities.

A coach will be faced with a myriad of questions about value, ethics, meaning and experience. Given that such questions are inescapable, it is better to be prepared to tackle them as competently as possible. Coaches should, therefore, be encouraged to use philosophical tools to develop a more logical and coherent understanding of the meaning, value, ethical and experiential dimensions of coaching in general, and of their own coaching in particular. Some specific questions a coach might want to reflect on include: What is coaching? What are the key values of coaching? Does coaching differ from teaching, if so, in which ways? Is coaching about the process or the product? Does coaching enrich children's lives? Ought coaches to specialise early or later? and Should all coaches be professionally accredited? These and many other issues are crucial for coaches and coaching organisations to address, because they help establish a clear agenda for both individual and collective aims, and the appropriateness of the manner in which such aims are to be achieved. There are no off-the-shelf responses to such queries, but there are better and worse answers. Philosophy and philosophical reflection can help coaches to establish a clear rationale for what they are doing and provide the tools to deal with these and other questions in a justified way (Drewe, 2000).

THE TOOLS OF PHILOSOPHY AND HOW THEY CAN BE USED IN COACHING

Our introduction attempted to emphasise that philosophy's contribution to coaching is an embedded and holistic one, which sees reasoned, principled and reflective thinking as essential for good coaching practice. Having said this, there are a number of philosophical concepts which, when understood better, can help to structure and guide greater self-awareness for practitioners. These concepts have already been mentioned, but what follows is an expanded account of how they might specifically relate to coaching practice.

Axiology (values)

All coaches must and will ask themselves at some stage what is good about sport? What is it about sport that makes them, players, and all others who contribute to the production of sports performances do what they do? After all, for most, coaching is a matter of choice as there are other, more lucrative, equally enjoyable ways of earning a living or spending free time. In answering this question, coaches may point to one or more things of value that can only be acquired by being a sports coach. In so doing, they will be engaged in discussing the branch of philosophy concerned with values, which is called axiology.

Once again, in order to further understand the concept of value and its relationship to sport and the coaching process, distinctions need to be drawn. It could be argued that there are two sources of value in both sport and coaching. First, there are subjective values which relate to what is of importance to individuals or groups of individuals, such as a coach or players. Second, there are objective values which relate to the importance and significance of things as objects in and of themselves, such as a hockey game, or the role of a coach. This distinction means, for example, that a coach may have personal or subjective reasons for wanting to coach which may or may not coincide with the objective values appropriate for the role of a coach. Conflicts of interest in coaching are often the result of a clash between objective and subjective values. Coaches choosing representative sides, for example, should ensure they use objective selection criteria to avoid any favouritism. The objective selection criteria used should be based on clear, justifiable and persuasive (to other coaches) accounts of what a good player looks like, and clear evidence (through the selection process) that those selected best fit such a description.

The distinction between subjective and objective values helps us to judge the appropriateness of different coaching motivations and practices. For example, a coach of a junior football side may value his or her role because it demands the application of certain qualities such as empathy, concentration, pedagogic skill, inspiration and motivation. This coach sees the coaching process as having intrinsic value (i.e. having a value in and of itself). Similarly, such a coach could regard football for the specific qualities of the skill, tactical acumen, cooperation, speed, and commitment required to play the game well. The coach gains satisfaction from getting players to do the best they can and to develop their football abilities in order to gain the enjoyment attached to playing well.

On the other hand, a rival football coach may value sport and the coaching process for very different reasons. For him or her, playing football might be seen in terms of a means to achieve other ends, such as demonstrating superiority by developing masculine values or achieving recognition through winning trophies.

A. Hardman and C. Jones

Similarly, the coach may be motivated by the social status or financial rewards and career opportunities that coaching provides. For such a person, coaching can become a vehicle for exercising power or achieving rewards external to football. This coach can be said to perceive football and coaching in terms of their extrinsic value. To borrow from psychology, it could be said that the first coach is intrinsically motivated to coach and fosters internal motivation in his/her players, whereas the second coach is extrinsically motivated to coach and encourages his/her players to focus on external or tangible rewards. Consequently, the respective coaches' sources of motivation and the reasons why they coach are different. From the given examples, playing and coaching sports can be said to be valuable in two ways. First, they have inherent value – that is, they can be said to be valuable for their own sake or in their own right (McNamee, 1997) – and second, they have instrumental value in that they may be used as instruments to secure a number of goals such as money, fame, esteem and so forth.

For the most part, individuals' motives to coach will be made up of intrinsic and extrinsic reasons. Consequently, they will appreciate both the values inherent to sport, and the manner in which it has instrumental value when used as a means to pursue other ends. While the mix is a legitimate one, it is important to understand how an emphasis on a particular set of values and motivations affects what is deemed important to coaches (Kretchmar, 1994). This reflects on how coaches make decisions in terms of what is emphasised and how they get their message across.

Ethics (morality)

The philosophical sub-discipline of ethics is closely related to axiology in that it deals with values. Ethics, however, focuses specifically on certain types of values, namely moral values. Moral values are, in essence, to do with how we treat ourselves and others, and what counts as good and bad, and right and wrong, in these contexts (there is an extended account of the importance of ethics in coaching in Chapter 8). Clearly, moral values play a central role in coaching given the interpersonal interaction involved. Ethicists attempt to articulate a value framework for a given practice (e.g. coaching) and identify a list of prescriptions (actions which are encouraged), proscriptions (actions which are discouraged) and qualities of character that promote and sustain that practice and those who participate in it. The ethics of coaching, therefore, is to do with what goals coaches aim for, and how they behave towards themselves and others in pursuing these goals.

Often a coach's moral obligations are outlined in a code of ethical conduct. A code of conduct is generally a list of do's and don't's that spell out the rights and duties of both the coach and the athletes. This focus on rights and duties is associated with a particular tradition in ethics called deontology (DeSensi and Rosenberg, 2003). Deontology defines the moral arena in terms of a number of entitlements that persons have. When an individual claims they have a right, it means that other individuals have corresponding duties that they must perform to ensure that such rights are granted. For example, a young player's right not to be bullied by the coach is closely related to the coach's duty not to act in a threatening and intimidating manner. Codes of conduct then, are essentially a list of rights and duties that aim to promote certain moral principles or values such as freedom, autonomy, fairness and justice. Such codes are useful, but knowing their content is not sufficient in itself. Knowing what is right is no guarantee of right action. Hence, additional qualities of character such as compassion, wisdom, courage, fairness, honesty and integrity may be required for such (i.e. right) action. For the deontologist, right and wrong are understood in terms of the inherent qualities of actions; for example, lying and causing physical harm are deemed inherently wrong, whereas honesty and fairness are inherently right.

Another branch of ethics, namely utilitarianism (often used interchangeably with the term 'consequentialism') approaches the nature of moral goodness from a different perspective (DeSensi and Rosenberg, 2003). For a utilitarian, actions are right insofar as the action contributes to an increase in overall goodness, pleasure or satisfaction, or a decrease in pain, suffering or badness. Actions are wrong insofar as they result in an overall decrease in good, pleasure or satisfaction or an increase in pain, suffering or badness. According to the utilitarian approach, the ends may justify the means. For example, a gymnastic coach may justify robust physical treatment of junior gymnasts in terms of the eventual overall pleasure and satisfaction that will be derived from their future success. In his autobiography, Andre Agassi (2009) reflects on the early coaching by his father. Without the intense, boring and repetitive coaching he received, he recognises that he would not have had the successful career, the financial stability or his eventual marriage to Steffi Graf. Nevertheless, he also recognises the cost of such intensive training on his mental and emotional health. In other words, he doesn't necessarily believe that the means are justified by the ends. Coaches face difficult decisions about the means they use to achieve their goals, and often may have to accept that playing and coaching sport comes with a price (missing school, being away from the family, unsociable hours, risk of injury). A utilitarian approach to the ethics of coaching might lead to the justification of all sorts of dubious training practices so long as the goal is achieved (East Germany pursued a systematic state-sponsored doping regime which produced Olympic success, but in doing so, failed to treat athletes with respect and dignity).

Another approach to ethics, namely virtue ethics, focuses more specifically on the qualities of individuals rather than right actions (McNamee, 1995). Virtue ethics aims for the development of good habits, character traits and dispositions such as courage, fairness and integrity (MacIntyre, 1984). A coach who is compassionate, fair, just, honest, committed and dedicated will try to produce a responsive moral climate when coaching, and will seek to cultivate similar dispositions in his or her athletes. Arguably, the coach's character, more than his knowledge, qualifications or playing history, is the most important asset. For example, Carwyn James' character, coach of the only British and Irish Lions rugby union team to have won a test series in New Zealand in 1971, is talked about fondly by those who played for him. His qualities are summed up by one of the star players, Barry John:

> Without him, it's very questionable if we would have done so well. He got from everybody, a tremendous respect – doctors, dentists, fitters, turners, miners – total respect, and that's an incredible achievement. So that, in the end, he gave players such belief, they were prepared to get hurt for him.
>
> (in Richards, 2002: 112)

One of the key questions a coach might ask themselves, then, is: What kind of example do I want to be to my players?

Ontology (the meaning of coaching)

Ontology is the branch of philosophy that deals with the nature of existence in terms of what actually exists. It asks fundamental questions about the meaning of life and, as such, ontological questions can be the most complex and frustrating of all. For the purposes of this discussion, however, we will focus on the ways in which coaching is a meaningful practice that can provide a rich and rewarding pursuit or vocation. Here, the notion of how coaching and being a coach might come to exemplify the so-called 'good life' or *telos* is an important consideration. Our overall outlook, then, in terms of ontology, seeks to understand and recognise how coaching can contribute to the pursuit of a meaningful life (Hardman *et al.*, 2010).

We find meaning in our lives through performing social roles or when engaged in certain social practices that we either have or acquire through choice. The idea of a social practice is that of a coherent, complex and meaningful human activity through which individual and collective goals and values are realised. Social practices are usually formally supported by institutional mechanisms such as associations, organisations or companies, whose responsibility it is to ensure that the well-being of such practices are safeguarded. Through related social interactions, communal bonds are formed which provide the fabric that underpins society. Social practices include such things as education, law, commerce and, for our purposes, sport, including the more specific practice of coaching. Such practices are supported by the respective institutions of schools and universities, the criminal justice system, banking and stock markets and, in the case of sport, by organisations such as the Football Association, the International Olympic Committee and, in coaching, by bodies such as sports coach UK.

In order for a social practice to thrive as a meaningful aspect of our lives, we undertake various social roles. Our most immediate and recognisable roles involve being a partner, son or daughter, brother or sister, and possibly a grandparent. These roles all derive their meaning and significance within the institutional framework of the family. Elsewhere, we may have other roles as a friend, a colleague or, in the context of sporting practices, as a player, a coach, a mentor, an administrator, an official or a supporter. The type and number of roles and practices that we undertake are likely to be products of a number of factors which may or may not be under our control. The roles and practices we choose will depend on the extent to which we have the opportunity and wherewithal to undertake them. For many, socio-economic circumstances, for example, may limit opportunities. Fortunately, for those who are interested in coaching, sport is, relatively speaking, socially inclusive, providing a mix of practices in which the vast majority of people can engage and find enjoyment. As a result, there are ample opportunities to become involved in coaching sport, particularly at its foundational levels.

Once we understand that coaching can, and perhaps should, be understood as a social practice, we begin to recognise that it can become a way of life for any who do it, affecting much of what they do and how they think of themselves. Rather than recognise coaching as a set of techniques and skills, therefore, coaching's ontological significance lies in the manner in which it has the potential to shape a coach's life and who he or she is as a person. While it is true that each individual coach – due to his or her personality, experience and particular circumstances – will be different in many ways, there will, nonetheless, be a core set of features to coaching which provide personal significance and a central source of meaning, self-understanding, social expression and self-esteem to that person. It is important, therefore, that the coach attempts to interrogate and understand what it is about sport that provides such a powerful personal sense of purpose and well-being; that is, why sport is central to their pursuit of 'the good life'. Part of that interrogation requires the coach to contemplate the nature of sporting activity and its unique characteristics. Here, beyond the contingencies of particular sporting contexts within specific historical times, such an investigation often reveals that a significant reason for sport's enduring magnetism is that it centres on game playing (Suits, 1995). Despite the tendency to under-value the play element in modern sports, it is important to understand that sport's principal attraction is that of experiencing a well-made game. Though many may play sport for the immediate psychological and material benefits of winning, sport's unique and enduring appeal lies in how it provides participants with opportunities to pursue a mutual quest for athletic excellence through challenge (Simon, 1991). In this quest, coaches have a significant role to play in maximising the tactical and technical attributes of the participants to allow them to overcome the obstacles that the game presents.

Following on from this point, it would appear important for coaches to fully understand the specific role that they play in facilitating quality sporting experiences for others. To do this, coaches should develop and nurture a lasting appreciation in their players and athletes of core internal goods that can only be acquired through diligent and committed attention to the demands of the sport in question. These internal goods include the development of fundamental skills, acquiring a sophisticated understanding of the tactical possibilities that the game presents, and also an understanding and respect for the proper social conventions of the game, including the observation of good sportspersonship. In our opinion, a good coach will ensure such aspects of sport are prioritised ahead of external goods such as the acquisition of financial rewards, fame and prestige.

Phenomenology

Phenomenology is a philosophical approach that deals with conscious experience. It differs from psychology in that it does not attempt to explain cognitive or affective antecedents of behaviour, but endeavours to understand experience from the perspective of a subject (person) as a lived body. Phenomenology might try to get to grips with questions such as: What is it like to be a coach, athlete or parent? What is it like to experience fear? and What does fear mean to an athlete (not as a general category, but for each individual)? Phenomenology is anti-reductivist. That means it does not attempt to gain understanding by analysing and breaking down ideas to other concepts. For example, a psychologist might try to understand performance in terms of ideas like stress, anxiety, motivation, coping, and so forth, while phenomenologists are keen to understand experience without reducing or simplifying it. A crude way of putting it, is that what is sought is knowledge of the experience 'as it really is', including the feelings, emotions and physical sensations. We can access our own phenomenological accounts of being coaches by using a first-person perspective to convey how coaching 'really is for us'. In this respect, it is important for a coach to reflect on personal experiences and practice as well as on the experiences of those they are coaching. Open mindedness, empathy and imagination are important for coaches, who should subsequently aim at an authentic understanding of what coaching is, what coaching is for them, and the experiences of those they coach. In the Andre Agassi example cited earlier, one might conclude that his father had little insight into the reality of the experience of coaching his young son, either for him or for Andre. The phenomenon understood by both at the time as 'coaching' might, in fact, have been a much more dysfunctional relationship.

The recent tragic death of the Wales football coach Gary Speed, brought to light issues related to depression and addiction in professional sport. What became immediately clear was that the external perceptions of success in sport do not always mirror internal affect and reality. The sad event also stimulated organisations such as the Professional Footballers' Association to encourage their members to talk about problematic feelings that they encounter, particularly those related to depression and isolation. Although this process may not be immediately recognisable as phenomenological philosophy, the link to better understanding of 'what it's like' to be a professional athlete (or coach) is clear.

APPLYING PHILOSOPHY TO COACHING

The following example attempts to demonstrate how an ability to reflect and articulate philosophical thinking may benefit coaches.

SCENARIO: THE ETHICS OF 'PLAYER-ORIENTATED' COACHING

You are a coach of an under-eights seven-a-side football team. There are significant differences in ability within your squad of ten players, and it is clear that the overall level of team performance depends on who is on the field of play at any given time. Though you want to ensure that all players have equal playing time, you know that doing so will mean losing games you could win. You wonder if you are doing the right thing.

Most coaches will find themselves initially coaching at a foundational level despite the fact that they may have been elite or sub-elite athletes themselves. Usually, this means working to develop young players during their formative experiences rather than fine-tuning high-level tactical and technical abilities. In such circumstances, a crucial starting point for philosophical reflection is to take into account the needs of various stakeholders (i.e. those who contribute to the coaching process generally). Here, while your interests as a coach and those of parents are important, we contend that the overriding concern is what is in the best interests of the players.

It is usually taken that, at a young age, the development of technical and tactical footballing abilities (for example) should be relatively minor aspects of a child's overall needs. This gives rise to the often used cliché that it is the development of persons that should be the primary focus of the coach rather than a specific set of footballing strategies. In practice, this means that the coach should focus on ensuring players have intrinsic enjoyment from football and begin to acquire an appreciation and understanding of the physical skills, competitive challenges and particular ethos of the game. Here, the coach tries to develop in children a commitment to, and love of, the game, from which a desire for technical and tactical improvement will grow.

This approach suggests that the immediate demands of competitive success are relatively unimportant. However, this need not necessarily be the case. What is probably more important is that the coach is able to judge the extent to which the competitive environment provides each individual player with an appropriate opportunity to develop, first, as a person and, second, as a footballer. Under such conditions, it is highly likely that any contest at this foundational level would warrant a coach sharing playing time equally among his or her squad of players. Nevertheless, in accordance with such a principle, this does not mean that it is appropriate to ignore all differences between individual players. A coach will still need to take into account such things as the physical, emotional, and technical differences among his or her players, and treat such variations accordingly. It is important to ensure that both stronger and weaker players gain as much from their playing experience as possible. Hence, they may be allocated proportionately more or less playing time, depending on the quality of the opposition. The same adjustments may also be needed for less physically developed players when playing against stronger or weaker teams. The coach may also need to identify both positional and tactical responsibilities that best suit certain players. Though it is preferable that all players gain experience from playing in different positions, such challenges ought to be developed first through coaching sessions and sensitively implemented in game situations when the stresses of other challenges are diminished. Subsequently, experimentation with playing position and team tactics could best be carried out against weaker opposition.

Fortunately, many junior football leagues recognise such ideals, and downplay competitiveness through regulatory structures (i.e. no need to report scores, no leagues or tables, no elimination competitions) and certain playing rules (no penalty kicks, unlimited substitutions). Furthermore, discerning coaches, recognising the range of abilities and needs of the individual players within their squad, will organise coaching sessions in an appropriate manner to cater for those different needs. Such coaches would possibly conduct aspects of practice in ability groups and, where exceptional talent is identified, seek out a further developmental environment for it (i.e. a regional academy). Within the context of the game, while playing time may be shared equally, this does not mean that time or playing position should be assigned randomly. Again, part of the coach's skill is to recognise which players, playing in which positions, provide effectual organisational structure to the team to enable as many players as possible to play effectively. Consequently, key players in core positions would get a little more playing time, while more limited players are played in positions and at stages in the game that aren't overly demanding.

CONCLUSION

The example of the under-eights football team is laden with philosophical significance, although no philosophical terminology was used. The most important guide for coaches should be to consider players' holistic development as persons. Philosophy provides a number of valuable tools and ideas to focus a coach's thinking and reflection towards this goal. If we accept that the holistic development of players as persons is the priority of coaches, the values which inform this goal must be identified. This is largely a process of philosophical reflection. We also suggest that the cultivation of moral values for coaches and players (such as honesty, courage, perseverance, commitment, respect) is more important than the cultivation of non-moral ones. Although the cultivation of non-moral values, such as skill, determination and the will to win, are central to coaching practice, philosophical and moral reflection can help a coach identify a value hierarchy that contributes to the flourishing of athletes as persons.

DISCUSSION TOPICS AND REVIEW QUESTIONS

1 Can you identify ways in which you have thought philosophically about your coaching?
2 Do you agree that coaching is first and foremost about developing persons? What, if anything, do children with poor sporting skills get from sport?
3 Can you make a list of important moral duties which are a prerequisite to being a good coach? Do coaches have any rights? If so, what are they and where do they come from?
4 Can you describe the difference between the internal and the external values of sport?
5 Describe ways in which a coach might help young athletes to appreciate both the internal and the external goods of sport.

110

6   The tragic death of the Wales football manager Gary Speed in 2011, prompted people to reflect on the pressures of elite coaching. How important is playing or coaching sport in your life, compared with your family, friends, and relationships?

7   Can you identify your own value hierarchy in relation to coaching; i.e. which are the most important values for you? Try to justify this hierarchy, remembering to ask yourself the two important questions: What do I mean? and How do I know?

8   How can philosophy help you to decide on a course of action if there was a conflict between values? Imagine that one of your star players was accused of spitting at an opponent in a match. Is there a conflict between loyalty to your player and respecting the opposition? How would thinking philosophically help you resolve this dilemma?

Web Resources

http://www.philosophybites.com/

This is an excellent website with a wide range of free podcasts in which important philosophical concepts are discussed by leaders in the field.

http://www.bbc.co.uk/ethics/

This link takes you to the BBC ethics page where there are a number of resources, including podcasts of radio programmes discussing a number of important ethical questions.

http://www.wikipedia.org/

Wikipedia is a useful resource for finding explanations of philosophical ideas very quickly. However, take care not to rely on Wikipedia for any assignments or projects.

http://www.philosophyofsport.org.uk/

This is the website for the British Philosophy of Sport Association. Here, you can find some useful links and information about the philosophy of sport.

http://iaps.net/

This is the website for the International Association for the Philosophy of Sport. Again, you can find some useful links and information about philosophy of sport here.

CHAPTER 8

ETHICS FOR COACHES

ALUN HARDMAN AND CARWYN JONES

Be more concerned with your character than your reputation, because your character is what you really are, while your reputation is merely what others think you are.

John Wooden, Head Basketball Coach, UCLA, 1948–1975

Everything I know about morality and the obligations of men, I owe it to football.

Albert Camus, philosopher and 1957 Nobel Prize Winner

INTRODUCTION: WHAT ARE ETHICS AND HOW CAN THEY HELP US UNDERSTAND COACHING?

Systematic enquiry into the practice of sports coaching is increasingly sophisticated. The growing resources allocated to ensure effective coaching and coach development are manifest through an ever expanding range of specialists who now contribute to almost every area of athletic performance. As one cruel jibe about the general preponderance of expertise goes,

> they are all specialists. Everyone's becoming better and better at less and less. Eventually someone's going to be superb . . . at nothing.
>
> (Williams, 1987)

It is certainly the case that the cult of expertise may have promoted a somewhat uncritical view of coaching as a largely functional and technical practice (Cross and Lyle, 1999; Lyle, 2002; Martens, 2004). The outcome is that there has been a traditional orthodoxy in coaching 'science', which endorses a view of the practice and the profession as one that aims at positivistic, empirical and quantifiable improvements in athletic performance.

113

From the point of view of ethics, however, coaching is fundamentally a moral practice. Such a perspective is grounded in the view that coaching involves human relationships. At any one moment, therefore, coaching not only affects the interactions between and among coaches and athletes, but also the values and attitudes athletes hold towards themselves, one another and their sport. Coaches work with people not machines; consequently, most, if not all, coaching exchanges have a moral dimension to them. If these premises are accepted, the moral dimensions of sports coaching are both unavoidable and, more significantly, may be at odds with the orthodox view of sport which exalts performance. A number of important implications follow if sport's coaching is understood as a moral enterprise.[1] First, it implies that coaching ethics are evident in the way that coaches decide what, who, why, and how they coach. This applies not merely in terms of enhancing tactical and technical proficiency, but more crucially in relation to how they treat those they coach – is it with consideration, respect and compassion, such that a shared sense of motivation and joyful meaning towards the sport in question is engendered? Or is it with callousness, recklessness and competitive ruthlessness, which may spread cynicism, disillusionment and cheerlessness?

In the coaching environment, the ethical dimension is considerable and has a strong presence. It is important, for example, to help our understanding of the coach–athlete relationship, and more generally in terms of thinking how coaches ought to best sustain both the integrity of participants and of the sporting practices in which they participate. One consideration for coaches might be how the fundamental Kantian principle, that all persons are first and foremost ends in themselves, can be safeguarded (Tuxhill and Wigmore, 1998; Fry, 2000). This issue is frequently at the centre of the relationship between coaches and their athletes, because despite (largely) shared goals, coaches and athletes may still struggle to agree as to how best such goals can be realised. Similarly, the nature of the relationship between coaches and athletes can lead to unhealthy power imbalances, that hinder the possibility of open discussion between both parties. Furthermore, much will also depend on the particular circumstances and the demands required in specific situations. Sometimes, advancing greater autonomy may stifle the development of performance, while at other times, allowing greater freedom for athletes can facilitate commitment to their sport. Ensuring the balance is right between exercising authority and allowing freedom of choice are the cornerstones of ethical discourse in the context of sports coaching.

As indicated in Chapter 7 ('Philosophy for coaches'), ethics is a philosophical sub-discipline, and is often considered the most (by some, the only) relevant sub-discipline to the study of sport (McFee, 1998). From an ethicist point of view, what really matters is how we treat ourselves and others, and how we evaluate good and bad behaviour in the context of sport. The role of ethics in sport coaching, then, is to provide legitimate underpinning and a clear framework for coaching behaviour – to establish which actions are to be encouraged and which are to be discouraged, and what qualities of character ought to be promoted and sustained through the coaching enterprise. According to such a view, a coach cannot ask if his or her practice requires an ethical approach (as if it were a perspective that could be accepted or rejected). Rather, it is something that is unavoidable, thus the option is that of 'doing' ethics for better or for worse (Kretchmar, 1994). The remainder of this chapter outlines how a sports coach might develop a clear and effective moral framework to underpin his or her practice. It does this in five parts. The first briefly presents a number of moral concepts important for coaches, before the second identifies what it means for a coach to adopt a moral point of view. The third section sketches a number of relevant theories that could be used to underpin a moral approach to coaching, while the fourth examines the process of coaching from an ethical perspective by focusing on the character of the coach. The fifth and final section provides an example of an ethical issue in sport.

MORAL CONCEPTS IN SPORT

In this section, we outline a number of related moral principles that are central to understanding sports coaching from an ethical point of view. We present and discuss them as a series of ideas that are grouped around related moral issues. We suggest that coaches need to develop some understanding of these moral clusters, as they almost inevitably encounter them in their practice.

Fairness, cheating and competition

Coaches have a significant influence on how athletes understand and abide by aspects of fair play. No coach will deny that fairness for all competitors with respect to playing conditions (i.e. that teams have equal numbers of players) is a central and undeniable principle of sport. However, what is more difficult to determine is where exactly each coach is willing to draw the line with regards to what constitutes an acceptable or unacceptable advantage in sport. Nowhere is this more apparent than in the influence coaches can have upon athletes' attitudes to the rules of competition and their application. Coaches might agree that it is important to abide by such rules but, in practice, some coaches may view the value of winning as the most important goal. The result is that coaches may be indifferent to the constraints established by the rules, and either actively encourage, or fail to condemn, players who cheat to secure a resulting strategic advantage.

Many coaches adopt a technical attitude towards the rules as a part of good strategy. However, from a moral point view, it is evident that such a purely instrumental approach may result in undesirable testing conditions. A technical outlook toward the rules of sport involves efforts to manipulate officials, break rules expediently, and undermine an opponent's competitive disposition. In this context, a good coach is more than one who develops players that demonstrate superior physical skills, technical abilities and strategic guile within the laws of the game. Rather, it is also one who is able to coach players to see the rules, officials and opponents as mere obstacles to overcome as expediently or as efficiently as possible. For many, such an approach to sport is not only an accurate description of coaching practice, but a perfectly acceptable moral account. The end of winning justifies the means used to achieve that end. According to such a perspective, beyond what is otherwise criminal, the rules of sport are viewed as 'prices' that are either worth or not worth the risk of paying, should one be so careless as to be caught out and penalised (Simon, 1991). A clear example of this view is the so-called 'professional' foul, where no effort is made to deceive officials. In such an environment, a contest may be won or lost as a result of matters beyond the ability to perform the physical skills constituted by the rules (Fraleigh, 1995). Consequently, when it comes to strategic rule breaking and outright cheating, a coach has an important role with regards to safeguarding the integrity of the game – a view that recognises that the central value of winning lies in "a mutual quest for excellence through challenge" (Simon, 1991: 23) – because the greatest sporting victories are ones achieved against the best opponents (Kretchmar, 1994). Coaches ought to be aware that victories achieved by whatever means necessary are of little worth; a principle which should guide their ethics.

Gamesmanship

The rules of games do not prescribe what is fair with regards to all contesting behaviour. In addition to physical skills, advantages can be gained by a wide range of strategies that exploit a competitor's weaknesses. In particular, players and coaches may develop ways to unsettle opponents psychologically – through verbal or physical intimidation, through frustrating their concentration and rhythm, through time-wasting, or through employing novel strategies which, while not forbidden by the rules of the game, are as morally dubious as they are strategically sharp. As there are no written rules in place to establish the moral standing of acts of gamesmanship, such strategies, if they help to win, often become broadly adopted by coaches. But are rules all that coaches have to work with when determining the moral framework as to what is, or is not, acceptable from their athletes? The overriding concern here, again, is to interrogate one's underpinning values, as they guide subsequent ethical actions.

116

Merit, admiration and luck

Coaches ought to have a clear understanding as to what comprises athletic superiority. Most often, we think that being good at sport simply reflects being better than one's opponent (on a particular day)! However, as Bailey and Toms (2010) point out, the factors that determine sporting success are largely out of our hands and are grounded in psycho-physical predispositions (e.g. aggression, competitiveness, strength and power). They argue that in terms of both nature and nurture, what brings elite level athletes to the competitive start-line is an extremely capricious or fickle process. Here, in addition to having the right psycho-physical blueprint, as Kay (2000: 151) summarises, "children are simply much more likely to achieve success if they come from a certain type of family". All of this raises the question of why we, as a society, admire elite sports performers and their achievements in the ways we do, if the advantages bequeathed upon them are the product of genetic and socio-economic luck? Coaches might respond to this criticism about the value of sport in society (and the role they play within it) in the following way. They could argue that there is 'objective' worth in displays of athletic excellence, because such efforts demonstrate the aesthetic significance of sport to human existence. Such a perspective is grounded in the belief that persons are moving beings whose lives are 'embodied' (Kretchmar, 1994): that is, people exist as physical beings in a physical world which constantly challenges, inspires and excites our physical awareness and capacities. The cultivation of physical games and formal sports provide novel and complex ways in which to respond to that embodied existence. This is evident in a range of activities, such as the aesthetic pleasures of dancing freely or the hardships of extreme marathon running. Team games such as football, cricket and rugby, also appeal to pursuing an embodied life through the complexities of physical skill and social interaction contained within them.

From a moral point of view, perhaps what is most important for the coach is that admiration in sport ought to be associated with *ethically significant excellences* (virtues) such as fairness, courage, generosity, self-control, perseverance and grace, rather than non-ethical (or non-moral) values such as wealth and power. In practice, this suggests that coaches should reward and compliment athletes in proportion to efforts rather than just on plain competition outcomes – a view reinforced within earlier chapters of this text (see, for example, Chapter 4 'Psychology for coaches').

Autonomy, freedom and paternalism

According to one school of moral thought, the best coaches are the ones who make themselves increasingly irrelevant and unnecessary (Vallerand, 2007).

This claim is based on the view that athletes, above all others, are able to determine what is in their own best interests. This goal is not always easily or perhaps ever achieved in sport coaching, and may take years to progress. The context is also an important consideration for coaches working with children who find themselves *in loco parentis*. Such coaches must protect their charges from harm, sometimes against the latter's wishes and in the absence of full understanding. Indeed, the need for coaching authority is evident in terms of assessing the physical, psychological and social well-being of athletes at whatever level of sporting competition. The guiding principle here for coaches is that they ought to prevent harm and foster effective development that is both in the short and long-term interests of athletes themselves. Identifying more precisely what those long-term interests are, and how best they can be achieved, are some of the most vexing challenges a coach faces. Added to the mix, more often than not, is also the influence of 'stakeholders' – namely parents, teachers and friends, who all (to varying degrees) have interests, duties and obligations to the young athlete in question.

David Archard (2004) has suggested that the concept of an 'open future' ought to be the normative goal for children in sport. The idea is that progress in sport, or any other activity, ought not to be pursued to the point that opportunities for development in a broad range of other activities and skills are neglected. Getting the balance right between specialisation and generalisation is notoriously difficult, and though the issue has received some attention in the context of sport, clear blueprints for effective policy and practice are embryonic. In practical terms, however, a good coach ought to ensure that, as ends in their own right, the interests of the athletes must take precedence over other external goals. This means that the coach–athlete relationship should progress as a dynamic, interactive one, where the athlete's emerging autonomy and increasing capacity to determine his or her own interests is the priority. Meeting this goal, while at the same time ensuring that athletes submit to the rigorous discipline of training, represents one of the more challenging aspects of coaching. However, there need be no contradiction here; the athlete who decides to submit him or herself uncoerced to the discipline of sport, is one who exemplifies the qualities of autonomy which the coach desires.

Equity, equality and justice

Issues of equity and equality are plentiful in the coaching context. Such matters affect basic features of coaching practice such as who is to be coached, how often and at what level of intensity. It is also evident in terms of how coaching success is to be evaluated and measured. Two core principles of justice can help in our understanding of this moral cluster. First, there are matters that relate to *procedural justice.* Here, the coach is interested in equality of opportunity, that is, securing athlete equity of access to the coaching process. In practice, this relates to the procedures the coach might put in place in order to determine what constitutes fairness in coaching. For example, is access to coaching, in the broader sense, open to all athletes regardless of their talents, age, gender, size, where they live (school catchment area), proximity to facilities and availability of equipment? Or, are there prerequisites to access such opportunities, such as how rich you are, being talented, having a certain level of commitment, being male or female, or having the correct equipment? In addition, there are matters of *distributive justice*, which concern how the coach fairly and equitably rewards (or punishes) on the basis of the outcome of available opportunities. An obvious example of this is how a coach selects players – are the criteria both appropriate and transparent, such that players who are rewarded the most (with selection and game time) are those who meet the criteria? Further questions to grapple with here include: Does the coach reward hard work and effort, or skill and effectiveness? Does the coach prefer physically adept players, or those who may be limited physically but understand the game well? Is youth more important than experience? With regards to managing players, does the coach insist on a set of team rules that players must follow? Do such rules apply all the time? To all players? and If a coach has established a 'no train, no play' policy, is it enforced consistently?

A MORAL POINT OF VIEW – THE OBJECTIVITY, SUBJECTIVITY AND NORMATIVITY OF SPORT COACHING

This section addresses the fundamental problem of what counts as a moral point of view. This is crucial for coaches, as we have argued that ethical matters in sport are not something that coaches can choose to ignore, but something they will do for better or worse. Progress in coaching ethics will depend on three things – curiosity, confidence and a commitment to a moral outlook on sport (Kretchmar, 1994.) These three ideas are now explained in more detail.

Moral curiosity is often the hook for coaches. It means that moral issues in sport look interesting, provocative, challenging and fun to deal with. A key issue for coaches, then, is the degree to which they see the moral issues they face – of ensuring fairness, of demanding effort, of requiring respect (between players, towards official and opponents) as crucial aspects of the coaching process. Moral confidence is the belief that there are solutions to moral debates – that ethics are not just a matter of discussion, but that correct behaviours and actions are the outcome of moral engagement. This provides the coach with the resolve to press on and be insistent, (often in the face of resistance) that moral principles should be sustained. Moral commitment relates to normative understanding. This demands that the coach consistently question his or her (often taken-for-granted) practice. It means that coaches must recognise that their ethical encounters are important, and that an appropriate course of action can be identified. Much is demanded of the character of coaches to demonstrate that, through deed and action, their daily coaching behaviours have a clear moral basis.

Types of ethics in sport

Having identified the various moral viewpoints available to the coach, and in particular what it means to adopt a particular moral point of view, this section details the different types of ethics a coach is likely to encounter in practice. There are five such types: meta-ethics, descriptive ethics, normative ethics, discourse ethics and applied ethics. Meta-ethics is the systematic study of establishing how best to understand moral terminology, moral theories, how to conduct moral debate and guide 'moral practice'. Meta-ethics is *not* ethics as such, and experts on meta-ethics may not be good ethicists themselves! A helpful analogy is that of a football pundit, whose expertise is different to that of a footballer. Meta-ethics is concerned with the language of morality (that is, what the moral terms used in coaching actually mean), what function they have, and in what way can we say there is truth in moral statements (such as 'cheating is wrong' or that was a 'good foul'). It is also concerned with the psychology of morality and, in particular, the sorts of mental states that are associated with different moral claims. For example, how do such psychological states as emotions and/or rationality affect the actions and behaviour of those involved in sport? Hardman *et al.* (2010), based on the work of Gilligan (1982) and Flanagan (1991), suggested that the competitive and momentary nature of some moral contexts, such as those encountered in sport, make the exhibition of moral action particularly improbable; namely, that we exaggerate what is possible morally in the context of sport. Such a perspective, however, begs the question: Is a coach largely ineffective in altering the moral outlook of his or her players in terms of how they act on the field of play? And relatedly: What can a coach realistically do in terms of affecting the moral decision making of his or her players? Meta-ethics is also concerned with the 'big-picture' metaphysics of examining whether there is any sort of moral reality, moral properties or moral facts? If so, what are they like? Do they occur naturally (innately) or are they constructed (socially)? If they exist, are they observable or verifiable in some way? Inevitably, such grand questions also depend on what sorts of reasons are provided for arguing about the existence, the nature and the purpose of ethics. Such arguments are matters of epistemology, where the concern is what sort of reason, if any, can be given in favour of moral claims.

Descriptive ethics is the study of people's actual beliefs about ethics. Hence, no attempt is made to assess or judge these beliefs. In the context of sports coaching, descriptive ethics is a matter of simply noting certain moral interactions between coaches, players and/or others who may be involved. This could mean, for example, that differing coaching behaviours are witnessed in differing contexts. One coach may berate, criticise, abuse and threaten players, while another is complimentary, encouraging and supportive. It may be possible to examine further the reasons for such contrasts and also to report the views of players on the (different) coaching styles they are subjected to. All such work, however, is purely descriptive, one of painting a picture of what one sees. No evaluation is undertaken here, as the task is one of presenting information. Such an approach may be taken seriously by some sociologists of sport, who see their purpose as one of uncovering the views, opinions, values, behaviours and practices of distinct sporting groups.

A number of sports philosophers have argued that descriptive ethics is all one needs, as, with an accurate narrative of coaching, meaning and significance can be inferred directly without the need for further intervention (Roberts, 1995; Burke, 2006). This view is motivated by several factors such as the desire to remain as neutral as possible and to avoid a subjective (and, therefore, potentially biased) account of coaching practice. Whether such a descriptive approach can ensure such neutrality is a key issue. This is because even in the act of description, the ethicist will selectively observe some events rather than others and see as worthy of description some observations and not others. In one sense, then, subjectivity is ever present, as narrative description is always somebody's description of something. For this reason, descriptive ethics is criticised because the kind of neutrality it wants to claim is just not possible. A far better approach, some suggest, is both to recognise one's biases and to acclaim that such subjectivity may provide the capacity to judge wisely (Morgan, 2004, 2003). So, far from accepting that all moral viewpoints are equal, it is possible for ethicists to argue that the existence of moral relativism does not preclude the possibility that some moral perspectives are better, and some are worse. Ethicists of this kind believe that examining coaching practice is a normative, rather than just a descriptive, enterprise.

Normative ethics is the branch of morality that examines issues which arise whenever we ask the question 'How ought I to act? In coaching, then, the normative is ever-present. This is because, as we have argued, coaching is inherently a moral practice where, at any moment, what the coach chooses or chooses not to do affects others. Normative ethics is distinct from meta-ethics because it examines standards related to the rightness and wrongness of coaching actions. Meta-ethics, on the other hand, studies the meaning of moral language and the metaphysics of moral facts as they relate to the sport coaching environment.

Broadly speaking, normative ethics can be separated into the sub-fields of moral theory and applied ethics. In the current context, this distinction is often blurred, as coaching sometimes presents applied problems rather than ones unique to the activity itself. Traditional moral theories are concerned with establishing moral principles that allow one to determine whether a (coaching) action is right or wrong. Classical theories of this type include deontology and consequentialism. These theories offer overarching moral principles to which one could appeal in order to resolve difficult coaching decisions. More recent forays into normative ethics have sought to highlight the morality of persons where, rather than concentrate on the rightness or wrongness of acts and actions, the focus is on the goodness or badness of individual people. The theoretical approach which takes this perspective is virtue ethics. A broad outline of deontology, consequentialism and virtue ethics is presented in Chapter 7 ('Philosophy for coaches').

Applied ethics involves the analysis of specific controversial moral issues. In contrast to abortion, animal rights or euthanasia, coaching is not inherently controversial, although there may be aspects of the practice that are. Examples are questions such as: Should coaches encourage players to hurt an opponent? Should coaches date their younger (female) athletes? or Is physical punishment ever justified as a coaching strategy? All court strong views. By contrast, the issue of whether a coach ought to be allowed to supply performance enhancing drugs to athletes is not an applied ethical issue, since everyone agrees that such action is grossly negligent and wrong. By contrast, the morality of the use of performance enhancing substances in adult sport would be an applied ethical issue, since there are significant groups of people who express different views on the matter.

To be an applied ethical issue, the coaching problem to be addressed must also be a distinctly moral one. On any given day, the media presents us with an array of sensitive topics such as the selection of England's next football coach, whether an autocratic coaching style is more effective than a democratic one, or whether high level rather than average athletes make better coaches. Although all of these issues are controversial and have an important impact on sports coaching, they are not all moral issues. Most are issues of sporting policy, some are related to coaching practice and others to (sporting) cultural taste and preference. Moral issues in sports coaching, by contrast, concern more universally obligatory principles. These could include our duty to avoid lying, harming others or accepting bribes, and are not confined to particular sporting groups.

Sometimes, issues of sporting policy and morality overlap, as with obligatory vetting checks of coaches. This is because the appointment of (serious) criminals as coaches is both socially prohibited and immoral. However, the two groups of issues are often distinct. For example, many would argue that, morally speaking, coaches ought not to openly chastise and criticise an adult athlete's perform-ance. However, they may well stop short of calling for sporting policies regulating such poor practice, let alone criminal laws punishing coaches for such conduct. In the case of children, however, the view changes because of the different context, as safeguarding children from harm is very relevant. Here, such a coaching style could constitute emotional abuse and can consequently be seen as morally wrong. Indeed, if severe enough, such action could also require the intervention of the police, as well as the sport's child-protection unit. To count as an applied ethical issue, then, the coaching matter at hand must be more than one of mere policy; it must be morally relevant as well.

In theory, resolving applied ethical issues in coaching should be easy. For example, in relation to the matter of hurting an opponent, we could consult our normative principle of choice, such as consequentialism. If a given strategy produces greater 'goodness' than 'badness' then, according to consequentialism, it would be morally acceptable for a coach to encourage a player to hurt an oppo-nent. Unfortunately, there are rival normative principles, some of which point to a different conclusion. Thus, the tension in normative ethics between conflicting theories prevents a single decisive procedure for determining the morality of a specific issue. The usual solution today to this stalemate is to consult several representative normative principles at once, and see where the weight of evidence lies. The procedure advocated by many to undertake such consultation is that of discourse ethics.

Discourse ethics (where 'discourse' is understood as an ongoing formalised discussion on a topic that is limited and framed by social conventions) is perhaps better understood as a method of doing ethics rather than orders for coaching. Consequently, discourse ethics does not prescribe a set of universal rules or prin-ciples of duty that have been decided in advance. Rather, it focuses on the pro-cesses of argumentation (i.e. what are the rules for debating moral issues), which themselves must satisfy each person's particular interests. The aim of discourse ethics, then, is to ensure that all participants in the debate can have their views fairly and impartially judged. In the case of coaching ethics, in addition to having a good understanding of morality, the coach must also be aware of the forces of socialisation and culture that inevitably affect the ways in which moral debate takes shape. Differences in power, authority and status are rife within the coaching process. Some of these are due to the inevitable difference between personalities, but others are the result of the structural forces that are inherent in sport (see Chapter 5 on 'Sociology for coaches' for a further discussion on these structural forces).

One practical effect of discourse ethics in the context of sports coaching, involves the role that representatives and representative bodies play in disputes. Most sporting bodies have various groups who lobby on behalf of distinct stakeholders – for example, in football, the Professional Footballers' Association (PFA), the League Managers Association (LMA) and the Premier League club owners all have representative groups. While these bodies have an overt function to resolve actual disputes, from the point of view of discourse ethics, their role is to establish, particularly where disagreement prevails, whose point of view is to count as important in the pursuit of agreements. On a more participatory level, the role that team captains, player representatives and child welfare officers play are all crucial indicators of the moral standing of a sporting organisation. Where these roles are carefully considered and constantly reviewed, effective discourse is, more than often, in place. The goal, then, of such discourse is not only to establish coaching as being receptive to issues and language associated with morality, but that the processes that allow such receptiveness are themselves morally commendable.

THE NATURE AND PRACTICE OF COACHING ETHICS

By now, it is clear that ethics in coaching is dependent on the effectiveness of both the structure and agency of human behaviour (this relationship is also identified in Chapter 5, 'Sociology for coaches'). In coaching terms, agency refers to the capacity of coaches to act independently and to make their own free choices. Structure, in contrast, refers to the recurrent patterned institutional arrangements which influence or limit the choices and opportunities available to coaches. While this relationship is evident across social life, from the point of view of coaching ethics, the focus is on how the capacity for the development of individual moral agency interweaves with the way in which sporting institutions establish good moral practice. With regards to agency, the ethics of coaching raises philosophical questions related to the identity of the coach and his or her specific role. The relationships between personhood, character and how coaches manifest these qualities in behaviour are all of crucial importance.

From the point of view of coaching ethics, the prevailing educative approach has involved an improbable abstract unpicking of hypothetical 'what ifs', where coaches are expected to provide well constructed moral responses to made-up scenarios. While there is some value to this approach, such methods tend to expose the gap between hindsight and foresight. The problem here is that reflecting on one's response to a moral dilemma in the past provides no guarantee as to how one will act in the future. There are two reasons for this. The first is that reflecting on past moral dilemmas is no guarantee that at some time in the future, a coach will be able to recognise where such reflection is most appropriately required. And, even if the coach does bring past experience to bear on the present, it will never be the case that two exact coaching situations ever re-present themselves in precisely the same way. While there is value to reflecting on past coaching decision making, crucially, it is important to recognise that such discussions are largely beside the point, for where good coaching ethics really count is in actual present practice.

This temporal or time-related displacement also fosters a cognitive disconnection; that is, *thinking* about good coaching and what one *ought* to do is a separate exercise from actually *doing* good coaching. The result is that discourse on what coaching ethics should be, in both academic and professional circles, often focuses on something other than actual coaching *praxis* (where praxis is taken as the application of ethical knowledge and understanding in action). The central problem which *praxis* reveals is that the 'doing' of good ethics (in sports coaching) is revealed through what happens, rather than by or because of what is planned, predicted or discussed ahead of any event. Because of the fluid complexity of coaching *praxis*, trying to prove that the goodness or badness of what actually happens in coaching is directly related to prior planning is difficult. While this does not deny the need for careful consideration and reflection, it seems that good coaching ethics is something that is revealed in the moment through perceptive self-awareness. For coaches, capturing exactly what happens in that 'good' coaching moment in such a way that it becomes a quality which the coach is aware of, understands and can subsequently refine, is a key to coaching success.

Understanding coaching as a moral enterprise has led a number of authors (Hemmestad *et al.*, 2010; Standahl and Hemmestad, 2011; Kristjánsson, 2005; Carr, 1998, 2000) to suggest the Greek virtue of *phronesis* (practical wisdom) as an appropriate and coveted coaching disposition. *Phronesis* is contrasted with the more familiar notion of *techné* – that (technical) aspect of coaching that holds means-to-ends relationships to be uncomplicated problems which can be addressed by scientific knowledge. The virtue of *phronesis,* on the other hand, allows coaches to respond to the unexpected human 'messiness' of coaching; perhaps a more realistic conception of what coaches actually do. Such responsiveness is far from a collapse into relativity, however, as it holds to considered 'good' ethical or moral coaching beliefs. In a similar vein, Loland (2011) has argued that a good coach is an 'enlightened generalist' – an individual who pursues the ideals of ethical perfectionism in terms of the Aristotelian idea of *eudaimonia,* or human flourishing. Such an approach, he argues, provides the coach with both the necessary perspective and *phronesis* (practical wisdom) to respond to the potentially excessive demands to succeed in contemporary competitive sport. Loland (2011) points to the significance of *phronesis* as an important virtue, but argues that, in order for the concept to develop greater authority and respect within the coaching profession, there is much more to be done to clarify what exactly *phronesis* is, and how it can be identified and transmitted effectively in coach education programmes. From the perspective of structure, the moral environment in which sports coaching ought to take place requires an understanding of coaching as a profession (McNamee, 1998). McNamee argues here that professionalisation is necessary in order to under-write the exacting moral standards that coaching practice requires. For the most part, the tendency for coaching organisations is to rely on unexamined and superficial usage of codes of conduct to do the bulk of their ethical work. If such codes are to be of any merit, they must be built on the central virtue of trust, which requires that coaches are not merely professional in name but that such central virtues carry over into the authoritative and regulatory functions of coaching institutions (see Cassidy *et al.*[2009] 'Understanding sports coaching' for an expanded discussion on this).

THE ETHICS OF SPORTS COACHING – EXAMPLE

In this final section of the chapter, we work through a specific example to illustrate the role of ethics in the practice of sports coaching. However, so as not to overlook much of what has been presented earlier, this discussion comes with a caution. The chapter has argued that coaching ethics is a phronetic activity and, therefore, may only reveal itself effectively through the exercise of practical wisdom that can only be properly perceived in real coaching situations. If this is the case, then an abstract discussion of a hypothetical example, no matter how representative it may be of coaching reality, will be of limited value. Good coaching ethics, though grounded in sound principles and pursued in a system-atic and consistent way, are marked by particular situational characteristics. If this were not the case, then we would have a formula for answering all moral problems. But in sport, as in other areas of applied ethics, things are rarely so straightforward. Here, therefore, what the reader can take from the following discussion are guidelines and a procedure to follow. Where such guidelines and procedures lead is for the individual coach to decide.

> **SCENARIO: THE ETHICS OF COACHING PHYSICAL AGGRESSION**
>
> *You are the coach of a professional academy contact-sport team. Your players are between 16 and 18 years old and are not professional athletes, though a few soon will be. The players are highly skilled and have an advanced understanding of the game and its ethos. They are aware of forms of gamesmanship that can give an advantage over opponents beyond the differences in technical skill. A key area which can determine competitive*

126

> *advantage is the level of physical aggression and dominance a player or team can exert over an opponent. You do not want your players to deliberately injure opponents and forbid 'cheap shots', but you do want your team to have a physical edge and accept the strategic benefit of injuries to opponents when they happen. How should you coach your players to approach physical aggression with this understanding of the game?*

The scenario admits to many possibilities and important variations. However, it is possible to discern three discrete moral perspectives one can take which will impact directly on the way one might coach aggression. The first position is that of 'lawful aggression'. A core consideration here is the role and status of the rules with respect to aggression in sport. In the specific example, the coach indicates some initial awareness of 'lawful aggression' through his intolerance of 'cheap shots', as they are prohibited by the rules. A further issue for consideration is whether that intolerance can hold firm and be consistent in the face of the possible instrumental benefits (if important opposition players are injured in this important game, we win), and where there is greater ambiguity with respect to the clarity of the rules in terms of the acceptability of certain forms of aggression and physical play.

A key guiding principle in this situation, depends on one's fundamental attitude to one's opponents. If opponents are seen exclusively as only means towards particular sporting ends, and not as valued ends in themselves, then it is more likely that the coach will objectify the opposition as obstacles to overcome as effectively as possible. While this efficiency may also include some consideration of the rules, the coach is also aware that the nature of the sport and the rules which constitute the game, do present occasions where maximal physical force can be exerted in ways that are injurious to opponents. In such situations, aggression is more likely to be coached proactively and instrumentally, where constraint is motivated by the need for discipline and avoiding penalties. One suspects that much of the everyday psychology of elite level sport might take this 'lawful-aggression' approach.

On the other hand, a coach may extend the view that other participants in the game are also persons who legitimately have genuine interests in competing, and that opponents have a right to pursue their sporting ends in ways that they would expect themselves. In this second approach, the principle of 'reciprocal-aggression' holds sway. Here, it is recognised that what makes the sporting contest acceptable is a level of equality that emerges in part through the rules, and in part through the ethos of the game. Reciprocal-aggression, through a social contract of sorts, underpins the narrative of the game. In such situations, a coach may condone aggressive play in line with what the prevailing ethos might allow. In other words, what becomes acceptable is not just based on the rules, but also the shared thinking of the participants. For instance, in pick-up games, children's contests and veterans' games, it is generally well understood that one should 'go easy' on opponents. Unfortunately, of course, such an approach is fragile and needs to be constantly reaffirmed through the actions of one's opponent. Similarly, there is also the prospect that reciprocity may mean participants actually agree to be more aggressive than the rules would otherwise permit.

'Ethical-aggression' represents a third approach. Here, it is necessary to establish clearly and unconditionally the type of aggressive attitude and approach one can legitimately pursue when one places the well-being and integrity of one's opponent as a priority. What is different here, is that the legitimate interests of one's opponents are appropriately considered in advance of any aggressive act. This does not mean, of course, that the game ought to lack aggressive intent or physical intensity – such qualities are, after all, also interests in which our opponents share – if we value such contests, we will want aggressive rather than passive opponents. What is does mean, however, is that coaching would focus on the technical demands of physical contact skills, and seek to effectively avoid situations which may leave participants vulnerable to injury, hurt and harm, even if it means choosing a less 'effective' technique. Furthermore, where coaches are able to identify effective ways to rule out such injurious and harmful scenarios, they have a further expectation to share such insights and present the game in its best light. This approach demands more of the coach, because it asks him or her to balance considerations of effective contesting, the integrity of persons and the aesthetic qualities of the game – not necessarily high priorities at any given time. But, one hopes, as coaches ought to be reflective on their practice, they should not be unmoved by the consequences of their actions. Hence, regardless of the formal rules and what goes for normal practice, they still hold a significant responsibility for the way aggression in their sport is directed.

CONCLUSION

Although this chapter has covered a broad spectrum of concerns, we believe a consistent message about the ethical nature and significance of sports coaching emerges in three significant ways. First, we consider that coaches who are reflective share a commitment to establish ethics as fundamental to, and at the forefront of, their practice. We have also argued that coaching is centrally a humanistic endeavour which involves the development of persons within and through movement practices. As such encounters require coaches to influence

128

the behaviour and values of athletes (and others), coaching practice can be considered to be a 'wilful' interaction. Coaches, therefore, need to be constantly aware of what they ought or ought not to do in their practice. Second, we have highlighted that discussion on the moral nature of coaching is important for practitioners and academics alike. We have presented a number of relevant concepts and principles in this chapter, and worked through a hypothetical example. Of far greater importance, however, is the need to capture accurately the moral engagements taking place in coaching. The need exists, then, for coaches and academics to be open and innovative in finding ways they can capture and record such experiences so that greater meaning and shared understanding of what 'good' coaching ethics is can emerge. Third, we would like to think that, in the same way that the coaching community invests significant time and resources into producing technical and tactical improvements, greater interest might be directed towards investigating how ethics can best work to improve coaching practice. Such issues, and the inevitable subsequent debate, ought to have a significant impact on the design and development of sport coaching curricula and the working practices of committed and reflective coaches, whether amateur or professional.

DISCUSSION TOPICS AND REVIEW QUESTIONS

1   Indentify and discuss some ethical issues for sports coaches. Try to ensure that your responses do not just reflect your personal experiences, but that they are considered alongside others in the context of the coaching process.
2   Identify your own moral perspective as a coach. Develop a list of all the do's and don't's you use as a coach. Identify which of these 'rules' are moral in nature. Are they related to any of the moral concepts presented in this chapter?
3   Discuss the ways in which you have been made aware of coaching ethics through your coaching qualifications. To what extent has such advice been helpful to you and changed your coaching behaviour? Are there any other ways in which you have become aware of 'good' or 'bad' coaching ethics?
4   Reflect on examples from your coaching experience where you have disputed the behaviour, values or actions of an athlete, another coach or a parent. What argument did you use to resolve the dispute? What did you learn from the experience (in the sense that you now think and act differently)?

Web Resources

Useful websites to further outline and stimulate ethical debate in sport and coaching include:

http://www.heacademy.ac.uk/assets/hlst/documents/resources/philosophy_ethics_sport.pdf

http://philosophyandsports.blogspot.co.uk/
http://iaps.net/

NOTE

1 As is often the case, the terms 'ethics' and 'morality' will be used interchangeably in this chapter. A broad distinction, however, is that while 'ethics' principally relates to the systematic (academic) study of right and wrong behaviour, 'morality' relates to the actual beliefs, motives and intentions behind human action.

CHAPTER 9

SPORTS DEVELOPMENT FOR COACHES

NICOLA BOLTON AND BEV SMITH

Coaching is central to sport development. In addition to enhancing the sporting experience for participants and performers, excellent coaches increase and sustain active lifestyles too.

Dr Tony Byrne, Chief Executive, sports coach UK

INTRODUCTION

Spend a couple of minutes thinking about your own sporting career, and consider the various sports you have both taken up and subsequently dropped. Ask yourself the following questions:

- How many sports have you tried?
- What were the reasons for trying out these sports and why did you drop them?
- Who did you rely on to be able to participate?

A typical response to the first two questions would be that you have tried numerous sporting activities, and that your decisions for participating and perhaps giving up were governed largely by a mix of personal, social and structural or opportunity-related factors (Torkildsen, 2011). The third question is of great significance to this chapter. Regardless of the opportunities or constraints affecting your choice of activity, you will have relied on others. Indeed, you will have been dependent on others to participate. There are some obvious examples to draw upon: school teachers providing extra-curricular opportunities, coaches taking sessions, facility managers providing venues, volunteers helping at clubs and, of course, parents and other adults prepared to provide transport and finance. When put together, sport becomes an intricate participation event, thus neither coaches nor sports development workers operate in isolation.

Participation in sport is affected by where you live, your background and wider personal and social influences (Horne *et al.*, 1999). Consequently, not everyone has the same opportunities either to participate or excel in sport. Collins with Kay (2003) provided a clear overview of the unequal participation patterns experienced by groups, and within certain areas, in the UK. Hence, there are many equality issues inherent within sport, and, for some commentators, sport both reflects the unequal social composition of society and perpetuates it (Jarvie, 2006; Collins, 2008b).

The role sport plays in society has grown in importance and is reflected in greater political involvement. Within the UK, the two principal aims for sport are to achieve international success (especially given the 2012 London Olympics) and to ensure that the UK population becomes more physically active. It should be noted that government policy (within government and between successive governments) has 'see-sawed' between these two aims. This has created tensions, as 'sport for sport's sake' competes for priority over 'sport for good' (Coalter, 2007; Collins, 2010a; Green, 2009), with the inevitable consequences of intermittent, rather than sustained, long-term development.

The purpose of this chapter is to explore issues associated with developing sport and how they help inform the coaching process. To address these issues, the chapter is divided into four sections. The first provides some definitions and discussion of the key concepts of sports development and community development. This is followed by a review of the main policy shifts relating to sport and, in particular, that related to two coaching initiatives, the UK Coaching Certificate (UKCC) and the UK Coaching Framework. Drawing on this contextual information, the third section provides insights into some of the issues associated with sports development and sports coaching and, in particular, how the former can inform the latter. The final section makes some concluding remarks regarding how coaching and sports development are distinct from each other but inextricably linked. The significance of the chapter lies in giving coaches an understanding of the wider political environment in which sports development operates and which, in turn, can impact on the coaching landscape – how coaching opportunities are defined, generated and provided. Such knowledge is important for coaches, as it can help them comprehend the often problematic and changing context in which they work, thus helping them to manage it more effectively.

KEY CONCEPTS

Sports development

Sports development is a contested area of sport studies (Bramham and Hylton, 2008), with no existing single definition. Collins (2010b) refers to some of the original definitions emerging during the early 1990s, which highlighted the importance of understanding sports development as a process with appropriate structures and systems to provide opportunities for both greater participation and improved performance. Bramham and Hylton (2008: 2) develop this further by writing, 'sports development is more accurately a term used to describe policies, processes and practices that form an integral feature of work involved in providing sporting opportunities and positive sporting experiences'. They go on to explain that this broad interpretation means that sports development embraces a wide occupational matrix that, among others, includes PE staff, teachers and coaches. Thus, sports development does not operate in isolation, by necessity it is dependent on others. Hence, partnerships, collaboration and shared funding are fundamental to achieving sports development outcomes.

A specific area of interest for sports development is the use of models which help depict the above definitions. In the first edition of this book (Bolton and Smith, 2008), three models of sports development were selected and presented – the traditional continuum developed by Derek Casey in 1988, the modified model of sports development continuum (Houlihan and White, 2002), and Cooke's 'House of Sport' (Cooke, 1996). The traditional sports development continuum sought to show how participants could move from foundation, through participation and performance, to excellence. This basic pyramid model was adapted in the early 1990s to reconsider the relationship between sport participation and performance. Here, greater recognition of the horizontal movement between participation and performance was made, taking into account 'changes in lifestyle, family and employment circumstances' (Houlihan and White, 2002: 42). The third model, Cooke's 'House of Sport,' provided a more realistic way of depicting the sports development process by outlining separate pathways for recreation (participation) and performance, and the addition of a third floor and penthouse which embraced increasingly elite levels of sport (Bramham and Hylton, 2008). It recognised that success is not predicated on a broad base of participation, and that many people are introduced to some sports for the first time in adult life.

Since then, the Long Term Athlete Development (LTAD) strategy has been a significant development, relevant to both sports development and coaching. Based on the work of Balyi (2001), the LTAD model represents a pathway which focuses on the long-term development of high performance athletes. It identifies six stages from 'FUNdamentals' to 'Training to Compete' and is considered a 'specialisation' model. It is heavily supported by governing bodies for sport in Canada, Ireland and the UK (MacPhail et al., 2010). Policy development work in Ireland has also drawn extensively on Côté and Hay's model of (young) people's socialisation into sport to produce a sports development framework or archetype of lifelong involvement in sport and physical activity (LISPA). The identified need for better alignment and integration of organisations providing sport and physical activity opportunities was a key rationale for this development (MacPhail *et al.*, 2010).

Community development

Probably the most contested term used in this chapter is 'community'. The word has multiple meanings and is used in very different contexts. Often it is used to define places associated by a range of characteristics including geographical size, population and socio-economic standards. However, Jarvie (2006: 328) writes 'communities exist beyond geography; they encompass a wide range of social ties and common interests that go beyond proximity or common residence'. In a similar vein, Hylton and Totten (2008) have concluded that the term 'community' implies some notion of collectivity, commonality, a sense of belonging or something shared. Indeed, the notion of investing in one another has been loosely referred to as developing social capital (Jarvie, 2006) although the evidence of sport creating social capital remains largely inconclusive (Collins with Kay, 2003; Coalter, 2007). So, community sport is often used synonymously with community recreation, and might refer to all kinds of organisations operating across the public, private and voluntary sectors.

Community sports development (CSD) is different both in terms of its historical background (Houlihan and White, 2002; Hylton and Totten, 2008; McDonald, 1995) and its approach. It seeks to address the social inequalities that permeate sport and the need to challenge these if the participatory franchise in local communities is to be extended (Bolton *et al.*, 2008). Hylton and Totten (2008: 83) refer to the fact that 'CSD does not exist in a 'sports bubble' as it requires an active engagement with social justice' and that the scale of involvement ranges from the local to the national, and even to the transnational. A key feature here, is the extent to which the policy and practice of CSD is implemented from a 'top-down' (externally imposed/deterministic) or 'bottom-up' (internally driven/ interactive) perspective, although recent research by Bolton *et al.* (2008) has called for a new understanding which focuses on interdependent relationships (citizens, communities and providers), a shared value system and a shift away from hierarchical conceptions of CSD.

POLICY CONTEXT

We contend that there is a close relationship between coaches and sports development workers. In one sense, all coaches are involved in sports development and thus, knowledge and understanding of context is essential. Furthermore, coaches are crucial to the delivery of sports development opportunities, and this is reflected in the increasingly differentiated roles that coaches perform. A partnership approach between these two emerging professions seems imperative (Lyle, 2008), and for this to be effective, coaches should look to sports development and the wider policy context to inform their practice.

In the UK, the fate of sport during the post-war years (i.e. since 1945) has been linked to the political priorities set by various governments (Henry, 2001). Not surprisingly, the importance of sport to government policy has varied during this time and, whilst a full account of these changes is beyond the scope of this chapter, other authors have tracked these historical developments (see for example, Houlihan and White, 2002; Henry, 2001). It should be noted, however, that the relationship between national policy and local delivery in relation to sport has rarely taken centre stage. Hence, sport continues to be a discretionary service of the local state (Robinson, 2004), with no mandatory requirement (unlike education and social services) for authorities to fully address its provision and opportunities. In reality, most local authorities have chosen to provide sport as a service, although its discretionary nature means the outcome has been a variable pattern of provision whilst always being under threat during periods of austerity.

Elected in 1997, the Labour Government produced a number of over-arching complementary English policy documents relating to sport between 2000 and 2002. Devolution has also affected sports policy, as both the Scottish Parliament and Welsh Government produced their own strategies for sport. Taken together, they provided a long-term framework for sport to be developed. Greater emphasis was placed on the contribution that sport could make to the wider cross-cutting agendas in England and the devolved home countries. Thus, sport was viewed by government as having value to the wider social and economic environment (Coalter, 2001).

In 2008, the Labour Government published 'Playing to Win' (DCMS, 2008), which signalled a significant shift in English sport policy from 'sport for good' to 'sport for sport's sake' (Green, 2009; Collins, 2010b). The importance of podium success and the responsibility of holding the Olympics led to the then Minister Andy Burnham stating, 'When you play sport, you play to win. That is my philosophy . . . It is a plan to get more people taking up sport for the love of sport; to expand the pool of English sportsmen and women; and to break records, win medals and win tournaments for this country' (DCMS, 2008).

There has since been a general election with a Conservative-Liberal Democratic coalition government in Westminster. Their priority is to tackle the economy by principally curbing spending, especially the public sector deficit. This resulted in a list of planned cuts which included England's free swimming programme and the PE School Sport and Young People initiative. In 2010, a plan for the Olympic legacy was published (DCMS, 2010), which focused on competitive school sport including the mounting of a 'School Games' and a new youth sport strategy (DCMS, 2012).

So, how does sports coaching fit into this wider policy context? Emerging from the Government's original 'Sporting Future for All' (DCMS, 2000) report, a Coaching Task Force (CTF) was established to undertake a detailed review of sports coaching. One of the issues that emerged was a lack of nationally recognised/transferable qualifications within, and in relation to, coaching. As a result, sports coach UK, the organisation responsible for coach development in Britain, was charged with addressing this issue and significant funding was made available. Two developments, the UKCC and the UK Coaching Framework were subsequently launched. Given the comments made earlier in relation to devolution, the fact that these initiatives were agreed on a UK level is important. Each initiative will be considered briefly, but students are directed to the sports coach UK's website to obtain more detailed information (http//www.sportscoachuk.gov).

The UK Coaching Certificate

Those within sports coach UK charged with creating the UKCC worked with a number of national governing bodies and key agencies in its development. Initially, five levels of coaching were considered and, after consultation, these levels were reduced to four, in order to align with European qualifications (sports coach UK, 2011a). The UKCC has been designed to help professionalise the role of the coach, to enable movement between the home countries and provide opportunities to relocate between sports through the inclusion of core components. It is important to note that the UKCC is not, in itself, a qualification. Rather, it is an endorsement, or a mark of the quality of a governing body with regards to its coach education programme. The current position of the UKCC is that thirty sports have engaged with it, and achieved the endorsement.

An extensive monitoring and evaluation programme in relation to the success of the new structure has been put in place. In 2004, Marketing and Opinion Research International (MORI) undertook a series of in-depth semi-structured interviews with coaches and other national stakeholders (such as the Sports Councils) with the twin objectives to evaluate the delivery planning process and to assess the ongoing functioning of the UKCC. Research was also conducted to determine enablers and barriers that the governing bodies faced regarding the implementation of the UKCC. In summing up the delivery-planning process, the perceived benefits included: better defining the sports coach's role, standardising coach education and qualifications, raising the profile of coaching, and producing knowledgeable and competent coaches. Similarly, the ongoing implementation study reported significant progress in several areas, including the identification of tutors, verifiers and assessors; the employment of extra staff; and greater support from governing body senior management and external agencies (sports coach UK, 2004). Perhaps most important, however, was the emergence of support for the new structure from existing coaches. On the other hand, increased demand on lead officers, a delay in guidance materials and poor networking between sports, emerged as barriers to progress. Subsequent reviews undertaken in 2008 and 2010, confirmed that coaching was perceived as being more coherent between all participating national governing bodies of sport. In addition, there was a belief that the differences between elite and other levels of coaching had narrowed. Other key benefits of UKCC endorsement included an industry-wide approach to development and the sharing of good practice (sports coach UK, 2011b).

The UK Coaching Framework

The UK Coaching Framework was formulated after an extensive period of consultation, and launched in 2008. It was developed to build on the work of the Coaching Task Force, the Home Country Sports Councils and respective governing body plans. The founding vision of the UK Coaching Framework was 'to create a cohesive, ethical, inclusive and valued coaching system where skilled coaches support children, players and athletes at all stages of their development and is world-leading by 2016' (sports coach UK, 2008: 11).

The UK Coaching Framework is seen as an important reference point for governing bodies, local coach networks and other organisations to support the evolution of coaching development systems. Students of sport development and coaching seeking more information can locate *The UK Coaching Framework: A 3–7–11 year action plan* document by visiting www.sportscoachuk.org/resource/uk-coaching-framework.

INSIGHTS FOR SPORTS DEVELOPMENT AND SPORTS COACHING

Since the turn of the twenty-first century, sports related employment opportunities have grown. This has been witnessed within the emerging professions of sports development (Collins, 2008b) and coaching (Lyle, 2002), suggesting that they are gaining parity with other professions, such as teaching. If one subscribes to the view that there is a pathway towards greater recognition of sports development and sports coaching as professions, then much can be learned from the work of Bayles (1988). He suggested three necessary conditions for a profession: extensive training, training that is intellectual in kind, and the delivery of an important service. Similarly, Chelladurai (2006) suggested four characteristics as defining a profession: an organised body of knowledge, professional authority, community sanction and a regulative code of ethics.

As students of sport, and in light of the above conditions and characteristics, you might spend a little time thinking about sports development and coaching and ask yourselves the following questions: Do you view either sports development or sports coaching in the same professional light as law, medicine or teaching? Alternatively, do you see either, or both, as a vocation or an occupation? Finally, what factors did you consider in coming to your conclusion?

Although some of you may consider both sports development and coaching to be professions, there are clearly areas of doubt. One of them surrounds the clear conceptualisation of what each involves. That is, do they meet Chelladurai's condition of being rooted in distinct bodies of knowledge? Indeed, the terms 'sports development' and 'coaching' are often used randomly and inappropriately; a tendency which undermines the credibility of both to be considered separate professions. This is particularly so when studying the relationship between sports development and sports coaching at the community level. Think of some adverts for jobs to develop sport in the community. Often they come with a mix of descriptors crossing the fields of coaching and sports development which serve to confuse potential candidates. Similarly, in practice, there is frequently a blurring of roles between sports development and sports coaching. An illustration of this is provided in the following scenario.

CASE STUDY

A graduate with a Masters qualification in a sports discipline is seeking employment. In addition to academic qualifications, she has a national governing body coaching qualification and experience of working with a sports team. She sees an advertisement for a sport specific development officer to work in an identified geographical area. Some of the key objectives for the post-holder, against which the applications will be measured, include:

- *Increasing the size of the governing body membership (participants, coaches, officials and clubs);*
- *Sustainable club development (increasing the capacity in clubs and identifying relevant training for club personnel); and*

▼

- *Increasing the size of the network (identifying and involving key partners to contribute to the sports development process).*

Having been the successful candidate, she is given considerable freedom in creating a work programme. Being enthusiastic and relatively inexperienced, she develops an extremely busy schedule, networking between various schools and clubs and working many unsocial hours. On a visit to one of the area's clubs, it became apparent that one of the teams was likely to disband because they were unable to find a replacement coach. The club Secretary made it quite clear that the best way a Development Officer (DO) could help them was to coach the team until they could find someone else. After much discussion, she, as the DO, agreed to find some extra hours in the work programme and coach the team for a period of three weeks, while the club looked for a replacement. In that period, the team made progress and attracted additional players whilst she thoroughly enjoyed working in the given coaching capacity. After three weeks, the club had still not found a replacement so she, as a DO, agreed to stay on indefinitely ('until another coach was found').

This illustration seeks to provide a real-life situation many sports development officers experience. Now consider the following two questions. First, determine two advantages and two disadvantages of undertaking the role of the coach in this instance; and second, suggest one or two alternative solutions the DO could have explored to resolve the situation she found herself in. It might be suggested that our graduate DO provided a good service to the club. Equally she may have taken this course of action as a form of self-promotion, working within her 'comfort zone'. We contend that undertaking the coaching position was in no-one's long-term interests, as she was focusing her energies on one club and neglecting to address the key objectives of her job. This is not to say that sport development officers should not be involved in coaching, and we support the work of Eady (1993), Lyle (2008) and Nesti (2001) who suggest that sports development workers and coaches have similarities, with both being considered agents of change. Both also seek to engage people in sport and physical activity, thus making a difference to people's lives. The significant distinction between them, however, lies in the fundamental roles they should play. For example, a sports development worker affects change in several places with many different groups of participants. This involves the employment or deployment of coaches and seeks a modification in the behaviour of individuals in the community. On the other hand, a coach affects change in one place at a time with a single group or individual participant through the delivery of specific sessions.

There is an ongoing debate in coaching that suggests important shifts are occurring: from instruction to pedagogy, and from a focus on the participant–performer divide to an emphasis on developing the individual (Jones, 2006a). Additionally, coaching is becoming increasingly recognised as 'an inherently non-routine, problematic and complex endeavour' particularly with regard to its complex leader–follower nature (Jones, 2006a: 3). There is also a debate within sport development. Nesti (2001) identified the personal and psychological qualities possessed by many sports development workers as creativity, empathy, commitment, presence and authenticity. Given sports development's rather unique role to be proactive and interventionist, Nesti (2001: 210) suggested close links to counsellors, psychotherapists and educators. This has resonance with some fields of knowledge that underpin the work of sport development professionals, which, according to Pitchford and Collins (2010), include health promotion, social work and physical education. Clearly, these two emerging professions (i.e. coaching and sports development) have commonalities and, given the current agenda, if developed in a complementary and meaningful manner, could be instrumental in contributing to a new sporting landscape.

Recognising their complementary nature, it is important to examine how sports development concepts can be used to support coaches in their practice. For example, for coaches to have a better understanding of their evolving role, it would appear relevant for them to have a firm grasp of governmental agendas as related to increasing sport and physical activity in the UK. An over-riding goal is to encourage greater participation, across all age groups and with specific reference to particular community sport. This will require sports development professionals and sports coaches to seek new participants, as an agenda that focuses on getting existing participants to do more, will be insufficient. For example, encouraging sport and physical activity to be undertaken at places of work could be a way forward in this regard, thus establishing employers as priority partners for the future. Such initiatives will run parallel to the primary and secondary school participation programmes already being implemented. Sports development, thus, should have a key role in developing sustainable opportunities within local communities; in essence, providing opportunities for sports coaches to work, or assisting coaches to develop such opportunities for themselves.

Sports coaches also need to determine their role within this wider agenda. Sports development workers will be seeking coaches to deliver sessions but, given that there will be new audiences, it is anticipated that sports coaching will be as much about engagement and retention as about performance and 'match' results. Hence, we believe there will be a need to look beyond an historic emphasis on coaching young people and performers, and to consider the needs of the wider population. The development menu of the future, then, needs to be varied, targeted and sustainable. Indeed, the UK Coaching Framework (sports coach UK,

140

2006) establishes some clear expectations that coaches should address if interest in sport is to be engendered and sustained. These include: welcoming children and adults into sport; making sport fun; building fundamental skills and improving sport-specific skills; developing fair play, discipline and respect; enhancing physical fitness and lifestyle; placing a high value on the development of the whole person; and keeping children, players and athletes safe. Such directives hold the potential to give coaches a clear future focus in relation to where they should concentrate their energies.

CONCLUSION

Since the beginning of the twenty-first century, the sectors of sports development and coaching have received unprecedented levels of attention and investment from central and devolved government. Sport is now recognised as a tool that can assist in partially delivering the related governmental social agendas. Furthermore, education and training for sports development professionals has been seen as a priority in official policy documents such as 'Sporting Future for All' (DCMS, 2000), whilst the recent launch of a new professional body, the Chartered Institute for the Management of Sport and Physical Activity (CIMSPA), has signalled a step-change in improving the stature and profile of its members. Unsurprisingly, then, sports development and sports coaching are growing occupations and emerging professions. Set within an overall policy context of increasing participation, it is important that their roles remain complementary but distinct. Each comes with its own challenges but shares the need to remain people-centred and people-focused as change agents within the sports industry. Knowledge of the sport development context and how it shapes coaching policy, then, is undoubtedly important for coaches, as it enables them to carefully consider their role as they respond to the wider developmental and social agenda.

DISCUSSION TOPICS AND REVIEW QUESTIONS

1   Discuss the models outlined in this chapter and identify their strengths and weaknesses.
2   Identify three differences between sports development and community sports development. How would these differences be reflected in any respective job descriptions and appointments for sports development and community sports development workers?
3   Identify three differences between coaching at the community level as compared to high performance coaching.

4   Drawing on the work of Chelladurai (2006), discuss whether you think either sports development and/or sports coaching merit the label 'profession' or 'emerging profession'. Give some reasons for your decision.
5   With reference to the 2012 London Olympics, consider the common goals between sports development workers and sports coaches to achieve an effective legacy.

Web Resources

Relevant websites to research further on this topic of sport development for coaches include:

http://www.cimspa.co.uk/

http://www.sportsdevelopment.org.uk/

http://www.sportscoachuk.org/

http://www.sportengland.org/

http://www.sportscotland.org.uk/

http://www.sportni.net/

http://www.sportwales.org.uk/

http://www.uksport.gov.uk/

PART IV

CHAPTER 10

BIOMECHANICS FOR COACHES

GARETH IRWIN, IAN BEZODIS AND DAVID KERWIN

Knowledge about biomechanical principles is critical in understanding and explaining suitable technique to athletes.

> Jon Grydeland, Head Coach, Norwegian Women's Beach
> Volleyball team (2006 European Championships
> and World Cup, Bronze medallists)

INTRODUCTION

This chapter aims to outline the value of biomechanics for coaches. Biomechanics is the application of mechanical principles to biological systems. In this context, the focus is on how these principles apply to the human athlete taking part in sporting activities. Gymnastics and athletics, both highly technical sports, are ideal to illustrate many of the concepts being presented and so feature strongly within the chapter. Other sports are referenced where appropriate, with several of the ideas being transferable. Many established texts exist that provide a well grounded scientifically rigorous explanation of the basic concepts relating to sports biomechanics (e.g. Hay, 1994; Hamill and Knutson, 2009; Robertson *et al.*, 2004; Watkins, 2007). The content of this chapter provides our perspective, and is supported by current research that has evaluated the link between the coaching process, training theory and the universal principles of biomechanics. In many ways, then, this chapter bridges the divide between science and coaching.

The first section introduces a conceptual model of technique and performance based on the article by Irwin *et al.* (2005), and includes a discussion of the ways in which coaches understand technique within the context of biomechanics. The second section introduces the notion of the coaching–biomechanics interface, which details how biomechanics can help coaches in their work. This is followed by a third section, which outlines different types of analyses in biomechanics that are currently practised in relation to sport. A note of caution, however, runs through the chapter concerning issues of (coach) interpretation and comprehension, particularly in relation to the use of new video-based technologies. Coaches, thus, should be aware that, at times, a false impression can be created, with the images alone appearing to provide answers when the reality is more complex. While not suggesting that some issues cannot be evaluated accurately and appropriately through video technology, we would like to emphasise the importance of understanding within biomechanics and its translation to coaching, which places biomechanical knowledge as a tool to be critically used by coaches. Finally, a brief view of future developments in biomechanics and coaching are presented to highlight the impact of new technologies on coaching practice.

THE CONCEPTUAL MODEL OF TECHNIQUE AND PERFORMANCE

Knowing how to successfully develop skills in athletes is a crucial aspect of a coach's knowledge (Zinkovsky *et al.*, 1976). To illustrate how elite coaches facilitate such improvements, Irwin *et al.*, (2005) recently developed a conceptual model (see Figure 10.1).

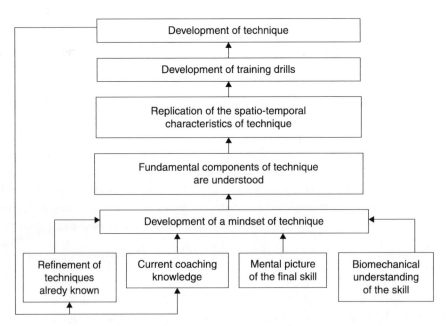

Figure 10.1 A conceptual model depicting how coaches develop skills in athletes. (Adapted from Irwin *et al.*, 2005)

G. Irwin, I. Bezodis and D. Kerwin

This model is consistent with others (e.g. Côté *et al.*, 1995), and represents a mental process illustrative of a coach's response to, and interpretation of, a specific situation. The research that underpins it was carried out on elite gymnastics coaches, and echoes previous findings within the more generic coaching literature (e.g. Gould *et al.*, 1990). A key feature of the model is the development of a 'mindset' for a coach, which represents a conceptual understanding of the technical aspects of a skill. Over time, coaches develop this conceptual understanding which they associate with successful performance. The components underpinning the development of this mindset are, first, the refinement of techniques that are already known. For example, when, in 2000, the gymnastic vaulting horse was replaced by the vaulting table (Irwin and Kerwin, 2009), coaches relied on refining the training drills from the old horse to the new table. The second component that contributes to the mindset is current coaching knowledge. The importance of this has been well researched (Gould *et al.*, 1990; Irwin *et al.*, 2004) with the significance of critical reflection and interactive mentorships being emphasised. The third aspect is to do with a coach's mental picture of the skill and is used to identify key phases, movement patterns and timings. Finally, a fourth component, biomechanical understanding of the final skill, relates to a descriptive grasp of how the performer organises his or her body segments to achieve a successful technique. The development of the mental picture and the biomechanical understanding (i.e. the third and fourth) components are often aided by technology (e.g. a frame-by-frame analysis). From the resultant mindset, a coach can generate an understanding of the key phases of the skill in question.

When developing training regimes, coaches often attempt to replicate key aspects of technique in the drills they use. This specificity allows adaptations to occur that assist in the effective and efficient development of skill. Importantly, Figure 10.1 also highlights the fact that the coach is managing the whole process, and decides how and in what order aspects of the desired skill are going to be addressed. This ability to arrange the process of skill development is fundamental, although naturally it relies heavily on technical knowledge being clearly understood in the first place. For example, an elite gymnastics coach would have precise knowledge of what he or she would expect from a gymnast in terms of the movement patterns and body positions to be performed (Irwin *et al.*, 2005). If, on the other hand, the technical understanding is not accurate, it would be impossible for the coach to select training drills that would be effective. The potential benefit of the model depicted in Figure 10.1, then, echoing the case made in Chapter 3 ('Skill acquisition for coaches'), lies in uncovering the mechanisms that control skill development in order that coaches can manage them better.

Similarly, the theoretically grounded science of sports biomechanics provides a mechanism that can help coaches better understand technique. It can do this through identifying the most effective skill development pathways, reducing the risk of injury and removing the trial and error of training. In essence, following the principles of overload and specificity (principles that are discussed in greater depth in Chapter 13 'Physiology for coaches'), sports biomechanics aims to make training more effective and efficient. Helping coaches to understand technique and, hence, providing the link between biomechanics and coaching has been a challenge for the last 30 years. Trying to address how biomechanics can help coaches and how the knowledge requirements of coaches can be harnessed has led us to what we have termed the coaching–biomechanics interface.

THE COACHING–BIOMECHANICS INTERFACE

The coaching–biomechanics interface is a term that we use to conceptualise how coaching can be informed from a biomechanical perspective. The process involved here is a continuous one, with each cycle starting and ending with the athlete. The process is based on a coach's tacit knowledge in relation to the practices that are routinely used to develop athletes' skills. This information, through systematic conversation with a biomechanist, is then turned into biomechanical variables which can either be measured or theoretically analysed. The key to these variables is that they are directly related to successful performance of the skill. Once understanding of the key aspects of skills and any associated progressions or drills has been understood, informed feedback can be delivered to the athletes via the coach. Integral to this process, is the communication between the biomechanist, and the coach and athlete. This cycle of extracting, processing and imparting new scientifically grounded knowledge or understanding, represents the whole or the actuality of the coaching–biomechanics interface. Sometimes, this new knowledge may simply reinforce existing practices; at other times, it can provide new insights which inform future skill development. The interaction between the coach and the biomechanist is depicted in Figure 10.2 which illustrates how the technical understanding of elite coaches 'interfaces' with the underlying biomechanical determinants of performance. The coach–biomechanist interaction provides the opportunity to identify meaningful information that is both biomechanically driven and coaching relevant. Coaches can use this science-based information to provide feedback while biomechanists can use it to develop technologies; all in the interests of improving athletic performance. This coaching–biomechanics interface, then, provides a catalyst for the effective, efficient and safe development of training drills, strength and conditioning programmes and skill learning.

The overall purpose of developing the coaching–biomechanics interface is to bridge the gap between biomechanical science and practice. The interface aims to make training more effective and efficient, particularly for athletes who are working near to their physiological limits. More specifically, the coaching–biomechanics

148

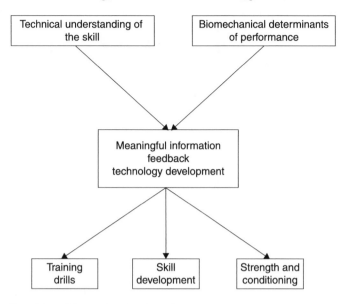

Figure 10.2 Coaching–Biomechanics Interface

interface can help coaches and the coaching process in five ways. Each will now be discussed in turn.

Enhancing coaches' technical understanding of skills

Input from biomechanics can enable coaches to gain a better appreciation of successful technique by providing an understanding of underlying principles of motion and how they apply to key phases of skills. In general, coaches' understanding of technique is based on a visual inspection of the skill in question. Here, in order to evaluate technique, a coach will look at the key aspects of performance which are considered to be directly related to success. For ease of interpretation, we shall call these variables performance indicators. These performance indicators fall into two main categories, continuous and discrete. The functional phases of the longswing in gymnastics have recently been shown to be good examples of continuous performance indicators (Irwin and Kerwin, 2006). The functional phases are characterised by a dynamic hip extension, (opening) to flexion (closing), and shoulder flexion to extension, as illustrated in Figure 10.3. The left graphic (in Figure 10.3) shows the start and end of the gymnast's hip functional phase (linked by a double-headed arrow), while the right graphic depicts the

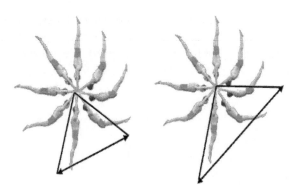

Figure 10.3 The functional phases of the gymnastic longswing (Irwin and Kerwin, 2007a)

corresponding phase for the gymnast's shoulders. The authors showed how both extension and flexion occurred as the gymnast passed underneath the bar and, consequently, that 70 per cent of the total musculoskeletal work needed for the longswing was completed during this time. As a consequence of such work, coaches could focus their attention on these phases of the swing, emphasising the extension and flexion of the hips and shoulders as the gymnast passes underneath the bar.

Discrete performance indicators are defined as single outcome measures, or measures at an instant in time during a skill, which are key to the successful performance of that skill. For example, Figure 10.4 illustrates a sprinter in the

Figure 10.4 Darren Campbell performing the sprint start showing extension into the 'thrust position': a key discrete performance indicator used by coaches as a measure of successful execution of the skill

150

thrust phase of his start. The thrust phase of the sprint start is the result of a large impulse which is needed to accelerate the athlete from the blocks. Ideally, a straight line should be formed from the ankle to the shoulder indicating that the drive is effectively transferred into a suitable forward and upward direction of motion.

Evaluating coaching practices to enhance skills

This area of work is potentially sensitive because a biomechanist can sometimes be seen as challenging a coach in relation to what the latter knows. This, however, should not be the case, as both should be working together to enhance each other's knowledge. For example, during the build up to the 2000 and 2004 Olympic Games, the sprinter Darren Campbell received biomechanical support for his sprint start technique. Based on the need to establish the most effective block setting, the coach, athlete and biomechanist devised a series of sessions that enabled them to determine which block setting (i.e. distance between the blocks and the hands) was most effective for Darren. In addition to this, a more detailed analysis of the thrust position (see Figure 10.4) and the forces and impulses produced by it was undertaken to enable the relationships between thrust mechanics and successful sprint start performance to be determined.

Evaluating training practices to develop skills

As opposed to the specific advice on certain aspects of performance given above, the primary aim here is to inform the selection of training drills or preparatory activities for the development of skills. One approach for coaches is to mine information from academic research relating to more effective training drills for the development of a particular skill. An example from our own work provides an illustration of this process in action. Here, a series of linked research studies were developed, based on the training principles of specificity and overload, focusing on developing the longswing in men's artistic gymnastics (Irwin and Kerwin, 2005, 2007a, 2007b). These studies involved the development of a method to identify more effective progressions (preparatory skills) for the development of the longswing. We had previously identified that UK coaches have at their disposal 49 different progressions for this skill (Irwin et al., 2004). Using biomechanical techniques, two categories of progressions were identified: those that exhibited similarities in movement patterns (kinematics and coordination), and those that required similar musculoskeletal work (kinetics) to the final skill. The progressions were then ranked within each category, enabling selection of appropriate progressions to each gymnast's current stage of development.

A second example comes from athletics, where sprint coaches routinely utilise the monitoring of 'flying 30' times (i.e. a 30m split time taken from the maximum velocity phase of the sprint) to assess changes in performance throughout training cycles. Biomechanical measurements taken from these runs can help explain any changes in velocity, which is the product of step length and step frequency. Our research has shown that within one training group over the course of several months, changes in velocity were closely linked to changes in step frequency (Bezodis *et al.*, 2008a). Furthermore, those changes occurred in conjunction with changes in the training programme. The sprinters created their highest velocities and step frequencies at times when the focus was on speed work, whereas lower velocities and step frequencies were created when the training programme involved high volume weight training. The weight training would have increased the strength of the muscle groups, and therefore their ability to impart force, but it was not until this was transferred to the actual skill of sprinting via the increase in speed work that the changes in velocity and step frequency were manifest. Such 'academically derived' knowledge has, unsurprisingly, proved very useful for coaches.

Facilitating the evolution of technique within sport (i.e. through the development of new skills)

Biomechanics has directed the development of sport in numerous ways. The most obvious instances lie within equipment design (e.g. new javelins, soccer balls and golf clubs) and innovative techniques. An example in relation to developing new techniques comes from the former Soviet Union (USSR) when it was decided that gymnastics was going to be an illustration of the country's superior political and social systems. Consequently, biomechanists and coaches worked together and theoretically derived a catalogue of skills that had never been attempted before (Malmerg, 1978). The most famous of these was the Tkachev (see Figure 10.5). The skill involves the gymnast rotatating clockwise around the bar up to the point of release before travelling backwards over the bar whilst rotating anti-clockwise to re-catch the bar on the downswing. The skill can be performed in a straddled, piked or straight body position, the shape adopted by the performer dictating the difficulty rating.

The skill was first performed in 1974 by the Russian gymnast Alexander Tkachev, after whom it was named. However, emphasising the link to biomechanics, it was first proposed not by a coach but by the Soviet biomechanist Smolevski in 1969. Nowadays, the Tkachev is commonly performed by elite male and female

152

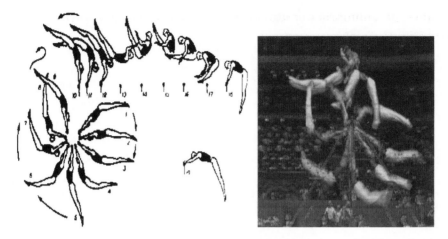

Figure 10.5 The Tkachev move: Left, the original Smolevskij drawing (1969). Right, stroboscopic image of a Tkachev, Olympic Games 2000

[source: Nissinen, M.A., Preiss, R. and Brüggemann, P. (1985). Simulation of human airborne movements on the horizontal bar. In D. A. Winter and R. Norman (eds.) *Biomechanics IX-B*. Champaign, IL.: Human Kinetics. pp. 373–376.]

gymnasts using different body shapes (straight, pike and straddle), and with extra twists during the flight phase. A recent example from female gymnastics (Kerwin and Irwin, 2010) showed how this skill has evolved and, more specifically, how gymnasts have adapted their technique to capitalise on the international governing body's decision to widen the uneven bars. The findings here demonstrated that changing the direction of the movement allowed gymnasts to gain greater height and generate larger angular momentum in the aerial phase (rotational capacity). Another key finding that has had a direct influence on coaching the amended Tkachev technique, was that the muscular work done during the old and new version of the skill is very different. Although the two Tkachevs appear visually similar, the muscle actions significantly differ and, as a consequence, the strength, conditioning and skill development requirements must be specific to the needs of the movement (Kerwin and Irwin, 2010). Such an example provides a clear illustration of the potential role of the biomechanist in supporting the coaching process.

Similarly, work by Hiley and Yeadon (2005) used computer simulation to address the question of whether a triple straight backward somersault dismount could be performed from the high bar. Their conclusion was that, although it is technically possible, the margins for error, in both the preparatory circle and the exact instant of release, are so minimal that it would be extremely risky for a gymnast to attempt the skill in competition.

Assisting in optimising performance (i.e. by theoretically justifying the modification of skills)

Computer models based on forward dynamics have been increasingly used to investigate and develop sports skills. For example, a forward dynamics model uses information on forces applied within the body to predict the subsequent body movements. Through such means, sports biomechanics can begin to address questions such as: What is the optimal technique for a particular performer? and What is potentially possible for the performer to execute? An example of how this has worked comes from a study by Kerwin *et al.* (1990). At the 1988 Olympic Games, (Seoul, South Korea) a famous Soviet gymnast Valeri Liukin (competitor #149 in Figure 10.6) performed his signature triple backward somersault dismount from the high bar. A simplified graphical reconstruction of this together with a recorded sequence from another competitor (#120) are shown in Figure 10.6.

To successfully execute a triple backward somersault, the gymnast needs to have generated substantial (i.e. enough) rotation (also known as angular momentum) as he releases from the bar (only male gymnasts carry out this manoeuvre). Importantly, once airborne, the magnitude of angular momentum will remain constant. The gymnast changes his body shape in order to control the somersault rate (also known as angular velocity), and whilst airborne, the rotation occurs around the gymnast's centre of mass. Because the gymnast needs to spin quickly to complete the triple somersault, he must grab his knees, thus pulling the body segments closer to the mass centre. This results in a reduction in the distribution

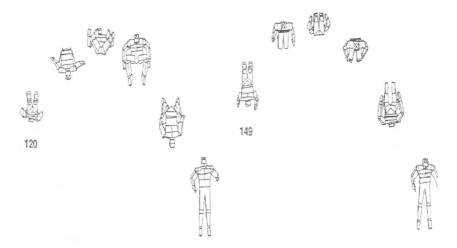

Figure 10.6 A graphical reconstruction of a triple backward somersault by Valeri Liukin (#149) and another gymnast (#120) at the 1988 Seoul Olympics

G. Irwin, I. Bezodis and D. Kerwin

of mass about the axis of rotation, with the reluctance to spin being decreased. This interplay between somersault rate (angular velocity) and resistance to rotate (moment of inertia) provides the performer with a control mechanism in flight. However, successful performance of this skill is dictated by the Fédération Internationale de Gymnastique (FIG) (the sport's international governing body), which states that the knees must not pass (i.e. be wider than) the width of the hips. Performer #120 in Figure 10.6 has the knees wider apart than the shoulders, whereas competitor #149 has adopted a (better) position with the knees being closer together. Officially, competitor #120 should lose marks; so, what can be done to help him? One way would be for the coach to just advise him to tighten or close the tuck shape to avoid this penalty, leaving the gymnast to work things out further from there. Alternatively, a much more detailed approach to solving the problem and help the gymnast achieve the desired aim, would be through the use of computer simulation. By developing a set of equations of motion for the gymnast (who is of known physical dimensions), it is possible to model the skill in question. Firstly, it is necessary to check that the model works; that is, that it reproduces an accurate representation of the skill performed. If this is satisfied, then it is possible to modify the movements made by the gymnast in subsequent 'runs' of the computer model. The biomechanist can then see what happens to the theoretical gymnast as a result of closing the model's legs together in flight. The precise measures that come from this form of modelling can determine how much the angular momentum (i.e. the capacity to rotate) of the gymnast around the bar prior to release would have to be increased to enable a modified triple somersault dismount to be achieved. We believe that this approach to examining technique and modifying performance is certainly preferable to putting an athlete at risk of injury from a failed move resulting from inaccurate advice. It is also preferable to wasting valuable training time on changes which ultimately may not improve performance.

TYPES OF ANALYSIS IN SPORTS BIOMECHANICS

There are many ways in which biomechanics can be used in a sports setting, but for the purposes of this chapter, they have been divided into three categories:

Qualitative analysis (e.g. matching to a mental image of a skill)

The increase in available computer and video technologies has provided opportunities for coaches to access a whole range of new techniques for analysis. As a result, areas of visual analysis which were once the province of the sports biomechanist have now become readily available to all interested parties.

Figure 10.7 A frame-by-frame depiction of the rugby place kick

As also mentioned in Chapter 11 ('Match analysis for coaches') commercial software (e.g. Silicon Coach™ and Dartfish™) suitable for this type of analysis can run on a standard laptop computer, and only require low cost digital video cameras for input. They enable instant replay, slow motion and frame-by-frame playback to be presented to the coach with ease. They also facilitate the production of sequential images of skills such as the rugby place kick (see Figure 10.7).

This form of video-based analysis is normally undertaken by coaches to inspect technical skills in detail or to compare performances from one session to another. It enables the coach to supplement and enhance his or her direct observational skills. As discussed in section two of this chapter, coaches develop an understanding of what they consider to be the desired technique and, by using new technologies they have additional ways of comparing the current performance with the mental image of the ideal performance. The effectiveness of any decisions made at this level of analysis, however, can only be as accurate as the coach's mindset or subjective perception. Hence, the coach may be able to see what is missing, but this does not necessarily result in understanding what needs to be changed to bring about a desired outcome.

Semi-quantitative analysis (e.g. analysis of angles and temporal aspects of movements)

This level of analysis is the first step to quantification, and provides an estimate of the key variables associated with performing any skill successfully. Care has to be taken when using semi-quantitative analyses, as only simple scaling (i.e. using a single object of known length to convert measures in the video image to real distances) can be achieved where movements are largely assumed to occur in a plane when, in reality, they are three-dimensional. Consequently, the inaccuracies arising from such an assumption are particularly evident when angles are being estimated (Rodano and Tavana, 1995). This leaves the validity of many measures recorded using semi-quantitative (and qualitative) analysis open to

156

question. Qualitative and semi-quantitative analyses then, whilst visually impressive and informative, do not provide coaches with the maximum benefit to be derived from such technology.

Quantitative analysis (e.g. full kinematic and kinetic analyses)

Kinematics is the general term used in biomechanics to describe temporal or sequential and spatial characteristics of movement. The variables in this category include position, velocity and acceleration of body parts (e.g. limbs) or the whole body mass centre. Kinetics, on the other hand, is the generic description of forces which cause motion. Knowledge of the physical size of an athlete is added to the information on externally applied forces to complete the study of kinetics. Examples here could include an analysis of muscular forces producing the joint flexion and extension necessary to determine the work done by specific muscle groups during dynamic activities such as jumping or landing.

For sport to benefit from quantitative analysis, close cooperation between coaches and biomechanists is necessary. The types of examination included here, range from 2D video analyses to measure linear and angular positions (i.e. kinematics) to 3D inverse dynamics analyses (i.e. kinetics) to determine internal joint forces, muscle powers and musculoskeletal work. A 2D video analysis might appear to be almost identical to one of the semi-quantitative studies listed above, but a true 2D video analysis needs very precise calibration of an image plane (Brewin and Kerwin, 2003). 2D quantitative analyses, then, can be used when the apparatus or environment constrains the movement, or when both sides of the body move simultaneously in the same direction, as in vertical jumping. A longswing on the high bar in gymnastics meets both these criteria, and so illustrates a situation where 2D analysis is sufficient (Irwin and Kerwin, 2001).

Biomechanists also use kinematics to describe and explain complex movement patterns involved in performances. This may be related to single joint analysis or to how joints and segments interact (Hamill *et al.*, 2000; van Emmerik and van Wegen, 2000). The joint and segmental interactions that occur, allow athletes to execute coordinated movement. This coordination, in turn, gives the performer the flexibility to accommodate changes that may suddenly occur in the task, the environment or their own body. Kinetic analyses of internal joint forces, on the other hand, are often used to produce insights into the musculoskeletal demand of movements. A recent example of such work from our research concerned the quantification of musculoskeletal demand, including joint power and work, in maximum velocity sprinting (Bezodis *et al.*, 2008b). The study combined 2D video with synchronised ground reaction force data to calculate joint kinetics.

This revealed that in maximum velocity sprinting, the muscles that cross the hip joint were net energy generators, those that cross the ankle joint were net energy absorbers, and those that cross the knee joint played a relatively reduced role energetically. The information gleaned here, provided insights not available from observation or kinematics alone.

By adding reflective markers to a person and combining images from multiple versions of high-speed video cameras, automatic 3D tracking systems are formed. These are commonly used in the film and television industries for motion capture (MoCap) as the basis from which computer-animated characters are created. Within sport, this approach generally uses passive markers attached to the performer. An alternative approach, based on active markers, is one in which the person being studied is fitted with miniature light emitting diodes (LEDs), whose positions are detected by cameras of varying types mounted in groups of three on a fixed base to facilitate triangulation. 3D tracking systems offer the facility to collect accurate 3D data on human movements, although their routine use in coaching settings is limited by the need to attach markers to athletes (not always an easy task for many reasons). A final form of quantitative biomechanics worth mentioning here, is the description of neuromuscular activity through the use of electromyography. This is a specialist area of biomechanics which can provide information on the electrical activity in muscles, thus informing biological function (Clarys, 2000; Komi *et al.*, 2000).

MODELLING IN BIOMECHANICS

The modelling most commonly referred to in biomechanics is the forward dynamic approach. The challenge in forward dynamics modelling is to build realistic and appropriate human body models with sufficient validity to enable techniques to be examined with confidence. A good example of this was developed by Wilson *et al.* (2006) who produced a forward dynamics model which enabled the fundamental mechanics of running jumps to be examined.

Ironically, from a mathematical point of view, modelling the airborne phase of a complex twisting somersault is actually easier than modelling a vertical jump take-off. The major reason for this, is that to model a takeoff or landing, the musculoskeletal system has to be represented. The human can be simplified within a model, but it still needs to be embodied as a system of rigid and wobbling mass parts linked by springs with varying stiffness and compliance characteristics (Gittoes *et al.*, 2006). The muscular contractions also have to be modelled to include complex dynamics in order to produce accurate skeletal muscle force profiles.

Even something as apparently simple as pushing off from the floor in a jump, is an immensely challenging computer modelling exercise. Despite such problems, computer simulation modelling offers great scope for future work in enhancing athletic performance. This approach has been used in a variety of sports (e.g. soccer [Bray and Kerwin, 2003], gymnastics [Arampatzis and Brüggemann, 1999; Hiley and Yeadon, 2005], athletics [Hubbard and Alaways, 1987; Wilson *et al.*, 2006] and tennis [Glynn *et al.*, 2006]) to address theoretical questions such as: What will happen if we change a certain aspect of the movement? or, What are the implications on wrist mechanics of changing the stiffness of a tennis racket frame? Computer simulation modelling represents a powerful tool, and is considered the only true method for identifying individualised optimal technique for a particular athlete performing a technically demanding skill.

CONCLUDING THOUGHTS: THE FUTURE

From a coaching perspective, it is likely that the future holds great innovation in terms of immediate feedback technology. These include visual replays via new graphical plasma display screens, and wireless linked laptop computers. This form of immediate post-event feedback will be a principal future means of athlete enhancement. For example, biofeedback derived from athlete-worn sensors will enable information on performance to be relayed to the athlete whilst training – greatly extending the simple measures in use today (e.g. heart rate). Additionally, the feedback timescale will stretch in the other direction to include overviews of seasonal and career-based tracking of performance. Athletes' training diaries will become totally electronic, and contain not just calendars and dietary information but also video records of performances. Trend analyses based on these electronic loggers and other biomechanical and physiological measures of performance will assist in the future development of training programmes and the planning of peaking regimes for optimising athletes' competitive performances.

From the biomechanics perspective, in addition to the developments and applications of simulation modelling, there are new technologies on the horizon in the fields of athlete-worn sensors which will impact sport. These new systems will expand the types of field-based measurements in qualitative and quantitative analyses, thus increasing the scope of activities which can be studied. The other impact of these new technologies will be a many fold increase in the volume of fine-grain data which should better underpin athlete performance profiling, and retrospective and prospective studies of injury, thus having the potential to greatly inform future coaching knowledge.

1　How do coaches develop an understanding of how skills work?
2　Summarise the role biomechanics plays in the coaching process.
3　What is meant by the term 'coaching–biomechanics interface'?
4　What are the advantages and disadvantages of using a qualitative approach compared to a semi-quantitative or quantitative one within biomechanical analysis of sport?
5　The chapter predicts a bright future for biomechanics within coaching. Do you agree or disagree? Why?

Web Resources

Coaches Information Service

http://www.coachesinfo.com/index.php

The CoachesInfo website is designed to deliver the latest information and education to sports practitioners including coaches, participants, physical educators and practitioners in the medical health vocations that have a sports focus.

International Society of Biomechanics in Sport

www.isbs.org/

This website, which is totally dedicated to Biomechanics in Sports, provides a forum for the exchange of ideas for sports biomechanics researchers, coaches and teachers. The society aims to bridge the gap between researchers and practitioners. Of particular relevance are the searchable proceedings of all ISBS conferences, which provide a useful resource for coaches and students.

Video Analysis for the Tennis Coach

http://en.coaching.itftennis.com/media/109788/109788.pdf

This article highlights how useful video analysis is to tennis coaching. The article illustrates how biomechanics can be applied to skill acquisition, technique refinement, visualisation, injury prevention and coach education.

CHAPTER 11

MATCH ANALYSIS FOR COACHES

PETER O'DONOGHUE

[Match] analysis has enabled Norway to maximise its limited resources, in terms of playing population and extreme weather conditions faced in the country, and compete with the best teams in the world.
                    Egil Olsen, Head Coach, Norwegian Soccer Squad
                                   (E. Olsen and O. Larsen, 1997)

INTRODUCTION

The use of notational analysis within the coaching process has been described in the first edition of this book (Hughes, 2008). The general principles of system development, operation and the use of the resulting analysis remain relevant today, despite the rapid changes in technology over the last four years. One such change, which deserves particular attention, is the need for feedback within the coaching process (Maslovat and Franks, 2008). Athletes receive feedback in two principal ways; through their senses and through augmented means. Sensory feedback includes sight, sound, tactile (i.e. physical) and proprioceptive information. Augmented feedback, on the other hand, comprises additional analyses often provided by a coach who observes their performances (see Chapter 3 for a review on feedback). With regard to the latter, there are limitations to the completeness and accuracy with which coaches can recall events within a performance (Maslovat and Franks, 2008). For example, in a recent study, UEFA qualified (football) coaches were only able to recall 59 per cent of critical incidents in a match (Laird and Waters, 2008). A further issue is the possibility of biased observation by coaches, or emotions influencing coach interpretation of performance (Maslovat and Franks, 2008). A principal point made in this chapter, then, is that augmented feedback provided by coaches should be supported by effective analysis of performance.

Performance analysis has different purposes including the analysis of technique, tactics and movement (Hughes, 1998). Since detailed analysis of athlete technique is covered in 'Biomechanics for coaches' (see Chapter 10), the current chapter will focus on the aspects of tactical analysis and technical effectiveness. The distinction between analysis of technique and technical effectiveness is as follows. Technical effectiveness is concerned with the broad quality with which events are performed; such events could include passes in team games, tackles in football or shots in racket sports. Technical effectiveness can also take the form of positive to negative ratios for event types, or winner to error ratios in racket sports. Analysis of technique, on the other hand, is concerned with the mechanical aspects of the way in which a skill or event is performed (O'Donoghue, 2010). The term 'match analysis' is used to represent the combined evaluation of both tactical aspects and technical effectiveness. In its structure, this chapter commences with general principles of system development before discussing the use of match analysis within coaching environments.

SYSTEM DEVELOPMENT

Overview of the system development process

The purpose of match analysis within the coaching process is to assist the decisions made by coaches and athletes in terms of how they prepare for competition. Therefore, match analysis activity should be dictated by the coaching process and its information needs, rather than the process being altered to incorporate a particular analysis system. There have been some technological developments, such as the use of video streaming on the internet, that have allowed communication between coaches and athletes to be accomplished in a more efficient way than before. Despite such advancements, the general principle remains; that systems should be developed to support the information needs of coaches and athletes, and not the other way around.

The system development process involves the following steps:

1   Requirements' analysis: determining the information needed and the raw sources of data that can be gathered, stored and analysed to provide this information. This can be thought of as determining 'what' the system (to be developed) must do.
2   Prototype development: creating manual and/or computerised means to fulfil the stated requirements for the system. These manual or computerised methods form 'how' the system will fulfil the requirements.

162

3   Reliability testing and end-user training to ensure the system (and its operation) is reliable enough for use in practice.
4   System operation within the coaching environment and maintenance.

The following section describes these phases in more depth.

Step 1: Requirements' analysis

This section is primarily concerned with the functional requirements of match analysis systems. These represent the information that needs to be produced, the raw data to be captured, the data to be stored and the processing functions. Non-functional requirements relating to the man–machine interface of computerised systems are also discussed.

The information required from match analysis systems takes a variety of forms, including match statistics, video clips and diagrammatic presentation of information (Carling *et al.*, 2005). Match statistics are referred to as performance indicators, where the variables are clearly important aspects of performance. Performance indicators provide an objective measurement procedure, a known scale of measurement, and some valid means of interpretation (O'Donoghue, 2010). A common misperception about performance indicators is that they have to distinguish between winning and losing performances. This may be true for indicators of technical effectiveness, such as winner to error ratios or percentages of events performed successfully. However, tactical aspects (to do with the way players and teams play) do not have to be associated with match outcomes. For example, in tennis, the percentage of times a player goes to the net during play may be an indicator of tactics or strategy, and not necessarily correlated with match outcome. On the other hand, the fact that this tactical aspect of play may not be associated with match outcome does not make it unimportant, as it could be crucial in understanding how opponents play as well as areas where they play effectively.

Performance indicators can be interpreted where there is common understanding of values associated with different types of performance. For example, it may be understood that a player should optimally get between 60 and 70 per cent of first serves in during tennis matches to generally dominate and win service games. Where the meaning of match statistics is not so well understood, norms can be developed to provide an understanding of these values. Performances, however, are clearly affected by the quality of opposition (McGarry and Franks, 1994; Lago and Martin, 2007; Taylor *et al.*, 2008; Tenga *et al.*, 2010a, 2010b). Therefore, different norms should be used for different types of matches. For example, in British National Superleague netball, four different sets of norms have been proposed to interpret performances between teams at the top and bottom of the league (O'Donoghue *et al.*, 2008). This approach is applicable where there are broad ranges of teams or players with respect to quality. However, the change in quality within a sport may be less obvious as one looks through the rankings of individual performers. Although such rankings can help to determine match-specific expected values (O'Donoghue and Cullinane, 2011), this is not practical in many situations where there are weak relationships between rankings and performance indicators.

Once performance indicators are specified, the raw data required to produce those performance indicators need to be identified. Consider a performance indicator for the percentage of service points in tennis where aces are achieved. The system needs to record the number of aces and the number of service points in order to calculate the performance indicator. This can be done by tallying the raw events (e.g. a service point) and their outcomes. While hand systems are both practical and efficient, the most important match information used in coaching today is video sequences. These contain rich and complex information that can be analysed in depth by coaches and players. Although there are systems that operate without video recordings, supporting video should be used wherever possible so that analysis is not limited to counts of events but is also about how such events are performed.

The usability of a computerised system depends on its interface. Performance indicator values can be presented in tables, charts or individually. Match information can also be presented on diagrams of the playing surface (Carling *et al.*, 2005). These diagrams can show movement patterns or event locations indicating tactical aspects. They can also be used to show event frequencies or technical effectiveness indicators in different zones of the playing surface. Interface issues are also important for data entry, hence, on-screen event buttons and labels should be arranged for efficient data entry using peripheral devices such as a 'mouse'.

Step 2: Evolutionary prototyping

After some initial requirements are discussed, a prototype system can be developed and used as a vehicle to elicit further requirements. This iterative process of requirements' elicitation and prototype development involves system developers, analysts and coaches. Where senior international athletes are being coached, they often have a say in the requirements for the system as well. This gives the whole team a sense of ownership over the system. This process should also include pilot work to assess the feasibility of desirable aspects, and the ability of operators to perform data entry tasks in real time. There are occasions where the final system is a compromise between coaches' and athletes' preferences, the technological constraints of match analysis packages, and the limits to what operators can deliver within set deadlines for feedback.

Despite the undoubted advances with regard to computerised systems for match analysis, manual notation systems continue to be used where computerised systems are either non-cost effective or are prohibited by tournament regulations. A key consideration in the development of a manual notation system is the information that is required from the system. Where temporal aspects of play are not important, a manual form can use event tallies as shown in Figure 11.1. Here, vertical strokes are used to record instances of events (i.e. shots in tennis) with each fifth stroke being placed diagonally or horizontally through the previous four to form a group of five. Those designing such systems should consider how the forms used can be optimally structured to aid both data collection and interpretation. Even if information were required for different sets of a tennis match, it is simple enough to use a separate form for each set. However, recording events in chronological order leaves analysts with more complex processing tasks to perform after the match has ended. Therefore, chronological event lists should only be used in manual notation systems where knowledge of individual events and sequences of events within the match is important.

Computerised systems allow event lists and automatic processing of those lists to produce accumulated totals. Generic database packages such as Microsoft Access can be programmed to record variables about events, including their chronological order, with immediate cross-tabulation of variables being possible. Such generic video analysis software packages include SportsCode (SportsTech International, Warriewood, Australia), Focus X2 (Elite Sports Analysis, Dalgety Bay, Scotland) and Dartfish (Dartfish, Fribourg, Switzerland), and integrate match videos with sequences of timed event records. Figure 11.2 shows the main components of the SportsCode system and the human operation processes involved during the data capture and match analysis phases. Figure 11.3 shows the SportsCode interface when used to analyse netball performance.

Figures 11.2 and 11.3 include important terms which are described as follows:

- Video capture window – the video capture window shows the match video frames as they are being recorded.
- Code window – the code window is used to input events. The code window contains buttons representing events performed (e.g. passes or tackles) as well as labels used to add other information about those events, such as pitch location, the players involved and/or the outcome(s)

Player	Serve	Deuce Court			Advantage Court		
		Left	Middle	Right	Left	Middle	Right
N. Djokovic	1st Serve	Played 卌 卌 卌 卌 |	Played 卌 ||||	Played 卌 卌 卌 卌 |	Played 卌 卌 卌 卌 卌 |	Played 卌 卌	Played 卌 卌 |
		Won 卌 卌 卌 |	Won 卌 ||	Won 卌 卌 |||	Won 卌 卌 卌 |	Won 卌 ||	Won 卌 |||
		16/21 76.2%	7/9 77.8%	13/21 61.9%	16/26 61.5%	7/10 70.0%	8/11 72.7%
	2nd Serve	Played 卌 卌 |||	Played 卌 卌 卌 |	Played 卌 |	Played 卌 卌	Played 卌 卌 卌 |	Played 卌
		Won 卌 ||	Won 卌 卌	Won ||||	Won 卌 |||	Won 卌 卌 |	Won |||
		7/13 53.8%	10/16 62.5%	4/6 66.7%	8/10 80.0%	11/16 68.8%	3/5 60.0%
R. Nadal	1st Serve	Played 卌 卌 ||||	Played 卌 卌 卌 ||	Played 卌 卌 卌 卌 卌 卌 卌	Played 卌 卌 卌 卌 ||	Played 卌 卌 卌 卌 ||||	Played 卌 卌 卌 卌 卌
		Won 卌 卌	Won 卌 卌 ||	Won 卌 卌 卌 卌 卌 ||	Won 卌 卌 卌 |	Won 卌 卌 ||	Won 卌 卌 |||
		10/14 71.4%	12/17 70.6%	27/35 77.1%	16/22 72.7%	12/24 50.0%	13/25 52.0%
	2nd Serve	Played 卌 卌 ||||	Played 卌 卌 卌 卌	Played 卌 卌	Played	Played 卌 卌 卌 |	Played 卌 卌 ||
		Won 卌 卌	Won 卌 卌	Won 卌	Won	Won 卌 |	Won 卌 |
		3/4 75.0%	10/20 50.0%	5/10 50.0%	0/0 N/A	6/16 37.5%	6/12 50.0%

Figure 11.1 A manual notation system for tennis showing the fraction of points won when serves land in different areas of the service box

Note: 'Left', 'middle' and 'right' refer to thirds of the service court where the served ball could land

166

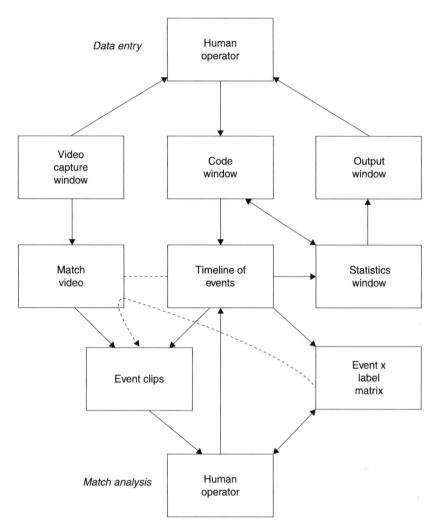

Figure 11.2 The main SportsCode components

- Timeline – the timeline in SportsCode is a timed event list which shows the start and end of each instance of each event type. The timeline is associated with a match video.
- Matrix – a matrix is a two dimensional table that has a row for each event type and a column for each label. The cells of the matrix show frequencies of labels recorded for each event type.
- Matrix organiser – very often the analyst and/or coach may wish to see the frequencies of events performed by a particular player in a particular area of the pitch where the result was a particular outcome. The matrix

Video display   **Matrix**   **Output window**

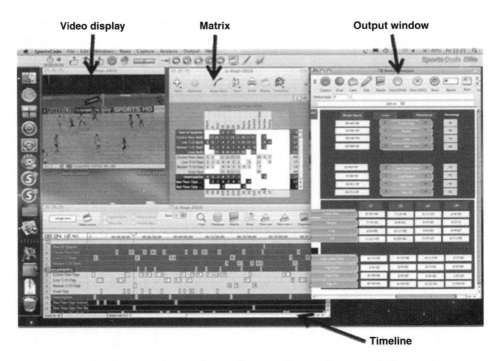

Timeline

Figure 11.3 The SportsCode interface (when used to analyse a netball game)

organiser allows matrices to be produced that are more focused than the default matrix.

■ Event clip – a clip is a video sequence. Video sequences can be accessed for events by direct manipulation of the timeline or the matrix.

■ Statistics window – the statistics window can be programmed to determine information from the raw event included in the timeline. The information produced by the statistics window can be sent to a user-friendly output window.

■ Script – a script is a sequence of executable instructions within a cell of the statistics window. The script is programmed to produce information using raw data from the timeline and other cells of the statistics window.

■ Output window – an output window displays summary match statistics.

Events are recorded with start and end times in SportsCode and, hence, have an element of duration. This is in contrast to Focus X2 where behaviour is modelled as a sequence of instantaneous events that have no duration. The benefit of abstracting sports behaviour to instantaneous events is that the volume of data entry activity for the operator is reduced. Events can also be linked, meaning that the entry of one event can activate a related event or turn a related

168

event off. For example, in badminton, we may have events representing rallies and inter-rally breaks which are toggled (i.e. the two states 'rally' and 'inter-rally break' are mutually exclusive, hence only one can be occurring at a time). Consequently, when the user enters an inter-rally break, the rally is automatically ended.

One of the most powerful features of SportsCode is the statistics window. This contains cells with scripts (e.g. a means to determine the percentage of centre passes in netball that result in a goal) that are executed when the timeline is changed by the entry of new events. The scripts can be programmed to inspect the timeline as well as other areas of the statistics window. As an example, the following script is used to determine the percentage of centre pass events in a netball match (a centre pass is the restart after a goal is scored) where the outcome is a goal.

```
$CentrePasses = count instances where row = "Centre Pass"
$CPassToGoal = count labels = "Goal" where row = "Centre Pass"
$PercentCPassToGoal = 100 * $CPassToGoal / $CentrePasses
$String=$CPassToGoal+"/"+$CentrePasses+"="+$PercentCPassToGoal
 + "%"
Show $String
Send $String to button "CPass Conversion"
```

The $ character is used at the beginning of local variables (e.g. $CentrePasses) within the script. The first line records the timeline to determine the number of centre pass events. The second line determines the number of centre pass events including a 'goal' label to represent the possessions starting with a centre pass that resulted in a goal. The third line evaluates the expression on the right hand side of the "=" sign, and assigns the resulting value to the variable to the left of the "=" sign ($PercentCPassToGoal). The fourth line produces a string of characters that represent the values in the form "6/12=50%". The fifth and sixth lines display the character string in the given cell of the statistics window and in the "CPass Conversion" display button of the output window respectively.

Any information that can be produced automatically from the data entered should be done by the statistics window to avoid the user having to do it. An example is the score in a tennis match. If we know the score at the beginning of a point and we know who served and who won the point, then the server and score at the beginning of the next point can be determined automatically. Additionally, the information produced by the statistics window can be sent to an output window, to events within the timeline, or to buttons within the code window to alert the user to conditions that may be emerging during the match.

An example of the type of information that can be sent to an output window is the percentage of passes that are successful in a soccer match. The area of the output window used to show this performance indicator can be coloured to indicate whether it (i.e. the performance aspect under analysis) is high, average or low each time it is updated.

Once the match video has been recorded and tagged (i.e. broken down and analysed, thus producing a timeline of related events), match analysis can take place. Here, the timeline can be accessed directly to look at a clip for any event. More commonly, the output window is used to identify areas of performance that require attention. For example, if fewer second service points to the advantage court in a tennis match were won than expected, the output window would alert the analyst to this. The matrix of events and labels can show the total frequency of such points that were lost but, more importantly, direct access to the matrix allows all relevant video clips to be viewed interactively. Additionally, any video clips identified using the matrix or the timeline can be saved in a movie file (Quicktime, for example).

Step 3: System reliability and validity

Validity is the most important measurement issue for a match analysis system. The system is considered valid if it is effective in producing useful information for coaches and players. If a system produces a series of output variables that are of no practical value or interest to coaches and players, it does not matter how reliable the system is, it will be ineffective.

The reliability of performance analysis systems is more important when the systems are being used within the coaching process rather than for academic research (O'Donoghue and Longville, 2004). This is because coaches and athletes will be making important decisions during match preparation and within matches based on the information provided by match analysis systems. The reliability of computerised systems can be improved using consistency checking. For example, in netball, centre passes alternate between teams, and teams scoring goals should be the teams taking possession just before goals are scored. Such event lists can be quickly examined after matches to identify any violations of these temporal constraints. This can be done by manual inspection, or computerised systems can automatically inspect event sequences, alerting operators where errors may have occurred. Where such errors exist, they can be rectified prior to the data being used by coaches and athletes. For example, if a user sees three centre passes in a row for the same team, they will know an error has occurred at this point and will be able to rectify it by checking the video.

170

Step 4: System operation and maintenance

Systems are used in different situations, for example, in week-to-week domestic league fixtures or in tournament situations. Some matches may be more important than others and this necessitates differing levels of analysis. Analysis of potential opponents can be an ongoing task used in preparation for matches. The time between matches here is a key factor in how much analysis can be done. For example, a netball team playing three matches in three days will focus on the most critical areas that need to be addressed, whereas a team with ten days between matches may do a more in-depth analysis of performance and utilise this information to a greater extent in training. Some analysts have manual versions of their computerised systems which they use where video recording of potential opponents is not possible.

A match analysis system rarely stays the same for more than one tournament, and, as such, systems are subject to continual adaptation and improvement. The enhancements may be due to emerging requirements as athletes and squads mature. These may result from changing systems of play which require different performance information to support decision making. Systems also change to keep abreast of developments in match analysis technology, such as the use of palmtop computers to record timed sequences of events at match venues, which can be integrated later with public domain footage of the observed games.

MATCH ANALYSIS WITHIN COACHING

The match analysis cycle

Coaching is the main application area for performance analysis. Several models of performance analysis within coaching have been proposed over the years, including the feedback models of Franks (1997), Winkler (1988), O'Donoghue (2006) and Mayes *et al.* (2009). Performance analysis processes used in coaching depend on a number of factors, including the nature of the sport, the level of the athletes and access to technology. This section will consider a model of match analysis involving video feedback, which includes the use of internet streaming and wireless communication. The rationale for this approach is that members of elite sports squads come from different geographical areas, thus reviewing match statistics and video sequences in preparation online allows training sessions to be used more productively.

There have been major technological advances in recent years (Kirkbride, in press). These advances have made data collection and analysis more efficient, and changed the way feedback is given. Video sequences can now be provided by internet streaming in a secure environment by systems such as Replay (www. replayanalysis.org). This allows coaches and athletes to make better use of training time, as feedback and discussion about areas of previous performance can be done online in the days before the next training session. This technology is especially useful for travelling athletes (such as tennis players on the ATP or WTA tours) or teams of players who live in different areas. Mayes *et al.* (2009) described how the use of performance analysis video streaming has enhanced the coaching process. The review of video sequences in this way can be accompanied by online discussion of aspects of play. Figure 11.4 shows the model used by Mayes *et al.* (2009) which presents match analysis as action research (Schön, 1983; Zuber-Skerritt, 1996). Hence, when a match is played, it is observed with events entered into a match analysis system live. The match video is indexed with events that are entered by the operator. The events are also labelled with outcomes and the players involved, allowing matrices to be produced during analysis. The matrix of events and outcomes can be pasted into a pre-programmed spreadsheet, allowing performance indicator values to be produced. Performance indicator values are compared to norms for matches against the level of opposition faced (O'Donoghue *et al.*, 2008). This allows problematic or successful areas to be identified.

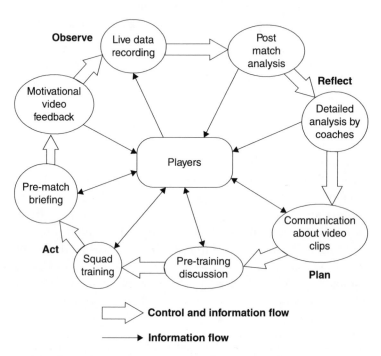

Figure 11.4 Match analysis as action research in a coaching context (Mayes *et al.*, 2009)

172

Instructional feedback

Instructional feedback helps athletes improve by identifying particular areas of performance that they need to address and monitor. Consider how Rafael Nadal might use the information presented earlier in Figure 11.1. The statistics suggest that Nadal's second serve to the advantage court may require attention. Other areas that may require work are his receiving of first serves to the outside and middle of both the deuce and advantage courts (the deuce court is the right side of the court for each player, the advantage court the left). Computerised match analysis systems support different levels of analyses within the coaching process and, typically, statistical information is produced identifying areas requiring attention. This quantitative analysis identifies 'what' needs to be looked at. The system can then be used to interactively examine video clips of relevant points. For example, Nadal could look at particular point types where he is not as effective as in others. Coaches and players will also see a great deal of qualitative visual detail within these clips. These can be replayed, paused and shown in slow motion during a process of communication between coaches and athletes about 'why' and 'how' any problem has occurred and 'how' it can be addressed. Therefore, the analyst often does not need to present events in great detail to facilitate coach and athlete discussion. The broad analysis of points and outcomes is often sufficient to allow coaches and athletes to focus on those areas requiring attention. It may also be counter-productive for analysts to examine in too much detail, as their understanding of the sport may be limited in comparison with elite performers and coaches. Hence, a broad analysis of possession outcomes is typically enough to facilitate productive coach–player discussion about areas of performance.

Instructional information can also be provided about forthcoming matches and particular opponents. This can be presented in the form of performance profiles (O'Donoghue, 2005) or form charts (Jones *et al.*, 2008). A profile is a collection of performance indicators representing different aspects of performance. In match analysis, a profile should include indicators of tactics as well as those of technical effectiveness. Sports performance is not a stable characteristic of an opponent and varies from match to match due to opposition effect and other factors. Therefore, O'Donoghue's profiling technique represented a typical performance over a set of matches as well as variability about that performance, allowing areas of consistency and inconsistency to be understood. Figure 11.5 is an example of such a profile for a male tennis player. The percentage scale used for each variable represents the percentage of players with lower values for each performance indicator than him. This shows that he executes a relatively low number of net points, but wins a relatively high number of points when he goes to the net. His most consistent area of play is the number of break points earned

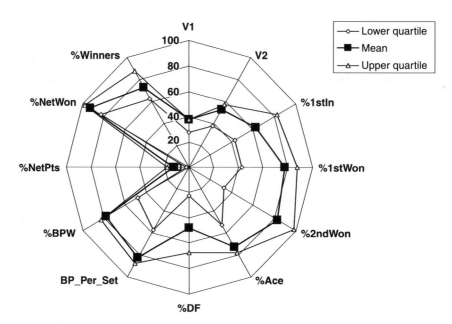

Figure 11.5 Normative performance profile for a male Grand Slam tennis player (13 matches). The lower quartile equates to the fact that 25 per cent of the player's performances have a lower value than this, while the upper quartile is the value such that 75 per cent of the player's performances have a value lower than this

per set, and his most erratic area of play is the percentage of points won when he requires a second serve.

Form charts can also represent recent performances showing trends in indicator values over a series of matches. The quantitative information provided in form charts and profiles can be supplemented with video sequences illustrating key tactical aspects of opponent play. Statistical information can also be incorporated into instructional videos, allowing the statistics and related video sequences to be presented synergetically.

It is important to recognise that coaches should use match information as they see fit. There may be some areas of performance that are deemed of concern by match analysis which may be of lower priority for coaches. For example, an evaluation study of match analysis in netball, found that squads would defer working on areas that required long-term attention, instead focusing on tactical weaknesses that could quickly be rectified within a match-to-match coaching cycle (Jenkins *et al.*, 2007). A further issue found by this study was that coaches would still focus on perceived key aspects in training, even if these were not areas of current concern in recent performances; data which again highlight the subjective role of perception in the area of match analysis.

CONCLUSION

Match analysis is primarily concerned with tactical aspects of play and technical effectiveness. A variety of information types can be used during match analysis including statistics and video sequences. Technological developments have enabled feedback to be provided on internet-based systems prior to training sessions. This allows coaches and athletes to make better use of training time with discussion of tactical aspects having previously taken place. It is likely that future developments in match analysis will include live statistical feedback to coaches during competition, as well as facilities to review key video sequences during competition. Other future developments could include the use of pervasive technology to record performance related information during matches, thus providing game-live information to coaches.

DISCUSSION TOPICS AND REVIEW QUESTIONS

1   Why is performance analysis used in coaching and what are the benefits?
2   Develop a hand notation system to analyse an important aspect of a sport of your choice. What information is produced and what data need to be recorded?
3   How can we interpret performance indicator values?
4   What is meant by a performance profile? How can a performance profile be used in coaching?

Web Resources

http://www.sportstec.com

Sportstec is the producer of widely used generic match analysis products that can be tailored for analysis of any sport.

http://www.prozonesports.com

Prozone is one of the suppliers of image processing-based player tracking systems used in professional soccer coaching.

http://www.ispas.org

The International Society of Performance Analysis in Sport is the professional body of the performance analysis profession.

http://www.ingentaconnect.com/content/uwic/ujpa

The International Journal of Performance Analysis in Sport publishes three issues a year on the latest research in sports performance.

CHAPTER 12

SPORTS MEDICINE FOR COACHES

ANDREW MILES AND RICHARD TONG

I am very concerned about injury preventive work. It enables me to challenge the specialists from a holistic perspective.
Per Mathias Høgmo, Director of Football, Norwegian Football Association; Head Coach, Norwegian National Women's Football Team (1997–2001); Gold medallists, Olympic Games, Sydney (2000)

INTRODUCTION

Traditionally, sport has been seen as both a competitive activity requiring intense periods of training and conditioning, and as a vehicle for the development of physical literacy and movement skills as part of school physical education curricula. The role of the coach and/or PE teacher in such contexts is multi-faceted, with the need to be one, or any combination, of: an instructor of new skills; a teacher of technical and tactical awareness; a physical conditioner preparing sportspeople for competition; and a developer of talent for the future. In recent times, increased financial support through National Lottery funding and a general increase in leisure time have created greater opportunities for mass participation in grass roots sport. Similarly, the high-profile professionalisation of many sports has been reflected in the desire for talented performers to train harder and for longer. The role of the coach has thus shifted to place a greater emphasis on the need for the regulation of the volume and intensity of training loads. There has also been a growing recognition of the wider role that sport and physical activity can play in enhancing society's general well-being and quality of life.

As a result of an ever-increasing prevalence of lifestyle related diseases (such as obesity, coronary heart disease, diabetes and cancer), health experts are turning to physical activity as a prevention and treatment intervention for patients and high-risk populations. In such instances, the role of the coach may need adapting towards becoming an exercise leader/instructor. The primary function here would be to motivate and support patients through planned and structured low-risk physical activity sessions, with the aim of developing health and well-being rather than skill and performance. Additionally, sport is regarded as a vehicle to address social issues such as exclusion, drug misuse and anti-social behaviour. In such cases, the role of the coach requires further adaptation to embrace the development of leadership and life skills, value and respect for others and oneself, and even offering sport as a distraction from life problems and related issues.

With the prospective increase in the training loads of sport participants and the uptake of sport and physical activity by previously sedentary populations, comes the potential for under-prepared individuals to embark on training without the necessary knowledge and support. Inevitably, this will lead to an increase in sport and physical activity related injuries. Sports medicine – especially its relevance for coaches, instructors and exercise leaders – is likely to become increasingly important, to manage the anticipated upsurge in such injuries. It is important that knowledge and awareness of sports medicine amongst practitioners (involved in the provision and management of sport and physical training) is developed in line with the potential increase in injury risk.

Medicine has typically been associated with the diagnosis and treatment of illness or injuries. However, with an improved understanding of the mechanisms and causes of injury, there has been a shift in emphasis towards the development of preventative approaches (Finch, 2006). Such a changing stance is based on the belief that, if society is to gain the desired benefits from increased involvement in physical activity and sport without overburdening existing provision, everyone involved in their organisation should be aware of the potential health risks associated with them. Hence, coaches should be able to plan physical activity sessions that are within the capability of athletes, participants or patients in order to elicit positive effects rather than placing such populations at risk of injury or to exacerbate existing conditions (Brukner and Kahn, 2007).

As the primary overseers of organised sporting activities, coaches should be aware that participation in sport can lead to injury. Accordingly, the sports coach, whilst not being expected to treat injuries, should have a good understanding of: (i) the factors and the causal mechanisms that can lead to injury, so that they can prevent them from occurring in the first instance; (ii) how an injury should be initially managed, in order to minimise the severity of the harm and enhance future recovery; and, (iii) how to support recovery and rehabilitation in order to reduce the risk of re-injury and to ensure effective return to health and fitness. Consequently, the purpose of this chapter is to highlight the value that such an understanding (of sports medicine and injury prevention, treatment and management) has for coaches. The chapter starts by defining sports medicine, before identifying and classifying common sports injuries. It then examines causal factors of such injuries and discusses strategies that coaches can utilise to reduce the risk of occurrence. Issues relating to the treatment of an injury will then be addressed, along with suggestions for the effective management of the recovery process.

WHAT IS SPORTS MEDICINE AND HOW CAN IT HELP COACHES?

Many authors have sought to define sports medicine. Hollmann (1988: xi) offered an early definition which was adopted by the International Federation of Sports Medicine (FIMS) as including:

> those theoretical and practical branches of medicine which investigate the effects of exercise, training and sport on healthy and ill people, as well as the effects of lack of exercise, to produce useful results for prevention, therapy [and] rehabilitation.

Hollmann (1988) further suggested that there are three facets to modern sports medicine, namely, prevention (which has come to play an increasingly significant role), diagnosis and treatment/rehabilitation. In a society which is becoming more and more dependent on technology and automation, whilst developing a fast-food culture, there is a distinct drift towards a lack of physical activity. Hollmann (1988) argued that the preventative aspects of sports medicine should use physical activity as a method to restore normal physiological conditions. Hence, appropriate training to produce physiological adaptations was seen as being able to prevent a range of diseases and age-related losses in physical capacity. Inevitably, injuries will still occur, and thus the need for diagnosis, treatment and rehabilitation remains. However, an increasingly effective prevention strategy can reduce the need for treatment.

A more contemporary definition, offered by Brukner and Khan (2006: 3), suggested that sports medicine should be defined as the 'medicine of exercise' or, perhaps more accurately, as the total medical care of the exercising individual. This was further expanded to define the discipline as comprising:

> Injury prevention, diagnosis, treatment and rehabilitation; performance enhancement through training, nutrition and psychology; management

of medical problems caused by exercise and the role of exercise in chronic disease states; the specific needs of exercising in children, females, older people and those with permanent disabilities; the medical care of sporting teams and events; medical care in situations of altered physiology, such as altitude or at depth; and ethical issues, such as the problem of drug abuse in sport.

Aside from the rather confusing use of the words sport and exercise, the most obvious observation arising from this extensive definition is the diversity of the discipline and the concept of total medical care provision. With this comes the recognition that any single practitioner is unlikely to be able to address all the issues associated with modern sports medicine. As such, almost all authors attempting to define modern sports medicine infer that the provision of good sports medicine services is characterised by a multidisciplinary approach; namely, that the sports medicine needs of an exercising individual are best met through a team approach, in which a number of specialists may be involved. Consequently, the traditional medical structure (Brukner and Kahn, 2007), such as that predominating in the UK National Health Service (where tiers of practitioner input exist, with a patient passing through a general diagnostic process before being referred to more specialist support), differs widely from the sports medicine model. In the latter, the athlete's primary point of contact in the event of an injury would, with the exception of emergency situations, be the coach. The coach would then refer the athlete to an appropriate specialist, for example, a physiotherapist, physiologist or masseur. Consequently, it is imperative for coaches to have a basic understanding of how to deal with injuries as they happen, and to whom they should subsequently refer an injured athlete.

According to Martens (2004), a coach's medical responsibilities are three-fold:

- To ensure that an athlete's health is satisfactory prior to participation;
- To determine whether an illness or injury is sufficient for an athlete to stop participation;
- To ensure that the athlete is ready to return to training and competition.

Arguably, however, Martens (2004) overlooks an important associated responsibility, namely, a coach's role in the prevention of injury. Therefore, an awareness of sports medicine concepts would appear to be important for coaches from a number of perspectives: from injury prevention, through referring injured or ill athletes to appropriate specialists, to monitoring and nurturing athletes' return to competition.

UNDERSTANDING SPORTS INJURIES

In order to effectively reduce the likelihood of injury occurrence amongst their athletes, sports coaches should be aware of the different elements within what Van Mechelen *et al.* (1992) termed the 'sequence of prevention' (see Figure 12.1). The first element of the sequence, 'Prevalence', suggests that coaches need to have an appreciation of the potential extent of sports injuries and an under-standing of the different types of injuries that can occur within their sport. Second, 'Causation' represents the need for an awareness of the main causal factors and mechanisms associated with the occurrence of these injuries. Finally, 'Prevention' refers to the introduction of measures targeting the reduction of risk to offset or reduce future occurrence and/or severity of injury. Thus, if a coach knows the typical types of injuries sustained in their sport and what may cause these injuries, he or she will be better placed to develop training programmes and practice strategies that can prevent them from occurring in the future. It would seem reasonable to suggest that the successful implementa-tion of preventative strategies would have a positive effect on reducing the subsequent prevalence of injuries. To assist coaches in understanding the impor-tance of this sequence, the following sections will now explore each step in more detail.

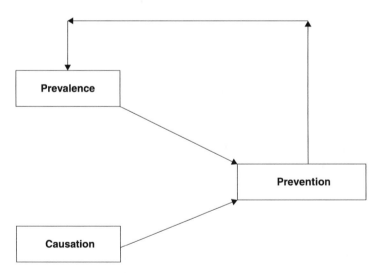

Figure 12.1 The so-called 'sequence of prevention' adapted from Van Mechelen *et al.* (1992)

Injury prevalence

Understanding the prevalence of injuries within a sport, requires defining, recording and classifying such injuries. This can be problematic, in that an examination of the literature reveals that there is no single widely accepted operational definition of a sports injury, either across the broad field of sports medicine generally (Van Mechelen *et al.*, 1992) or at a sport specific level. For example, reports from both football (Dvorak and Junge, 2000) and rugby union (Fuller *et al.*, 2007) suggest that no consensus regarding the definition of injury has yet been reached. Instead, the literature offers a range of definitions suggesting that a sports injury can be anything from the occurrence of a new symptom during training or competition, to decreased athletic performance as a result of reduced functioning of a body part, to the cessation of participation which necessitates contact with medical personnel (Caine *et al.*, 1996). Consequently, if defining what exactly constitutes a sports injury is so difficult, it is little wonder that recording the occurrence of sports injuries and detailing their exact causes and nature is an issue with which sports injury epidemiologists are constantly grappling (Caine *et al.*, 1996).

To record the prevalence of sports injuries, injury surveillance or epidemiology studies (i.e. the study of the characteristics and prevalence patterns of injuries or disease) are undertaken. Although the literature is awash with such studies, the only universal observation that can be made regarding them is that there is no consistent approach to data collection or to the definitions of different types of injury. Some researchers argue that injury surveillance studies are only truly effective if consistent, valid and reliable definitions and methods of data collection are utilised (Finch, 1997; Junge *et al.*, 2004; Schmikli *et al.*, 2009). Data are, however, often difficult to compare, given the various ways in which the information is collected and the different categorisations of injuries which are deployed. Whilst this apparent lack of agreement on terms and consistency of reporting strategies has complicated the determination of injury rates (Pelletier *et al.*, 1993), there have been moves by some sporting bodies to standardise the procedures used for collecting injury surveillance data.

For instance, a study undertaken by FIFA (Junge *et al.*, 2004) sought to try to make sense of injury occurrence data during major international football tournaments by developing an easy to use injury-reporting system to analyse the incidence, circumstances and characteristics of injury. The study, which captured data from 12 major tournaments, concluded that high-quality data could be collected, and consequently, a standardised injury-reporting system has been implemented as a matter of course in FIFA tournaments. Subsequently, a consensus statement on injury definitions and data collection procedures for studies of injuries in football was published (Fuller *et al.*, 2006). Work by the

International Rugby Board (IRB) led to a similar statement for rugby union injuries being published a year later (Fuller *et al.*, 2007). Such an approach within football and rugby, supports Finch's (1997) view that standardised collection methodologies are crucial for improving the comparability and interpretation of data.

Variations in data collection procedures and definitions aside, epidemiological studies are a useful means by which the prevalence of injuries can be identified. Analysis of a selection of studies shows that the research tends to report injury occurrence data from four major perspectives:

i)   Population specific – data can be collected from clearly defined and identified populations on the occurrence of injury over time within that population (e.g. young athletes, females or disabled athletes) (Gallagher *et al.*, 1984; Dirix *et al.*, 1988; Goldberg *et al.*, 2007).
ii) Sport specific – extensive studies have surveyed injury occurrence within sports or groups of sports. For example, Powell and Barber-Foss (1999) examined injury patterns in ten US high school sports across three seasons; Edwards and Ridgewell (2011) collected data from Welsh regional rugby players during a playing season; whilst Targett (1998) collected similar data from a Super 12 rugby squad, again, over a season.
iii) Tournament/competition specific – data can be collated from tournaments or competitions to establish a picture of injury occurrence in a particular competitive environment. For example, Cunningham and Cunningham (1996) gathered data from the 1994 Australian Universities Games, whilst Junge *et al.* (2004) gathered information from 12 major FIFA and Olympic football tournaments.
iv) Body part specific – focus can also be placed on common physical sites for injury in order to determine whether particular activities lead to a greater prevalence of such injuries. For example, Fong *et al.* (2007) undertook a systematic review of research that reported ankle injuries over a 28-year period, whilst Lian *et al.* (2005) looked at the prevalence of 'jumper's knee' across different sports.

Each perspective can offer different insights into injury prevalence within specific groups or contexts. The studies cited here also offer further comment on how and why injuries occur, rather than simply reporting their number. Such an approach can begin to offer detailed information relating to causal factors and mechanisms of injury.

The wide variety of injury surveillance studies and methodological approaches make it difficult to provide definitive data on the frequency and, hence, the risk of injury amongst sportspeople. However, some comprehensive studies have sought to quantify prevalence within certain sports. For example, Dvorak and Junge (2000) reported that, notwithstanding issues of competition, training, age, sex and level of play, the prevalence of injury in football is between 12 and 35 per 1000 hours of match play. This equates to between 1.5 and 7.6 per 1000 hours of practice for male players, whilst figures for women and adolescents are lower. In rugby, the figures reported are higher. For example, Targett (1998) discovered an injury rate of 120 per 1000 hours of match play in New Zealand, whilst Brooks *et al.* (2005) reported 91 injuries per 1000 hours of English Premiership rugby. At the other end of the spectrum, Bak *et al.* (1989) reported 0.9 injuries per 1000 hours of swimming amongst Danish swimmers. Using a different approach, McKay *et al.* (1996) looked at Australian netball players and reported an injury rate of 17.3 injuries per 1000 participants during competition. It is therefore, apparent that different sports have a greater or lesser risk of injury. However, as suggested previously, meaningful comparisons can only be made between those studies which utilise similar reporting methods and criteria for what actually represents an injury.

In terms of the most common sports injuries and the most prevalent injury sites, the literature suggests that the knee and ankle and their associated soft tissues are the predominant areas for sport related injury (Caine *et al.*, 1996). For example, Dvorak and Junge (2000) reported that in football, the ankle and knee joints and the muscles and ligaments of the thigh and calf were the most affected by injury, concluding that between 61 and 90 per cent of all injuries occurred in the lower extremities. On the other hand, the study by Brooks *et al.* (2005) into rugby union, suggested that thigh haematomas, anterior cruciate ligament and hamstring injuries accounted for the most absence (in days) from training. Interestingly, however, in the New Zealand rugby context, the most frequently injured body parts were the head and face, although the majority of significant injuries were musculo-tendinous sprains or strains (Targett, 1998). Finally, McKay *et al.*'s (1996) study of Australian netball, highlighted that injuries largely occurred to three body parts: the ankle (30.2 per cent), hand (20.9 per cent) and knee (17.8 per cent). It is of little surprise that in those sports which involve running, jumping and landing, it is the lower extremities that are at most risk from injury.

Given the complexity and depth of the epidemiological data, it is of little wonder that authors, researchers and practitioners have failed to arrive at a standardised approach to the classification of sports injuries. Arguably, the easiest approach to adopt is to simply report the injured body part and to distinguish whether the injury has occurred to bone, soft/connective tissue or to an organ or other structure (e.g. skin). In practical terms, this is a logical classification, yet it is really only uni-dimensional, in that it simply states the exact location of the injury rather than offering an insight into the cause of, or mechanisms behind, injury occurrence. Adding to this, the exact nature of the injury (e.g. fracture, tear,

184

sprain, lesion or haematoma) begins to tell us a little bit more about it. However, for such data to be meaningful, there is also a need to consider the context: the sporting activity in which the injury occurred. For example, quantifying the number of fractured wrists in distance runners is of less use than doing so amongst football goalkeepers.

Some studies categorise injuries with reference to where, in an environmental sense, the injury occurred. These could record and compare indoor versus outdoor venues, hard (e.g. concrete) as opposed to soft surfaces (e.g. grass), as well as other factors such as climate, equipment and altitude. Further classification suggestions include those in terms of when an injury occurs (e.g. in training as opposed to competition, or during a warm-up as opposed to a fatigued state) or in terms of severity and impact on training (e.g. the duration and nature of the treatment required, the amount of training or playing time lost, and whether there is permanent damage). These, and similar forms of categorisations, have some usefulness in trying to identify possible causes of injury, but tend to be binomial in nature, in that they are either one thing or the other. Since most injuries tend to occur as a result of a combination of factors, only recording one of them has limited value.

To be more effective, classifying sports injuries requires a multidimensional approach. To fully understand sports injuries, the most meaningful categorisation is one which includes all aspects of how, where, when, and in what context the injury was sustained. For example, many professional football clubs across Europe use video footage to examine the factors associated with an in-play injury. They may observe, amongst other things, what a player was doing when an injury occurred (e.g. landing from a jump, being tackled or running), what position their body or limbs were in at the time (e.g. extended, flexed, turning or under stress), the player's state of fatigue (e.g. how long into the game the injury occurred, or how far the player had run prior to the injury), or whether the player was executing a technique correctly or had been tackled illegally.

The literature widely utilises the terms 'acute' or 'sudden impact' to describe those injuries which have arisen as a result of some single traumatic incident. Similarly, the terms 'gradual onset', 'chronic' or 'overuse' are used to describe those injuries which have occurred from repetitive exposure to a stressor and have manifested themselves over a period of time. Acute injuries are caused by one-off events which lead to a body part being damaged. Such injuries can be further classified as being 'extrinsic acute' (a result of contact with an external force, typically being struck by, or colliding with, another person, some equipment or implement, or the ground) or 'intrinsic acute' (the result of some excessive internal force, such as a stretch, twist or pull, which can lead to strains, sprains, ruptures or dislocation). In contrast to those injuries which occur as a result of a sudden event, there are numerous injury types that may take time to elicit symptoms. As with acute injuries, chronic or overuse injuries can be further sub-classified according to the nature of the predisposing factor. Extrinsic chronic injuries are those which typically result from continued exposure to a factor that lies outside the body (e.g. excessive training loads, particularly on hard surfaces). Alternatively, intrinsic chronic injuries may result from some internal overstressing due to, for example, muscular weakness or imbalance. Figure 12.2 gives a summarised categorisation of the most common sporting injuries.

Injury causation

Through whatever method we classify and categorise sporting injuries, there is still a need to try to understand why and how an injury occurred, in order to identify potential preventative measures. The literature again adopts the terms *intrinsic* and *extrinsic* to categorise the main causal factors of sports injuries. Taimela *et al.* (1990) and Van Mechelen *et al.* (1992) suggest that intrinsic causal factors are person-related and are associated with the biological or psychosocial characteristics of a person. These could include their age, joint stability, muscle strength, tightness or asymmetry, previous injuries and rehabilitation effectiveness, and stress or fatigue. Conversely, extrinsic causal factors are related to environmental variables such as level and position of play, exercise load or

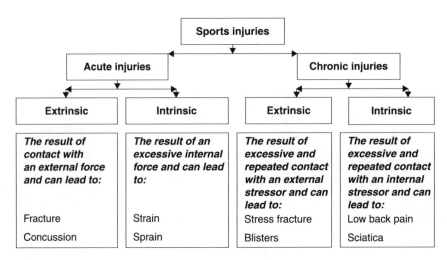

Figure 12.2 A categorisation of the most common sports injuries

186

intensity, training volume, protective equipment, playing surface, rules and foul play.

Once again, the epidemiological studies that seek to identify the most prevalent causes of injury, offer varied conclusions. Junge *et al.* (2009) collated information from injuries occurring in the Summer Olympics in 2008, and identified that 72.5 per cent of injuries occurred in competition. One third of these injuries were caused by contact with another athlete, 22 per cent through overuse and 20 per cent as a result of non-contact incidences. Also, individual sub-groups of the athletic population have been found to have unique and distinctive risk profiles (Watson, 1997). In this regard, it is of little surprise that contact sports would seem to have the highest injury risk. In Junge *et al.*'s (2009) Olympic study, injuries were reported from all sports, but their incidence and characteristics varied substantially. Here, the risk of incurring an injury was highest in football, taekwondo, hockey, handball, weightlifting and boxing (all ≥ 15 per cent of the athletes), and lowest for sailing, canoeing/kayaking, rowing, synchronised swimming, diving, fencing and swimming. Additionally, Dvorak and Junge (2000) suggested that within a football context, previous injuries and inadequate rehabilitation are the most important intrinsic factors, whilst the overall most common mechanism of injury is direct contact with other players. Junge *et al.* (2004) reported a total of 901 injuries in 334 major international football matches, (2.7 injuries per match), with 86 per cent of the injuries arising from contact with another player, and approximately half of all injuries being caused by foul play. Bahr and Holme (2003), however, suggest that injuries are rarely caused by a single factor, preferring to suggest that injuries result from a complex interaction of multiple risk factors and events. For example, anterior cruciate ligament injuries may occur as a result of a combination of landing and twisting actions on the part of the athlete, an interaction between footwear and playing surface, and/or underlying personal structural weaknesses or fatigue.

A coach's knowledge of the potential risk factors associated with sports injuries is vital in helping him or her to play a preventative role. For example, whilst coaches can do little about players' ages, he or she can ensure that players train and compete within safe thresholds for their ages, abilities and skill levels. It is to these issues of injury prevention that we now turn.

Injury prevention

With the increased understanding of the prevalence and causes of sports injuries comes an enhanced appreciation of the importance of preventative measures. Many national and international sporting organisations have begun to focus on the need to promote initiatives to reduce the prevalence of injuries. The most obvious adaptations that are made at an organisational level are rule changes to either reduce dangerous and foul play or permit greater use of protective equipment or clothing. Aubry *et al.* (2002), when discussing the occurrence of concussion in sport, suggested that rule changes may be appropriate where a clear-cut mechanism is implicated in a particular sport. They also stated that rule enforcement is a critical aspect of such approaches, and that referees play an important role. Coaches too should play a crucial role in rule enforcement and the maintenance of fair play.

The sport of rugby is a clear example of how these two approaches can be adopted. Here, Wales' 2011 Rugby World Cup semi-final defeat to France included a red card for the Wales captain for a so-called 'spear tackle'. Such a tackle is outlawed by the rules of the game to reduce the risk of serious injury to the tackled player. Although controversial in terms of the match outcome, in upholding the laws of the game, the referee raised the awareness of the dangerous nature of such a tackle. Also, whilst the introduction of helmets and mouthguards in rugby was intended to reduce the risk of head injuries, Aubry *et al.* (2002: 9) suggest that,

> whilst in sports in which high speed collisions can occur or which have the potential for missile injuries, there is published evidence that the use of sport-specific helmets reduces head injuries. For other sports such as soccer and rugby, no sport-specific helmets have been shown to be of benefit in reducing rates of head injury. Some believe that the use of protective equipment may deleteriously alter playing behaviour so that the athlete actually increases his or her risk of brain injury.

Whilst the arbitrators of sport play a key role in prevention through the development of rule changes, the responsibility for the use of protective equipment and other strategic approaches to injury prevention must lie at a more local level. The coach's role in injury prevention is to ensure that his or her actions appropriately prepare the performer and the coaching environment for prevention within both training and competition.

The risk and severity of injury has been shown to vary with the level of performance and the type of population (Dvorak and Junge, 2000). For example, the incidence of injury in professional rugby is far higher than in amateur rugby, due to the speed and intensity with which the game is played. At both levels, however, coaches need to be aware of typical injury sites, so that they can develop fitness and skill levels that reduce the likelihood of such injuries happening. Similarly, coaches of young children need to be aware of the developmental factors affecting their charges' participation in sport. For example,

188

intensive training of young children can delay the onset of puberty and skeletal maturation, thereby increasing the risk of damage to the heads of the bones (epiphysis). Additionally, in young women, heavy training increases the risk of the female triad syndrome of amenorrhea, osteoporosis and eating disorders (Birch, 2005). It is important that coaches understand these and other complex syndromes and recognise their symptoms, thus lessening the likelihood of occurrence. For those interested in more detail here, Dirix *et al.* (1988) provide a useful overview of sports injury perspectives in certain sporting populations, such as children, women, the aging athlete, and athletes with disabilities.

Detailed knowledge and understanding of the physical (and mental) demands of their sport is important for coaches as it enables them to develop and design relevant training programmes. This is necessary, as inappropriate training can have a negative impact at three levels. First, inadequate technique or fitness levels and/or excessive training loads may lead to fatigue, a state which makes athletes increasingly susceptible to injury (Gabbett, 2004). Second, continued high training loads and insufficient recovery time may result in athletes over-reaching in training or competition. This, in turn, can lead to greater injury susceptibility (Kreider *et al*, 1998). Additionally, sustained heavy training loads with inadequate recovery periods can result in the development of the pathological condition known as over-training, or unexplained underperformance syndrome (UUS). Indeed, Budgett (1998) reported that 10 per cent of endurance athletes per year experience over-training symptoms which, in turn, further increases the risk of injury.

Since sport is much more to do with training than competition, most injuries occur during the former. When preparing the training environment, then, the coach should be aware of any potential risks that may exist. For example, poor quality training facilities can result in trivial injuries which can be easily avoided. Also, coaches should familiarise themselves with emergency procedures and facilities both on and off the training site. Finally, in this context, whilst it is not essential, it is highly desirable for a coach to have basic first aid and life-support training, as it is often the coach who is the first person to attend to the injured athlete. Swift actions here can often save a life or reduce the severity of athlete injury. Recent high-profile cases within football have highlighted the need for prompt life-support equipment and expertise to be available.

Selection of the most appropriate equipment and training terrain is also important for injury prevention. For example, the shoe an athlete trains in should not only be dependent on the type of sport and the surface on which the training occurs, but also on the individual's specific mechanical characteristics. The prevalence of injury to footballers' metatarsals (i.e. foot bones) has highlighted the influence that inappropriate footwear may have on increasing the possibility of injury. Indeed, Ekstrand and Gillquist (1983) ascribed two-thirds of overuse injuries in football to poor quality shoes, whilst Vilwock *et al.* (2009) demonstrated that football playing surfaces and shoe design affect rotational traction which may be a potential mechanism for injury. Other examples of inappropriate use of equipment include using the wrong grip-size in tennis which promotes tennis elbow, or incorrectly sized cycle frames which increase the risk of back injury in cycling. Likewise, in contrast with the role of a running shoe (shock absorption and rear foot control), a tennis shoe is designed for lateral and cutting manoeuvres. Therefore, either running in a tennis shoe or playing tennis in a running shoe, increases the risk of injury.

Although coaches are often responsible for the organisation of medical provision, the type of sport and level of competition influences their role in this regard. For example, at most major international competitions or mass participation events, medical cover is normally provided by the organising body or sponsor. Here, it is the responsibility of the coach to be aware of the existing medical cover and how to access it. However, at the lower levels of competition, it is less likely that medical cover will be provided, leaving the coach personally responsible for organising medical support.

In terms of preparing an athlete for training or competition, there are a number of steps a coach can, and perhaps should, take to minimise the risk of injury. In addition to ensuring that the training undertaken matches the capabilities of athletes, coaches should also ensure that athletes are physically prepared for a training session through an effective warm-up routine. It is widely accepted that a general warm-up to elevate the heart rate and body temperature to optimal functioning levels, followed by a specific warm-up to mimic the joint actions and muscle contractions to be performed during training, can help reduce injuries (Gleim and McHugh, 1997). Further, whilst stretching is often reported to help prevent injury, the causal relationship here has yet to be definitively proven (Smith, 1994). In line with the increased awareness by sport governing bodies with regards to preventative measures, FIFA have developed a standardised warm-up routine which they term the 11+ programme and is designed to reduce the risk of injury in football players. Teams that performed this programme at least twice a week were found to have 30 to 50 per cent fewer injured players (Soligard *et al.*, 2008).

As has been suggested previously, the increased role of sport and physical activity in society has resulted in an increase in the number of people who have become physically active. Consequently, an escalation in implicit risks has occurred, which hitherto had been largely overlooked by sports coaches. Health screening is an increasingly important issue in exercise and sport, and can be essential, not only in previously non-athletic populations who take up or return to sport, but also in diseased populations who are prescribed exercise as a potential medical intervention through GP Referral and Exercise Prescription programmes.

A coach is unlikely to have detailed knowledge of the exercise history or medical background of new participants. Consequently, and regardless of previous exercise habits, individuals may arrive with muscle imbalances, joint instability or underlying health problems which could result in minor injuries or major clinical problems when exercise loads are too intense or inappropriate. Coaches, therefore, need to be aware of the potential risks that participants carry, and the need for some form of medical approval or screening prior to participation in exercise programmes. In addition, some form of functional screening may be necessary to assess athletes' suitability for the activities to be undertaken. Such an approach may involve ensuring that athletes are fit enough to participate by, whenever possible, checking their medical histories. This includes becoming familiar with key indicators such as a personal history of cardiovascular disease, cholesterol levels and blood pressure. Additional factors which should be considered include previous head and musculoskeletal injuries, exercise-induced asthma, diabetes and heart-related illness (Scuderi and McCann, 2005). For contact sports such as rugby, American football and boxing, there are clear guidelines regarding pre-screening as well as the amount of time before athletes can return to competition following a head injury. In many other sports, however, the guidelines are less prescriptive, making increased awareness very salient to coaches.

The recent collapse of Bolton FC footballer Fabrice Muamba during an FA Cup tie, and the death during a match in Italy just weeks later of the Livorno midfielder Piermario Morosini, once again brought to the world's attention the risk of sudden cardiac death. Here, apparently healthy young athletes succumbed to heart disease with little or no warning. As a result, many sporting organisations now require regular cardiac screening of participants to try to identify potential hidden risks within athletic populations.

INJURY MANAGEMENT

Successful return to play and restoration of normal function is usually the primary objective following occurrence of an injury. Underpinning this is the effective management of the injury from its initial occurrence through to complete recovery. This section will examine the key stages in injury management and identify the differing roles that coaches and others play in this process.

There are several stages in the management of a sports injury. The first of these is immediate management. Here, either first aid is administered or an initial diagnosis and treatment are performed. This is followed by early management, where a more informed diagnosis is carried out with appropriate treatment administered soon after the injury. The third stage is that of detailed diagnosis, where an in-depth analysis is completed which may require arthroscopic surgery or X-rays. The penultimate phase is rehabilitation, where the athlete undertakes exercises to strengthen and rehabilitate the affected area. The final stage involves the return to play, with the athlete being passed as fit again. Each will now be outlined in more depth.

At the immediate management stage, it is often the coach who takes the initiative. This may involve a decision related to the condition of the athlete in relation to continuing participation or the need for medical treatment. In some cases, coaches fail to realise the significance of the injury and allow the athlete to continue, often resulting in greater trauma to the injury site. For serious injuries to the head, neck or chest, additional specialist medical support should immediately be called for. To assist coaches in this context, Steele (1996) produced a useful textbook entitled 'Sideline help: A guide for immediate evaluation and care of sports injuries', which readers may wish to access to further their knowledge.

The early management phase tends to happen either on the field or in the changing/medical room. It is normally completed either by a coach, physician or physiotherapist and can result in referral to a specialist. This initial treatment is usually in response to one of four injury categories: wounds, fractures, soft tissue, and head or neck injuries. The coach should be aware that for wound management, the key aim is to reduce contamination and prevent blood loss. This is often done by dressing the wound. The initial treatment of fractures involves immobilising the joint, possibly using some form of splint. For soft tissue injuries, the goal is to reduce or control swelling. The most effective approach here is described by the acronym R.I.C.E.: Rest-Ice-Compression-Elevation. Generally, ice should be applied for 15 minutes every 1 or 2 hours in the 24 hours immediately after the injury occurring, whilst compression should be adequate enough to apply pressure but not to cause pain. Head and neck injuries normally require immobilisation via the application of a neck brace or spinal board.

During the detailed diagnosis stage, a specialist may become involved; this is often dependent on financial considerations rather than the severity of the injury. The diagnosis itself may require an X-ray or MRI scan, whilst for serious or complex injuries, several opinions may be required. The resulting treatment could be surgery, the use of therapeutic drugs such as cortisone steroids or other anti-inflammatories, ultrasound stimulation, manipulation or massage. Biomechanists, nutritionists, podiatrists or other specialists, could also be called upon at this stage to contribute to the overall management of the process. Such individuals can facilitate understanding of the underlying causes of injuries, and can often provide advice or interventions which may help prevent reoccurrence. For example, knee, hip and Achilles tendon injuries in runners, are often the result of wearing the wrong type of running shoe. A podiatrist/biomechanist can analyse a runner's gait to determine any mechanical issues that need addressing and, consequently, can prescribe orthotics or specially designed running shoes for the athlete in question. The final phase of rehabilitation and return to play will be covered in more detail in the next section. Suffice to say, this basically comprises a combination of treatments as outlined in the detailed diagnosis phase, combined with exercises to strengthen and regain flexibility in the injured region(s).

THE REHABILITATION PROCESS

This section will examine the key issues associated with rehabilitation from injury, and consider the processes involved in restoring full use to an injured body part. For successful rehabilitation to occur, a coach needs to appreciate that an injured athlete should be able to return to competition without any increased risk of the initial injury reoccurring. To achieve this, a rehabilitation programme needs to adhere to the general principles of training, with specific focus on progression and individuality.

The manipulation of key training principles for injured athletes involves paying particular attention to safe progression for each athlete in terms of frequency, intensity, overload and time. Unfortunately, there is no magic formula to achieve this. Consequently, these principles will vary with each case, since injuries are unique, whilst every individual also has specific needs to ensure successful recovery. However, all rehabilitation programmes have a common aim: to allow the athlete back to full functional ability at the earliest possible opportunity with minimal chance of recurrence of the original injury. According to Brukner and Kahn (2006), factors that influence the rehabilitation process include the:

- type and severity of injury;
- circumstances surrounding the injury;
- external pressures (pressure to return to play by the coach/media/team);
- pain tolerance of the athlete;
- psychological attributes of the athlete;
- coach–athlete support system.

In terms of this last point, the coach's role in supporting an injured athlete cannot be underestimated (Robbins and Rosenfeld, 2001). Here, the coach's knowledge of the athlete's self-esteem and attitude to training adherence is essential, as all athletes respond differently to being injured. Those with high self-esteem and motivation levels often respond well to rehabilitation by focusing on their desire to play again (Lampton *et al.*, 1993). These individuals normally follow any rehabilitation programme religiously, although they may also try to progress too rapidly during the initial stages of recovery. In contrast, athletes with low levels of self-esteem and poor adherence to training, often fail to follow strict exercise regimes, resulting in a longer rehabilitation phase (Lampton *et al.*, 1993). An injured athlete who understands what and why they are doing something, and who has easy access to facilities and support, is more likely to adhere to a reha-bilitation programme. Additionally, the setting of realistic and achievable targets by coaches will assist athlete compliance and adherence to the set course of action (Tracey, 2003). The use of sports specific activities can also help to main-tain athlete interest and motivation, thus allowing the injured athlete to recover more rapidly.

According to Brukner and Kahn (2006), a rehabilitation programme can be divided into four stages: initial, intermediate, advanced and a return to com-petition. A coach needs to recognise and understand each of these stages so that he or she can support the athlete's return to full fitness. The initial stage involves getting the athlete to be pain free and have a full range of move-ment. This phase is often very frustrating for injured athletes, as the required rehabilitation exercises are often highly repetitive and non-sports specific. Consequently, in team sports, it is sometimes useful to allow injured athletes to involve themselves in other ways to ensure they continue to feel part of the team. For example, they could help coach the less able athletes/players, or work with the development squads. Alternatively, some players rehabilitate better when isolated from distractions. Thus, they may benefit from attending specialist training/rehabilitation centres away from the home club. Naturally, these alternatives also depend on the nature of the injury and the availability of resources.

The main purpose of the intermediate stage is for the athlete to regain any defi-ciencies in strength/muscle imbalances associated with inactivity. Here, it is often useful for injured athletes to join specialised training groups. For example, professional soccer and rugby players often complete this stage in conjunction with other sportsmen/women who often focus purely on strength rather than skill or technique development. Alternatively, at the advanced rehabilitation stage, the injured athlete should be engaged in conditioning specific to the activity or sport in which they compete. The role of the coach is important here in ensuring that the rehabilitation exercises are sports specific, thus placing

194

the injured body parts under similar stresses to those encountered during competition. Finally, the coach has an important function in the return to competition stage of a rehabilitation programme by testing the player's capability to return to full training and competition. This may involve setting up simulated match practice or getting the athlete in question to initially compete at a lower level than normal. For example, it is usual for games players to start the return to competition stage by playing in the reserves, with a gradual transition to playing a full match for the first team. Likewise, international athletes often compete at local club competitions prior to returning to the intensity of elite sport.

SUMMARY

Injuries, whilst being very prevalent in sports participation, are, in many instances, preventable. A coach can assist in this prevention by developing a good understanding of the physical demands associated with their sport, and the different types and causes of injury that may occur within those sports. Such an understanding can help coaches reduce the potential risk of injury. In some instances, however, injuries will still occur. Here, coaches should be aware of the necessary steps to take, both to reduce the severity of, and facilitate the recovery from, such injuries. Careful management of an injury will aid an athlete's recovery and subsequent return to training and competition. Once an athlete is on the road to recovery, the coach should give consideration to how and when the athlete will be reintroduced to normal training. Similarly, the possible causes of the original injury should be reflected upon to prevent the same injury occurring again. Developing such sports medicine related knowledge, then, as associated with the prevention, treatment and management of injuries, allows the coach to better protect the health, well-being, fitness and, hence, the ultimate performance of athletes.

DISCUSSION TOPICS AND REVIEW QUESTIONS

1   Why is an understanding of sports medicine important for sport coaches?
2   What are the three elements of the 'sequence of prevention', and how are they inter-related?
3   How can an understanding of injury causation and injury prevalence be used by a coach?
4   How can a sports coach use the principles of fair play to reduce the risk of injuries?
5   How can a coach gauge whether a performer is ready to return to play?

Web Resources

http://www.basem.co.uk/

http://www.amssm.org/

http://www.acsm.org/

These three sites are the web pages of the professional bodies for sports medicine practitioners in the UK (British Association of Sport and Exercise Medicine) and the United States (American Medical Society for Sports Medicine, American College of Sports Medicine). They offer an overview of sports medicine in both contexts.

http://www.nhs.uk/conditions/sports-injuries/Pages/Introduction.aspx

This site is produced by the NHS and gives some basic information about sports injuries and how they can be prevented and treated.

http://www.nhs.uk/Conditions/Sports-injuries/Pages/Causes.aspx

This website outlines the most common sport injuries in both amateur and professional sport and offers some informative links to additional information.

http://f-marc.com/11plus/

This website offers details about the FIFA F-MARC 11+ Injury prevention programme. At this site you can (i) read the background and the scientific papers supporting the use of the 11+, (ii) watch the 11+ Exercises, (iii) scroll through the 11+ Manual and (iv) download the 11+ Material.

http://www.powerbar.com/articles/175/avoiding-sports-injuries-what-every-coach-should-know.aspx

This article gives a straightforward summary of some key issues that coaches should be familiar with.

http://coachr880.com/id42.html

This site gives a useful overview of key aspects of the healing and rehabilitation process. Whilst it is aimed primarily at athletics coaches, the information is applicable across most sports.

CHAPTER 13

PHYSIOLOGY FOR COACHES

MICHAEL G. HUGHES, JOHN L. OLIVER AND RHODRI LLOYD

A working knowledge of physiology is essential for all good coaches. You have to know how different kinds of training affect the body so you can develop the optimal preparation programme for players.
Julia Longville, Welsh National Netball Coach (2002–2006)

INTRODUCTION

Sports physiology is concerned with how the body reacts to physical training and competition. Many physiological characteristics affect an athlete's performance, ranging from visible factors, such as gender and body size, to the complex biochemical processes that cause muscle contraction at the molecular level. While a coach may not need to have an in-depth knowledge of all these processes and reactions, a grasp of the key aspects of physiology and how they relate to sports performance is essential for the optimal preparation of athletes. This knowledge stems from an appreciation of the physiological demands of the sport relative to the needs of the athletes. The aim of this chapter is to demonstrate how an understanding of physiology may help coaches to maximise the fitness and performance levels of their athletes. This will be achieved by, first, outlining the physiological components of sport performance, then by providing an overview of sport physiology, before moving on to discuss principles of training to enhance that performance. The chapter concludes with a section which focuses on aspects of sports physiology relevant to children.

THE PHYSIOLOGICAL COMPONENTS OF SPORT PERFORMANCE

Although it is important for coaches to observe performance in their sport from a holistic perspective, it is also crucial for them to be able to compartmentalise aspects of performance, especially when improvements are needed in those specific areas. This approach (of appreciating distinct components) is vital when aiming to improve physiological aspects of performance. For most sports, it is valuable to consider the extent to which some basic fitness elements are needed. For example, most sports require power, speed and endurance capabilities. However, the degree to which they are needed will vary significantly between (and in some cases, within) sports. Beyond that, individual athletes will have their own specific fitness needs which are dependent on a wide range of additional factors.

Coaches should, therefore, be well acquainted with the demands of their sport and the individual needs of their athletes. The use of performance analysis has been covered elsewhere in this book (see Chapter 11), and is a valuable tool for enhancing the appreciation of a sport's physiological demands. Indeed, comprehensive related knowledge is available on a variety of sports which can be used to have a direct impact on improving the training and competitive performance of athletes (Deutsch *et al.*, 2006; Bradley *et al.*, 2009). When combinations of performance analysis and physiological measures (Murias *et al.*, 2007; Mohr *et al.*, 2004) are used, even more comprehensive information can be gained.

With an appreciation of the physiological components which affect performance, a coach should be able to identify individual strengths and weaknesses of all athletes, allowing for the development of individualised training. For example, if agility is considered as a fitness component within a sport, those players deficient in agility can be given directed training to enhance this area. However, it is also important to appreciate that a variety of factors will affect agility, and that poor agility may be down to a variety of other fitness elements such as strength, power, movement technique or high body fat. It is, therefore, of great value to have knowledge of a wide range of fitness indicators so that identification of 'normal' results for each sport can be used to identify strengths and weaknesses.

AN OVERVIEW OF SPORTS PHYSIOLOGY

The contraction of muscle is fundamental to all exercise performance. It is initiated by nerve signals that promote movement, provided that sufficient chemical energy is available to the muscle fibres. Indeed, exercise represents a challenge to a muscle's energy stores, with many physiological reactions combining to replenish and mobilise such stores so that exercise can continue. The energy-releasing reactions range in complexity from very simple ones within the active muscle, to highly complex ones that require the coordinated responses of the muscle and the respiratory, metabolic, cardiovascular and hormonal systems.

198

An understanding of these systems and how they impact on different kinds of activity, both in competition and in training, will help coaches who wish to improve the fitness levels of athletes; some of these issues are discussed in the rest of this section.

Initiation of movement

The performance of very short-duration activity involves relatively few physiological processes. Nerve signals initiate a series of reactions which cause contraction in a muscle, resulting in force production and movement. If exercise lasts less than a couple of seconds, then energy stores within the working muscles are sufficient to meet the demands of the activity. The very short duration of such activity negates the need for other more complex energy-producing processes to be activated. Consequently, muscle produces its highest possible force and power when exercise is very short. Table 13.1 lists a series of sports events of contrasting exercise duration. It should be appreciated that sporting events with the shortest duration are also those that require the highest force production. The limiting factors for very short-duration exercise are mainly the muscle's maximal strength, size and power (Kraemer *et al.*, 2002).

Table 13.1 Sporting events and the physiological factors that limit their performance. (Number of '+' signs indicates relative importance)

Exercise duration	Examples of sport/ activity	Main physiological factors that determine performance		
		Muscle size, maximal strength cardio- and power fitness	Anaerobic energy production and fatigue resistance	Aerobic energy production and respiratory fitness
Up to 2 seconds	Shot putt, discus, weight-lifting	+++++	+	−
Up to ~ 15 seconds	60m and 100m sprints (run), bobsleigh	++++	++	+
~ 15–60 seconds	400m run, 50m and 100m swim	+++	++++	+++
1–10 minutes	1500m run, Alpine skiing, figure skating programme, rowing (2000m)	++	+++	++++
Longer than ~ 10 minutes	5000m running and above, triathlon, cycle stage races,	+	++	+++++

Strength is the ability to exert force against a resistance, and is fundamental to sports performance through its association with power and speed. Muscles can produce force while they are shortening, lengthening or maintaining a static position. The ability to produce force is governed by both structural and neural properties within the muscle, which vary according to age, gender, genetics and the training history of an athlete. When an athlete begins a training programme designed to enhance strength, early performance gains will primarily result from an increased ability to recruit more muscle fibres at the initiation of contraction. The development of structural adaptations, however, – that is, the increases in muscle size – can take up to five weeks to appear.

Power is perhaps the most significant physiological variable within sport, because the ability to produce high forces at speed is desirable in nearly all areas of athletic performance. Although it is usually advantageous to have high levels of strength, maximal strength is rarely produced in sporting activities. For example, rugby players are only likely to produce near-maximal force in sustained activities such as scrummaging, whereas the time when forces can be applied is much less in other typical activities such as sprinting, jumping, kicking and striking. In these latter cases, power becomes the most important factor in performance. The power-producing capabilities of muscles are dictated primarily by the 'force–velocity relationship'. This describes how high forces are possible only with slow movements and, conversely, that the fastest movements can only be achieved with a relatively low force production (see Figure 13.1). However, where movement velocity is high, there is insufficient time to recruit all of the available muscle fibres and the highest force produced is relatively low. The relationship between power and force is also shown in Figure 13.1, demonstrating that maximal power is achieved when both the force and velocity are sub-maximal.

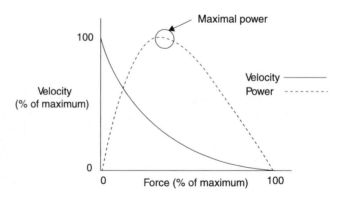

Figure 13.1 The force–velocity and force–power relationships for concentric contractions of muscle

Note: Maximal power occurs at sub-maximal values of force (F_{max}) and velocity (V_{max})

200

The maintenance of muscle activity

Once exercise lasts more than a couple of seconds, the need to continually supply the working muscles with energy begins to limit the levels of perform-ance. For all exercise intensities, strength and power remain very important, but as exercise duration increases, their relative importance to exercise performance is somewhat reduced. Figure 13.2 shows the power output during sprint running, illustrating the point that, once exercise lasts more than a couple of seconds, the performance of the muscle declines. In effect, muscles are already experiencing fatigue even after three seconds of sprint exercise because their most immediate supply of energy is beginning to be compromised, resulting in a decline in performance. This development of fatigue has important implications for training, a topic which will be considered later in this chapter.

The processes that the body uses to supply the energy needs for exercise are usually classified into two broad categories: aerobic and anaerobic. Anaerobic processes refer to energy-producing reactions that happen without the need for oxygen at the muscle. Conversely, aerobic metabolism refers to energy-producing reactions that require oxygen. As identified previously, muscle produces its highest possible levels of performance when activity is performed over very short periods. However, once exercise lasts more than two seconds or so, muscle performance is increasingly limited by the activity of the aerobic or anaerobic processes.

Anaerobic reactions convert energy within the working muscle, thus allowing movement to continue. These are relatively simple reactions, so can happen very

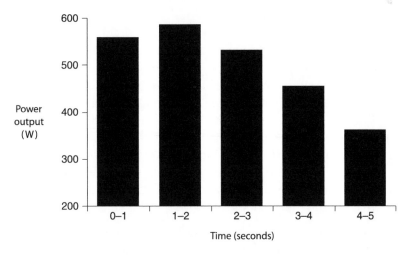

Figure 13.2 Power output during 5 seconds of treadmill sprinting

quickly. However, a consequence of such reactions is the development of fatigue due to the accumulation of metabolic by-products such as lactic acid. Because the energy stores are limited, anaerobic exercise cannot last for very long. As a consequence, because of fatigue and a relatively limited energy source, anaerobic processes are most important for short periods of high-intensity exercise. Aerobic processes, on the other hand, require the integrated response of the lungs, heart and circulation (i.e. the cardio-respiratory system) to take oxygen to the working muscle. This delivery of oxygen from the lungs merely provides for the energy-producing reactions at the muscle site which, in turn, maintain aerobic activity. Because of these complex requirements, aerobic processes cannot supply energy as quickly as anaerobic ones, although much greater energy stores can be accessed aerobically. This is partly because aerobic metabolism is associated with the release of energy (as fats and carbohydrates) from all over the body, not just from the muscle site. Consequently, aerobic metabolism provides access to more energy stores with which to fuel prolonged exercise. The compromise of using aerobic as opposed to anaerobic metabolism is that only relatively low-intensity exercise is possible. The factors that mainly limit the performance of aerobic activity, then, are the capability of the cardio-respiratory system and the speed of the aerobic energy reactions at the muscle site.

Intermittent muscle activity

The physiological demands described so far have focused on a situation where just one exercise bout of a specific duration is performed. However, many sports require athletes to perform several bouts of short-duration high-intensity exercise, interspersed with periods of relative recovery. These 'repeated-sprint sports' include football, hockey, rugby, basketball, volleyball and the racket sports. It has already been discussed how the performance of a single short-duration high-intensity bout of exercise is mostly determined by muscle strength, power and the anaerobic energy system. Consequently, these factors are also essential for success in repeated-sprint sports, but the speed of recovery from such high-intensity bouts is related to aerobic fitness (Glaister, 2005). So, not only do these sports require the strength, speed and anaerobic fitness for short-duration activity, they also require high levels of aerobic fitness in order to promote recovery. Owing to this variety of physiological requirements, it is important that a wide range of training session activities are provided for athletes who participate in the repeated-sprint sports.

In summary, it is essential that a coach understands the 'pay-off' between exercise intensity and duration. With very short-duration exercise, the body can produce its highest levels of performance. However, as exercise duration

202

increases, the delivery and maintenance of energy to working muscle tends to limit performance. Aerobic activity tends to be associated with the lower exercise intensities but longer exercise durations. If periods of high-intensity activity are interspersed with lower-intensity exercise, a combination of energy provision from the anaerobic and aerobic systems (in conjunction with strength, power and cardio-respiratory fitness) is required for optimal performance. An understanding of these issues is important in enabling coaches to devise training sessions that maximise the development of fitness.

TRAINING TO IMPROVE PHYSICAL PERFORMANCE

General considerations

One of the essential roles of a coach is to facilitate the development of fitness levels so that athletes can compete effectively. In some sports, the physical development of an athlete may be the main function of a coach. This is especially so where the technical or tactical demands of a sport are relatively low, and where success is judged by time or distance (e.g. athletics, swimming). In other cases, the non-physical demands of a sport may be so high that a coach may devote a smaller percentage of time to athletes' physical training. Irrespective of the sport, however, there are a number of key principles of fitness training that a coach should be able to understand and apply; these include the principles of overload, variation and specificity.

The human body is highly adaptable and, with sufficient training, significant gains can be made in all kinds of exercise performance. A key to achieving improvements is that a training programme must overload the physiological processes required for competition. A training programme which includes the overload principle will incorporate planned attempts to increase one or all of the key training variables (i.e. intensity, duration and frequency). For example, a training programme for an athlete who can only run for 30 minutes at a slow pace, and wishes simply to complete a marathon race, will predominantly involve an overload of the duration of training sessions. If the same runner wants to run the marathon in under three hours, then he or she would have to be additionally trained for maintaining the significantly faster speed required. In this case, the overload would need to be imposed in relation to the intensity of exercise as well as the duration. Similarly, the frequency of training could also be increased to provide an overload (e.g. from three sessions per week up to a target of five over a period of a few months).

Although small changes can happen over relatively short periods of time, the development of high fitness levels can take many years. If training only involved the performance of activity that was the same as the athlete's sport, the repeated stresses of this activity could lead to increased injury risk, while the athlete could become bored and unchallenged by their training schedule. It is essential, therefore, that an athlete experiences variation in training. Variation can be achieved by the use of alternative activities as well as by planning for periods of training that differ in intensity, frequency and duration.

In addition to the general considerations of overload and variation, a coach should also be aware of the principle of specificity when physically preparing athletes for competition. The principle of specificity dictates that training should be relevant to the demands of the sport and the athlete in question. Once the demands of the sport are understood, optimal fitness development is achieved by focusing on each element of physical performance in isolation. Specificity also dictates that the physiological demands of an event should be replicated in training. For example, if a sport requires short, highly intense bursts, training should be planned to include such activity. Specificity is further enhanced when the movement characteristics of a sport are matched in training. For example, many sports (e.g. tennis, rugby and squash) involve repeated changes in direction. Hence, the strength and speed training for these sports should include some activities that promote the required braking forces and leg muscle explosiveness that allow for quick directional changes. The remainder of this section will examine speed, strength and power development in more detail before going on to discuss the value of tailoring training towards anaerobic and aerobic energy provision.

Specific considerations

Increases in movement speed can usually be achieved by improvements in muscle power and movement technique, and potentially by a reduction in body mass. As discussed earlier, maximal speed can only ever be achieved over extremely short durations (see Figure 13.2). Hence, if the principle of specificity is to be applied to the development of speed, such training should incorporate very short periods of repeated maximal effort activity interspersed with long recoveries. Consequently, sprinters in athletics often have at least three minutes rest to allow for complete recovery after each short exercise bout. Similarly, for most sports players, maximal speed training should involve sprints of approximately five seconds followed by around one minute of recovery before the next sprint is performed. The fact that speed is essential in many sports, means that this type of training is an important component in developing the fitness of many athletes.

Training to enhance maximal strength is rather like that for speed, in that heavy demands are placed on the working muscles for very short periods of time. Also, like speed training, strength training requires short bouts of activity followed by longer periods of rest that allows the muscle's energy stores to be replenished. Only when the muscle can produce relatively high forces in training will it adapt to become stronger in the long term. The development of strength is likely to be beneficial to athletes in all sports, due to the fact that muscle strength provides protection from injury via improvements in general muscle control. For optimal strength development, it is important that the training load (resistance) is sufficient to recruit the majority of the fibres within a muscle. Therefore, the training intensity (external load) should exceed around 85 per cent of the load that can be lifted in a single repetition (i.e. one repetition maximum: 1RM). Typically, when training to develop strength, a Strength and Conditioning coach would prescribe 3–5 sets of 4–6 repetitions within around two minutes between sets. However, in order to overload the neuromuscular system and to elicit further strength adaptation, the training intensity should be increased with a concomitant decrease in volume (e.g. 3–5 sets of 1–3 repetitions using a 90–95 per cent 1RM load). Such training prescription would begin to develop maximal strength. However, during a long-term training plan, the intensities and volumes used by athletes should be manipulated to ensure continued improvements. Methods of strength training could include: free-weight resistance training, machine-fixed resistance training, weight-lifting (the snatch, and the clean and jerk), and resisted sport-specific movements (e.g. elasticated training bands, hill sprints).

For the development of power, a range of training methods exist, including: weightlifting exercises (again, the clean and jerk, and snatch movements), traditional resistance training exercises (light load squats and deadlifts), ballistic exercises (squat jumps and bench throws) and plyometrics. All of these exercises require the athlete to accelerate throughout the entire propulsive phase, which replicates the movement patterns inherent within sprinting, jumping and changing direction. With the exception of plyometrics, all of the other training methods typically involve some form of free-standing weightlifting equipment (i.e. a barbell and bumper plates). In contrast, plyometrics are characterised by jumping, hopping or rebounding against the ground, and require a rapid stretching and recoiling of the muscles. The intensity of plyometrics (which use body weight as the resistance) is manipulated by increasing the stretch rate of the muscle via increases in drop height. For athletes requiring high-power outputs against high external loads (e.g. rugby players), heavy-load power training is preferable (e.g. weightlifting or light-load resistance training exercises). However, where athletes require high-power outputs against light external loads (e.g. jumping, sprinting and striking), ballistics and plyometrics can serve as an effective training modality. Owing to the large neural contribution to power exercises, and the need to maintain rapid movement speeds, rest is essential during and between training sessions. At all times, coaches should strive to

Training goal	Load (%1RM)	Target repetitions	Force output	Movement speed
Power	30–80	1–6	Moderate/high	Rapid
Strength	≥85	1–6	Very high	Slow

ensure the quality of movements instead of focusing on the quantity of repetitions. Table 13.2 provides a summary of training prescription guidelines for strength and power development.

Training to enhance anaerobic energy provision requires adherence to similar principles as those for the development of strength and speed. Consequently, a training session to enhance anaerobic fitness could comprise repeated bouts of short exercise (e.g. 5 to around 30 seconds), with the interval between these being around 5–10 times the length of each bout (see Table 13.3). The main aim of anaerobic training is to improve the ability of the athlete to perform sustained high-intensity activity for events such as 200m running, 50m swimming or even sports like rugby and football where short, high-intensity bursts are interspersed with longer periods of low-intensity activity. Anaerobic fitness is also essential as a component of longer-duration events such as rowing, middle- to long-distance running and road cycling, where a sprint finish may be required towards the end of a race. When performing exercises to enhance anaerobic fitness, the use of the aerobic energy system should be low. By interspersing periods of work with long rest periods, there is less contribution from the aerobic system which, in turn, allows anaerobic processes to be the main providers of energy. It is essential that anaerobic training is performed at a very high intensity. Consequently, the athlete must work as hard as possible during the exercise periods.

Table 13.3 A selection of training (running) sessions to enhance anaerobic fitness

	Intended aim of session	Sprint duration	Rest between sprints	Number of repetitions
Short-sprint duration	i) Repetition of very-high-quality sprinting	5 seconds	90 seconds	10–15
	ii) Fatigue-resistance and speed-endurance	5 seconds	45 seconds	15
Long-sprint duration	i) Repetition of high-quality, sustained performance	20 seconds	150 seconds	6
	ii) Fatigue-resistance in sustained performance	20 seconds	90 seconds	10

Table 13.4 Selection of (running-based) training sessions to enhance aerobic fitness

	Intended aim of session	Details of session
Short-duration interval	To improve aerobic fitness at very high movement speed	5 sets of 10 repetitions (one repetition to include 10 seconds hard run, 20 seconds walk recovery), 2 minutes rest between sets
Medium-duration interval	To improve aerobic fitness at sustained high running speeds	6 repetitions (of 3 minutes hard run, interspersed with 2 minutes walking recovery)
Continuous exercise	To improve general aerobic fitness and endurance	45 minutes of low-intensity, continuous exercise

Aerobic fitness is a requirement of most sports. For example, long-duration events where activity is maintained at a relatively constant low intensity (such as triathlons, a 10,000m run or a 1500m swim) are almost exclusively aerobic. However, in repeated-sprint sports, aerobic requirements are also high. This is because aerobic fitness promotes recovery between high-intensity exercise bouts. Hence, most exercise will improve aerobic fitness, even strength and sprint training (Dawson *et al.*, 1998; Kraemer *et al.*, 1995; Burgomaster *et al.*, 2005). Although the traditional way of enhancing aerobic fitness has been to perform low-intensity exercise over prolonged periods of time, a whole range of activities can be used for its development. A common factor in doing so is the necessity to provide an overload of both exercise duration and intensity. Therefore, rather than just exercising at a low intensity for a longer time, optimal development of aerobic fitness also requires sessions where higher-intensity work is interspersed with rest periods (i.e. 'interval training'). This allows for more use of fast-contracting muscle fibres and greater stress on the cardiovascular system (Helgerud *et al.*, 2007). In turn, the fast-fibres and the cardio-respiratory systems adapt to the training and, with time, aerobic fitness improves. The differences between interval training sessions for aerobic and anaerobic fitness are that aerobic interval sessions are not usually performed at a maximal intensity, while the rest period between exercise bouts are usually a little shorter. Table 13.4 shows a selection of training sessions that would be suited to the development of aerobic fitness.

PHYSIOLOGICAL ISSUES IN EXERCISING CHILDREN

The physiological considerations of children during exercise deserve special attention, as their responses often differ from those seen in adults. For example, the anaerobic processes of children are usually less well developed than in adults, meaning that most exercise has a greater aerobic contribution for them. Additionally, children tend to recover more rapidly than adults during intermittent activity. As a child progresses from infancy to adulthood, fitness develops in a non-linear manner, with periods of relatively little change and periods of rapid development. Two periods of rapid development have been identified during childhood: the pre-adolescent spurt and the adolescent spurt (Viru *et al.*, 1999). The former occurs around the ages of 5–9 years old and is associated with rapid gains in central nervous system development, enabling a child to improve all aspects of fitness, but particularly those with a substantial motor control basis, such as skill, speed and strength. The adolescent spurt is associated with the onset of puberty, with performance gains observed around or after the time of the growth spurt.

Sexual maturation around puberty coincides with the release of sex and growth hormones that promote rapid changes in muscle and internal organ size, structure and function. These changes are particularly associated with rapid development of endurance and strength, although all components of fitness can continue to develop during this period. Prior to puberty, both genders exhibit similar performance levels. However, post-puberty, there is a divergence in performance, with females experiencing the disadvantage of increased fat mass while males experience the benefit of increased circulating anabolic hormones (e.g. testosterone). During these periods of rapid development, the underlying physiological processes may be more responsive to training-induced adaptations, so knowledge of a child's developmental status is valuable in the prescription of exercise training.

Training in children

Physical conditioning of children has been the subject of much debate over the years. However, there now appears to be consensus amongst scientists and professional organisations (e.g. the International Olympic Committee, the National Strength and Conditioning Association, British Association of Sport and Exercise Science) that children can safely engage in and benefit from sports training. For example, the belief that resistance training is unsafe or can stunt growth in children is considered inaccurate, provided training is appropriately structured and supervised (Faigenbaum *et al.*, 2009). The fact that children naturally engage in explosive and intermittent type activities suggests that they can safely engage in these types of exercise.

Evidence suggests that all aspects of fitness can be trained to some extent at all stages of childhood and adolescence. However, there may be distinct periods when responsiveness to training is increased. In this respect, few people would argue against the benefits of developing movement skills during the early years (and refining these skills in later years). Prior to adolescence, training should focus on factors associated with neural development, such as movement proficiency, sport-specific skills, speed of movement and explosiveness. These can continue to be trained throughout adolescence, but the growth spurt marks the start of a period where a child may be more responsive to endurance-related adaptations and increased muscle mass, with the latter normally observed after puberty when children (especially boys) naturally begin to add more muscle mass to their growing skeletal frame.

Maturational status

Maturation is a fundamental consideration when assessing the fitness of a child, as maturational status will have a significant impact on performance. For instance, if testing for talent identification purposes, it is unfair to compare results of two children of the same chronological age if one of those children is an 'early maturer' and the other a 'late maturer'. So, to know the maturational status of a child is desirable, but it tends to require laboratory techniques that are inaccessible to most. More practically, it is possible to measure standing height over time (e.g. three-monthly intervals) to establish growth rates and peak height velocity (PHV). PHV is defined as the peak growth rate in standing height (expressed as centimetres per year) and is associated with reaching biological maturity (i.e. puberty). This can provide a useful point around which to design training programmes. For example, for a child who has yet to reach their PHV, it is unlikely that a strength training programme would induce substantial hypertrophy. However, the same child may be far more susceptible to the acquisition of movement skill at the same age. In this way, coaches can individualise the training of children according to maturational status.

A disadvantage with identifying PHV is that it is a retrospective measure and requires multiple measurements over time, which may not always be possible. However, researchers have developed an equation that allows a prediction of how close to PHV a child is at any single time-point, which is measured as years before or after PHV (Mirwald *et al.*, 2002). The equation is based on the different growth rates observed between the limbs (e.g. leg length), which experience an earlier growth spurt, and the trunk which experiences a later growth spurt.

An understanding of the different developmental rates of children is of significance to coaches, as maturational status influences both technical and physiological development. For example, children may experience periods of rapid limb growth owing to physiological changes, but these can have a marked impact on their ability to coordinate their changing body dimensions. This process is known as 'adolescent awkwardness' and may significantly affect a child's performance.

In summary, coaches should appreciate that training children may require contrasting strategies and techniques compared to working with adults. Beyond the broad differences evident, coaches should appreciate the significance that contrasting maturational rates may have on developing performance, even between children of the same gender and chronological age.

CONCLUSION

The aim of this chapter was to highlight how an understanding of sports physiology can help inform coaching practice. It is intended that the issues presented may enable a coach to make decisions regarding the best strategies for enhancing the fitness of athletes in order to optimise their competitive performance. Although it is beyond the scope of the chapter to provide definitive answers regarding precise fitness questions in relation to individual athletes and the sports they perform, through applying the principles discussed, it is hoped that all coaches can approach the development of their athletes' fitness with a greater level of knowledge and confidence.

DISCUSSION TOPICS AND REVIEW QUESTIONS

1   A range of training types has been shown to enhance performance in aerobic activities. Speculate which physiological processes are enhanced as a result of:
    a)   high-intensity (sprint) interval training
    b)   continuous low-intensity training
2   What justifications are there for the use of strength training for the development of performance in endurance sports?
3   Competitors in 'repeated sprint sports' require a range of fitness attributes. If you are coaching a team which only trains using matches to promote fitness, why may this lead to sub-optimal development of fitness?
4   The performance of very-high-intensity activity (such as maximal strength and sprint exercise) will induce fatigue very rapidly.
    a)   How should coaches incorporate this factor into developing athletes' strength, power and speed?
    b)   How should coaches incorporate this factor into their plans for assessing fitness?
5   Your sport has a policy of selecting junior squads based on the best players within each age group between the ages of 10 and 18. These groups are

purely based on chronological age. Why may this policy be counter-productive in terms of developing these players into successful adults?

6 What approaches may a coach take to gain an increased understanding of the physiological requirements of their sport?

Web Resources

The websites cited below give a further indication of the value of physiological knowledge for coaches.

English Institute of Sport – Sport Physiology:

http://www.eis2win.co.uk/pages/physiology.aspx

Peak Performance – Physiology:

http://www.pponline.co.uk/encyc/physiology.htm

PART V

CHAPTER 14

TYING IT ALL TOGETHER

ROBYN L. JONES AND KIERAN KINGSTON

INTRODUCTION

In this book, we have introduced readers to the sport sciences that underpin coaching. No doubt it is somewhat at odds with previous introductory type books, which have tended to portray coaching as a rather simplified sequential activity. In this respect, for some it could be troublesome with previously familiar concepts rendered strangely complex (Perkins, 1999). We make no apology for this, as coaching is often problematic and hard to manage. To portray it otherwise would do the subject and those who study it an injustice. The book is also not intended to be an ending, but a beginning; a first passport into the developing field of coaching where numerous knowledges are constantly drawn upon by practitioners in attempts to improve the experience and performances of athletes. We've tried to make most of these knowledges explicit, in particular looking at how they may affect coaching.

Although, in terms of presentation, we have divided the disciplinary areas that underpin coaching along sport science lines, this was done in the interests of clarity and not because we view the subject as a fragmented or multi-disciplinary one (i.e. including distinct, separate disciplines which don't intersect). On the contrary, we see coaching as being predominantly inter-disciplinary in character, with practitioners needing to draw on several knowledge sources simultaneously to address both anticipated and unforeseen issues. Importantly, we also view coaching as a personal activity, with every coach having his or her own ideas about what works best for them. This is not to say that we endorse a philosophy of 'anything goes'; the preceding chapters present plenty of lines of good, researched practice. Such information, however, should be used to think with, rather than to apply in every situation without question or thought to the consequence. Here, we hope that readers actively engage with the information presented, thus helping to shed some light onto the misty world of coaching.

Doing so should further dent the myth that good coaches are born and not made. Indeed, while no doubt some practitioners have more aptitude than others for the job, with hard work and an inquiring mind, we consider that most can become competent, even good, coaches.

Although we've highlighted specific notions within the book that we believe can help coaches to develop, the personal nature of coaching was brought home to us by just how difficult we found it to write this final chapter. Naturally, we agree on many things regarding coaching, but when it came to deciding what to emphasise in this conclusion, our individual differences and perspectives soon emerged. For example, while one of us chose to highlight the importance of knowledges that can be more directly accessed and, hence, applied, the other considered that a social scientific perspective deserved a higher billing. The following problematic coaching scenario, and how both of us approached it, provides an illustration of the case in point.

DIFFERING VIEWS OF COACHING KNOWLEDGE

You are the relatively new coach of James (a highly gifted 16-year-old junior tennis player) who aims to make a successful transition to open age tennis in the near future. In appraising him, you notice he has a strong serve-and-volley game which has worked successfully in junior competitions. You also observe that James has neglected his backcourt game due to the ease with which he has succeeded so far with the aforementioned serve-and-volley tactic. To develop his game further, you focus on improving his ground-strokes while encouraging him to carefully craft points during a rally. Although seemingly acknowledging the strategy, James has struggled in recent competitions. This has frustrated him. Last week, during practice with a 'baseliner' who continuously kept the ball deep in the court, James openly displayed frustration and impatience by aggressively venturing to the net repeatedly, even when inappropriate. He was plainly unhappy. Following the session, he complained to you and anyone who would listen that he already had a successful game plan and didn't need to change things to succeed. After another first round loss earlier this week, James' father called saying that James was threatening to quit the sport. Apparently, he was disillusioned and losing his motivation to compete. He was no longer enjoying playing tennis and was blaming you for his gloomy state of affairs. James' father reminded you that before you became his coach,

216

> *James was a highly ranked junior and very intense about his sport. He now appears to have lost this intensity. You are, not unnaturally, stung by the criticism, which you consider unfair. Still, the facts seem unavoidable. How should you react? Where do you go from here?*

Kieran's interpretation

I am sure that few will be surprised (having read the earlier chapters to which I contributed) at my proposed approach in addressing the scenario outlined. As someone involved in two of the more traditional sport sciences (i.e. sport psychology and skill acquisition), I undoubtedly have a bias towards those areas. Consequently, if I was the coach in question, there seems to be obvious mileage in accessing knowledge regarding sport psychology (to help address the motivation and enjoyment issues) and skill acquisition (e.g. in terms of adopting an appropriate attentional focus to help James' execution of ground strokes). This is because I believe they can directly impact upon the antecedents or precursors to James' emotional state (and perhaps his father's interpretation of the situation). Furthermore, support could also be sought from performance analysts to evaluate any potential technical or strategic deficiencies in James' game, whilst using 'models' to help address James's reluctance to adopt any change in strategy. Accepting that the aforementioned approach reflects my training, I can also see great benefit in having or developing a deeper understanding of the sociological framework in which James as the performer and the sport exists. This understanding helps to provide me with a context for James' responses, and for reflecting on how my personal philosophy, both as a coach and a human being, influences my interpretation and the decisions I make.

On the face of it, my initial focus (as a coach) may appear overly narrow. In response, I'd argue that we live in the real world, with coaching decisions being made on the availability and applicability of existing resources. Therefore, while the objective of this text is to illustrate the multiple knowledges that could and should be applied to coaching, the reality may be that coaches make a judgement call (implicitly) on the relative tangible benefits and logistics of seeking, 'expert' guidance (both in person and from written resources). In this situation, then, I would argue that a coach is more likely to access what he or she considers more concrete information based on perceived need and potential impact. Naturally, I assume that such information would then be couched in a sensitive yet realistic coaching philosophy. That philosophy should be based on a sound moral and ethical code, an understanding of effective coaching styles, and an empathy with the sociological and historical factors that impinge on the athlete and the context.

This view of accessing certain types of information arguably implies a hierarchy of status comprising two tiers of knowledge: the concrete tangible 'known', and the softer social science-based theories, which appear a little more abstract. This is certainly not my intention as, although layers are evident, no judgement is made as to their importance, with both needing each other if coaching is to be accurate, informative, dynamic, empathetic and socially appropriate. Rather, the structure given is founded on issues of access, with coaches being more familiar and, hence, comfortable with what they already know and can retrieve directly. This would include information related to physiology, performance analysis (including biomechanics), psychology and skill acquisition. The second tier, then, might consist of disciplines that indirectly contribute to coaching, or which are pervasive in good coaching practice. These might include a personal philosophy of coaching (inclusive of ethics), an understanding of the historical and social context of the athlete and the sport in question (history and sociology), the organisational structure of the sport (sport development), and sports medicine in terms of managing injury risk.

Robyn's view

In many ways, I agree with the above interpretation. I acknowledge that a number of knowledge sources need to be drawn on here to deal with this problematic scenario. These include those from the realms of psychology (related to intrinsic and extrinsic motivation), biomechanics and performance analysis (carefully examining James' technique), skill acquisition and pedagogy (in terms of learning and feedback), and sport development (in locating coaching practice within wider political initiatives), among others. However, from my perspective, it would also mean drawing on sociological and historical knowledge to a much greater degree, particularly in terms of understanding what James has invested in his tennis identity and how he feels now that this identity is under threat. Like Kieran's admission above, this betrays my sociological roots in relation to what I think is important within coaching. The difference, then, between Kieran and myself, lies in my belief that knowledge from the so-called softer or social sciences can and should be made explicit to, and therefore directly accessed by, coaches. Much of this knowledge has often been seen as obvious, or taken-for-granted. However, as I have argued elsewhere (Jones *et al.*, 2011), making these social competences something concrete, to be learned and developed, can help coaches achieve their goals. This is because understanding and generating better working relationships with athletes (which don't have to be expressed in fuzzy 'arm-round-the-shoulder' language and actions) overrides concerns relating to planning, fitness and technique. Such knowledge has the capacity to directly influence coach–athlete interaction and not exist as some assumed common-sense or 'art' of coaching. Indeed, being taught to think with social, historical and philosophical tools is crucial if a fruitful relationship between coach and athlete is to be established. This is necessary so that knowledge and conversations about how hard to run (physiology), what to focus on mentally (psychology) and movement-wise (biomechanics) can be appropriately couched, enabling the message given to be accepted as intended. Indeed, recent research has highlighted that coaches consider how they interact and generally 'get on' with athletes to engender the latter's respect to be the most crucial aspect of their practice. After all, if the relationship between the coach and athlete is a dysfunctional one, then no matter what the information given by the coach, the chances are that athletes will simply disregard it. What comes into play here, of course, is the issue of power; something which we all know exists in coaching, but is rarely engaged with in the more 'straightforward' or scientific subjects. This relates not only to coaches' power, but also the power held by athletes over coaches; a form of power clearly indicated in James's story. Coaches, then, need to have knowledge about power and its workings to understand context and get the best from athletes (and other stakeholders!). As I said, where I differ principally from Kieran is my view that the interaction responsible for relationship building is a skill and knowledge that can and should be explicitly discussed, learned and worked on. It is only then, or rather in tandem with it, that other more sports specific coaching strategies can be considered and tried.

FINDING AGREEMENT: CONCLUDING THOUGHTS

Presenting these differing interpretations highlights what an individual activity coaching is; that there is no right answer to every scenario that one faces as a coach. As we talked through these differences, we came to realise that the important thing was not to find absolute agreement on every issue, but to experience the process of thinking about how to react in different situations, while being bound by general expectations of what the job of coaching actually entails. The information and concepts given in the chapters are presented as useful resources to deal with the unique problems that coaching consistently presents. Indeed, when we consider the variety of knowledge sources available to (and required by) coaches, and their interaction in the activity of coaching, we can see that there is much more to coaching than can be contained in fashionable, simplistic buzzwords or sound-bites. This is in line with our belief that there is no ideal model or coach-by-numbers formula to be had (even though some would still have us believe it is so). Rather, a requirement exists to think insightfully about how to solve problems that present themselves in each particular context. Consequently, even with the resources presented in this book (and others), there is still a need for you, as students of coaching, to address every issue faced with imagination, creativity and rigour (Stones, 1998). Indeed, the drive for creativity within coaching (and education more generally) is slowly gathering momentum, accompanied by a belief that its development cannot simply be left to chance. It is largely for this reason that a growing call now exists for its inclusion in coach education programmes, so that coaches can learn to thrive as well as survive in what is often rocky terrain (Shaheen, 2010). It is a strategy aimed at enabling coaches (and students of coaching) to think creatively and critically, to solve problems and to make a difference for the better. Similarly, as both of us had a different approach to managing the coaching scenario outlined, you are also encouraged to make your own decisions about how to negotiate coaching's choppy waters. After all, such decision making is really what coaching is all about. We hope that the information contained in this book will enable these decisions to be made from a more informed perspective.

Finally, we provide two additional scenarios for you, as students, to think about, discuss and engage with. They can be done individually or within groups. The task, however, is to carefully consider what are the predominant issues contained within them, then, why you think that, where you can find information or research to help you address these problems, and then to go ahead and do just that.

SCENARIO 1: THE INJURED RUGBY PLAYER

Andy is a biochemistry student in his third year at university. He also has a contract to play professional rugby for one of the country's leading clubs in his university town; this has been his ambition since he was 12. He finds it difficult to juggle his studying and sport commitments, especially with exams coming up, but so far he has managed well. Unfortunately, he has just suffered a major injury to his thumb which required surgery to insert a steel pin and several screws to keep the bones in position until they heal. He's still in a lot of pain and his confidence has taken a knock, but he is determined to maintain his fitness levels. The Chairman of the rugby club has asked you, as Head Coach, to write a fully referenced 1500 word report on how you intend to handle Andy's return to full fitness, and hopefully the 1st XV, for an upcoming shareholders' meeting. The report should deal with what you perceive to be the principal issues facing Andy's return and continued development, and how you intend to address them.

220

SCENARIO 2: THE 'TIRED' ROWER

Regan, a promising 18-year-old rower in her school's senior eight crew, told her coach that she was feeling 'tired all the time'. However, the National Championships are in six weeks' time and, therefore, keeping training intensity high before tapering is of great importance. It is also the time of year where Regan is studying hard to achieve the 'A'-level grades she requires to enter university and a rowing scholarship. There has correspondingly been a drop in her performance, which has affected the dynamics of the crew. Regan, believing she is now being 'picked on', has lost faith in her coach and the trust that had been developed over many years has begun to disappear. As the assistant to the Performance Director, you have been requested by her to produce a fully referenced 2000 word report highlighting the possible problems that are causing Regan's drop in performance and how they can be addressed.

REFERENCES

Agassi, A. (2009). *Hope: An autobiography*. London: Harper.

Al-Abood, S.A., Bennett, S.J., Moreno Hernandez, F., Ashford, D. and Davids, K. (2002). Effect of verbal instructions and image size on visual search strategies in basketball free throw shooting. *Journal of Sports Sciences*, 20: 271–278.

Ames, C. (1992a). Classrooms: Goals, structures, and student motivation. *Journal of Educational Psychology*, 84: 261–271.

Ames, C. (1992b). Achievement goals and the classroom motivational climate. In J. Meece and D. Schunck (eds.), *Student perceptions in the classroom*. Hillsdale, NJ: Erlbaum. pp. 327–348.

Ames, C. (1992c). Achievement goals, motivational climate, and motivational processes. In G.C. Roberts (ed.), *Motivation in sport and exercise*. Champaign, IL: Human Kinetics. pp. 161–176.

Anderson, A.G., Knowles, Z. and Gilbourne, D. (2004). Reflective practice for sport psychologists: Concepts, models, practical implications and thoughts on dissemination. *The Sport Psychologist*, 18: 188–203.

Anderson, B. (2005). *Imagined communities* (3rd edn), London: Verso.

Arampatzis, A. and Brüggemann, G.P. (1999). Mechanical energetic processes during the giant swing exercise before dismounts and flight elements on the high bar and the uneven parallel bars. *Journal of Biomechanics*, 32: 811–820.

Archard, D. (2004). *Children: Rights and childhood* (2nd edn). London: Routledge.

Aubry, M., Cantu, R., Dvorak, J., Graf-Baumann, T., Johnston, K., Kelly, J., Lovell, M., McCrory, P., Meeuwisse, W. and Schamasch, P. (2002). Summary and agreement statement of the first International Conference on Concussion in Sport, Vienna 2001. Recommendations for the improvement of safety and health of athletes who may suffer concussive injuries. *British Journal of Sports Medicine*, 36: 6–7.

Bahr, R. and Holme, I. (2003). Risk factors for sports injuries: A methodological approach. *British Journal of Sports Medicine*, 37: 384–392.

Bailey, R. and Toms, M. (2010). Youth talent development in sport: Rethinking luck and justice. In A. Hardman and C.R. Jones (eds.), *The ethics of sports coaching*. London: Routledge. pp. 149–164.

Bak, K., Bue, P. and Olsson, G. (1989). Injury patterns in Danish competitive swimming, *Ugeskr Laeger*, 151(45), 2982–2984.

Balyi, I. (2001). *Sport system building and long term athlete development in British Columbia*. Vancouver: SportMed BC.

Bandura, A. (1977). Self-efficacy: To ward a unifying theory of behaviour change. *Psychological Review*, 84: 191–215.

Bandura, A. (1997). *Self-efficacy: The exercise of control*. New York: Freeman.

Battig, W.F. (1966). Facilitation and interference. In E.A. Bilodeau (ed.), *Acquisition of skill*. New York: Academic Press. pp. 215–244.

Battig, W.F. (1979). The flexibility of human movement. In L.S. Cermak and F.I.M. Craik (eds.), *Levels of processing in human memory*. Hillsdale, NJ: Erlbaum. pp. 23–44.

Baumeister, R.F. (1984). Choking under pressure: Self-consciousness and paradoxical effects of incentives on skilful performance. *Journal of Personality and Social Psychology*, 46: 610–620.

Baumeister, R.F. and Leary, M.R. (1995). The need to belong: Desire for interpersonal attachments as a fundamental human motivation. *Psychological Bulletin, 117*: 497–529.

Bayles, M.D. (1988). The professional-client relationship. In J.C. Callaghan (ed.), *Ethical issues in professional life*. Oxford: OUP.

Beilock, S.L., Carr, T.H., Macmahon, C. and Starkes, J. (2002). When paying attention becomes counterproductive: Impact of divided versus skill focused attention on novice and experienced performance of sensorimotor skills. *Journal of Experimental Psychology*, 8(1): 6–16.

Bell, J.J. and Hardy, J. (2009). Effects of attentional focus on skilled performance in golf. *Journal of Applied Sports Psychology*, 21(2): 163–177.

Bennett, S.J. (2000). Implicit learning: Should it be used in practice? *International Journal of Sport Psychology*, 31: 542–546.

Berger, P. (1963). *Invitation to sociology*. New York: Anchor Books.

Bergmann-Drewe, S. (2000). Coaches, ethics and autonomy. *Sport, Education and Society*, (5)2: 147–162.

Bernstein, N. (1967). *The co-ordination and regulation of movement*. London: Pergamon Press.

Best, D. (1978). *Philosophy and human movement*. London: Allen and Unwin.

Bezodis, I.N., Salo, A.I.T. and Kerwin, D.G. (2008a). A longitudinal case study of step characteristics in a world class sprint athlete. In Y.-H. Kwon, J. Shim, J.K. Shim and I.-S. Shin (eds.), *Proceedings of XXVI International Symposium on Biomechanics in Sports*, Seoul, Korea: 537–540.

Bezodis, I.N., Kerwin, D.G. and Salo, A.I.T. (2008b). Lower-limb mechanics during the support phase of maximum-velocity sprint running. *Medicine and Science in Sports and Exercise*, 40: 707–715.

Billig, M. (1995). *Banal nationalism*. London: Sage.

Birch, K. (2005). Female athlete triad. *British Medical Journal*, 330: 244–246.

Bjork, R.A. (1988). Retrieval practice and the maintainance of knowledge. In M.M. Gruneberg, P.E. Morris and R.N. Sykes (eds.), *Practical aspects of memory* (Vol. II). London: Wiley. pp. 396–401.

Bolton, N. and Smith, B. (2008). Sports development for coaches. In R.L. Jones, M. Hughes and K. Kingston (eds.) *An introduction to sports coaching: From science and theory to practice*. London: Routledge.

Bolton, N., Fleming, S. and Elias, B. (2008). The experience of community sport development: A case study of Blaenau Gwent. *Managing Leisure*, 13(2): 92–103.

Boutcher, S.H. (1990). The role of performance routines in sport. In G. Jones and L. Hardy (eds.), *Stress and performance in sport*. Chichester: Wiley and Son Ltd.

Bower, G.H., Monteiro, K.P. and Gilligan, S.G. (1978). Emotional mood as a context for learning and recall. *Journal of Verbal Learning and Verbal Behavior*, 17(5): 573–585.

224

Brackenridge, C. (2001). *Spoilsports: Understanding and preventing sexual exploitation in sport.* London: Routledge.

Brackenridge, C. (2002). '. . . so what?' Attitudes of the voluntary sector towards child protection in sports clubs. *Managing Leisure*, 7(3): 103–123.

Brackenridge, C. (2004). Women and children first? Child abuse and child protection in sport. *Sport in Society*, 7(3): 322–337.

Brackenridge, C.H., Bishopp, D., Moussalli, S. and Tapp, J. (2008). The characteristics of sexual abuse in sport: A multidimensional scaling analysis of events described in media report. *International Journal of Sport and Exercise Psychology*, 6(4): 385–406.

Bradley, P.S., Sheldon, W., Wooster, B., Olsen, P., Boanas, P. and Krustrup, P. (2009). High-intensity running in English FA Premier League soccer matches. *Journal of Sports Sciences*, 27: 159–168.

Brady, F. (2004). Contextual interference: A meta-analytic study. *Perceptual and Motor Skills*, 99(1): 116–126.

Bramham, P. and Hylton, K. (2008). Introduction. In K. Hylton and P. Bramham (2nd edn) *Sports development: Policy, process and practice.* London: Routledge.

Bray, K. and Kerwin, D.G. (2003). Modelling the flight of a soccer ball in a direct free kick. *Journal of Sports Sciences*, 21: 75–85.

Brewin, M.A. and Kerwin, D.G. (2003). Accuracy of scaling and DLT reconstruction techniques for planar motion analyses. *Journal of Applied Biomechanics*, 19: 79–88.

Bringer, J., Brackenridge, C.H. and Johnston, L.H. (2006). Swimming coaches' perceptions of sexual exploitation in sport: A preliminary model of role conflict and role ambiguity. *The Sports Psychologist*, 20(4): 465–479.

Brooks, J.H.M., Fuller, C.W., Kemp, S.P.T. and Reddin, D.B. (2005). Epidemiology of injuries in English professional rugby union: Part 1 match injuries. *British Journal of Sports Medicine*, 39: 757–766.

Brucker, B.S. and Bulaeva, N.V. (1996). Biofeedback effect on electromyography responses in patients with spinal cord injury. *Archives of Physical Medicine and Rehabilitation*, 77(2): 133–137.

Brukner, P. and Khan, K. (2006). *Clinical sports medicine.* Sydney: McGraw-Hill.

Brukner, P. and Kahn, K. (2007). Sports medicine: The team approach. In P. Brukner and K. Kahn (eds.), *Clinical sports medicine* (3rd edn). Sydney: McGraw-Hill.

Budd, C. (2011). *The growth of an urban sporting culture: Middlesbrough, c.1870–1914.* Unpublished PhD, De Montfort University.

Budgett, R. (1998). Fatigue and underperformance in athletes: The overtraining syndrome. *British Journal of Sport Medicine*, 32: 107–110.

Bull, S.J., Shambrook, C.J., James, W. and Brooks, J.E. (2005). Towards an understanding of mental toughness in elite English cricketers. *Journal of Applied Sport Psychology*, 17: 209–227.

Bunker, D. and Thorpe, R. (1982). A model for the teaching of games in secondary schools. *Bulletin of Physical Education*, 18: 5–8.

Burgomaster, K.A., Hughes, S.C., Heigenhauser, G.J.F., Bradwell, S.N. and Gibala, M.J. (2005). Six sessions of sprint interval training increases muscle oxidative potential and cycle endurance capacity in humans. *Journal of Applied Physiology*, 98: 1985–1990.

Burke, M. (2006). Response to Dixon and Davis: Answering realists with anti-epistemological pragmatism. *Journal of the Philosophy of Sport*, 33(1): 78–100.

Burton, D., Naylor, S. and Holiday, B. (2001). Goal setting in sport: Investigating the goal effectiveness paradox. In R.A. Singer, H.A. Hausenblas and C.M. Janelle (eds.), *Handbook of sport psychology* (2nd edn). New York: Wiley. pp. 497–528.

Cain, N. (2004). Question time for the coaches: The six men plotting their countries' fortunes on the best and worst of their jobs. *The Sunday Times*, Sport Section (2): 19.

Caine, C.G., Caine, D.J. and Kindner, L.J. (1996). The epidemiologic approach to sports injuries. In C.G. Caine, D.J. Caine and L.J. Kindner (eds.), *The epidemiology of sports injuries*. Champaign, IL: Human Kinetics.

Carless, D. and Douglas, K. (2011). Stories as personal coaching philosophy. *International Journal of Sport Science and Coaching*, 6(1): 1–12.

Carling, C., Williams, A.M. and Reilly, T. (2005). *Handbook of soccer match analysis: A systematic approach to improving performance*. London: Routledge.

Carpenter, P.J. and Morgan, K. (1999). Motivational climate, personal goal perspectives, and cognitive and affective responses in physical education classes. *European Journal of Physical Education*, 4: 31–41.

Carr, D. (1998). What moral educational significance has physical education? A question in need of disambiguation. In M. McNamee and S.J. Parry (eds.), *Ethics and Sport*. London: Routledge.

Carr, D. (2000). *Professionalism and ethics in teaching*. London: Routledge.

Carr, W. and Kemmis, S. (1986). *Becoming critical*. Melbourne: Deakin University Press.

Carrington, B. and McDonald, I. (eds.) (2001). *Race, sport and British society*. London: Routledge.

Carron, A.V., Hausenblas, H.A. and Eys, M.A. (2005). *Group dynamics in sport* (3rd edn). Morgantown, WV: Fitness Information Technology.

Cashmore, E. (1982). *Black sportsmen*. London: Routledge and Kegan Paul.

Cassidy, T., Jones, R.L. and Potrac, P. (2009). *Understanding sports coaching: The social, cultural and pedagogical foundations of coaching practice* (2nd edn). London: Routledge.

Chambers, K.L. and Vickers, J.N. (2006). Effects of bandwidth feedback and questioning on the performance of competitive swimmers. *Sport Psychology*, 20(2): 184–197.

Chandler, T.J.L. (1991). Games at Oxbridge and the public school 1830–1890: Diffusion of an innovation. *International Journal for the History of Sport*, 18(2): 171–204.

Chelladurai, P. (2006). *Human resource management in sport and recreation* (2nd edn). Leeds: Human Kinetics.

Chollet, D., Micallef, J.P. and Rabischong, P. (1988). Biomechanical signals for external biofeedback to improve swimming techniques. In B.E. Ungerechts, K. White and K. Reichle (eds.), *Swimming science* (Vol. V). Champaign, IL: Human Kinetics. pp. 389–396.

Clarys, J.P. (2000). Electromyography in sports and occupational settings: An update of its limits and possibilities. *Ergonomics*, 43(10): 1750–1762.

Coad, D. (2008). *The metrosexual: Gender, sexuality and sport*. Albany: SUNY Press.

Coakley, J. and Pike, L. (2009). *Sports in society: Issues and controversies*. Maidenhead: McGraw-Hill Education.

Coalter, F. (2001). *Realising the potential for cultural services: The case for sport*. London: Local Government Association.

Coalter, F. (2007). *A wider social role for sport: Who's keeping the score?* London: Routledge.

Cobb, P. (1996). Where is the mind? A coordination of sociocultural and cognitive perspectives. In C.T. Fosnot (ed.), *Constructivism: Theory, perspectives and practice*. New York: Teachers College, Columbia University.

Collins, M. (2008a). Social exclusion from sport and leisure. In B. Houlihan (ed.), *Sport and society: A student introduction*. London: Sage.

226

Collins, M. (2008b). Public policies on sports development: Can mass and elite sport hold together. In V. Girginov (ed.), *Management of sports development*. Oxford: Butterworth-Heinemann.

Collins, M. (2010a). From 'sport for good' to 'sport for sport's sake' – not a good move for sports development in England? *International Journal of Sport Policy and Politics*, 2(3): 367–379.

Collins, M. (2010b). Introduction. In M. Collins (ed.), *Examining sports development*. London: Routledge.

Collins, M. with Kay, T. (2003). *Sport and social exclusion*. London: Routledge.

Collins, T. (1998). *Rugby's great split: Class, culture and the origins of Rugby League Football*. London: Frank Cass.

Collins, T. (2009). *A social history of English rugby union*. London: Routledge.

Cooke, G. (1996). A strategic approach to performance and excellence. *Supercoach: National Coaching Foundation*, 8: 10.

Côté, J. and Hay, J. (2002). Children's involvement in sport: A development perspective. In J.M. Silva and D. Stevens (eds.), *Psychological foundations of sport*. Boston: Allyn and Bacon.

Côté, J., Salmela, J. and Russell, S. (1995). The knowledge of high-performance gymnastic coaches: Competition and training considerations. *The Sport Psychologist*, 9: 76–95.

Cronin, M. (1999). *Sport and nationalism in Ireland: Gaelic games, soccer and Irish identity since 1884*. Dublin: Four Courts Press.

Cropley, B., Hanton, S., Miles, A. and Niven, A. (2010a). Exploring the relationship between effective and reflective practice in applied sport psychology. *The Sport Psychologist*, 24: 521–541.

Cropley, B., Hanton, S., Miles, A. and Niven, A. (2010b). The value of reflective practice in professional development: An applied sport psychology perspective. *Sports Science Review*, 19, 3–4: 179–208.

Cross, N. and Lyle, N. (1999). *The coaching process: Principles and practice for sport*. Edinburgh: Butterworth-Heinmann.

Cunningham, C. and Cunningham, S. (1996). Injury surveillance at a national multi-sport event. *Australian Journal of Science and Medicine in Sport*, 28(2): 50–56.

Cushion, C. (2007). Modelling the complexity of the coaching process. *International Journal of Sports Science and Coaching*, 2(4): 395–401.

Cushion, C. and Jones, R.L. (2006). Power, discourse and symbolic violence in professional youth soccer: The case of Albion F.C.. *Sociology of Sport Journal*, 23(2): 142–161.

Daniels, F.S. and Landers, D.M. (1981). Biofeedback and shooting performance: A test of disregualtion and systems theory. *Journal of Sport Psychology*, 3: 271–282.

Dawson, B., Fitzsimons, M., Green, S., Goodman, C., Carey, M. and Cole, K. (1998). Changes in performance, muscle metabolites, enzymes and fibre types after short sprint training. *European Journal of Applied Physiology*, 78: 163–169.

Deci, E.L. and Ryan, R.M. (1985). *Intrinsic motivation and self-determination in human behavior*. New York: Plenum Press.

Deci, E.L. and Ryan, R.M. (2000). The "what" and "why" of goal pursuits: Human needs and the self-determination of behavior. *Psychological Inquiry*, 11: 227–268.

Deci, E.L., Koestener, R. and Ryan, R. (1999). A meta-analytic review of experiments examining the effects of extrinsic rewards on intrinsic motivation. *Psychological Bulletin*, 125: 627–668.

Del Rey, P., Whitehurst, M., Wughalter, E. and Barnwell, J. (1983). Contextual interference and experience in acquisition and transfer. *Perceptual and Motor Skills*, 57(1): 241–242.

den Duyn, N. (1997). *Game sense: Developing thinking players*. Canberra, Australia: Australian Sports Commission.

Denison, J. and Avner, Z. (2011). Positive coaching: Ethical practices for athlete development. *Quest*, 63: 209–227.

Department of Culture, Media and Sport (DCMS) (2000). *A sporting future for all*. London: DCMS.

Department for Culture, Media and Sport (DCMS) (2002). *The coaching task force – Final report*. London: DCMS.

Department of Culture, Media and Sport (DCMS) (2008). *Playing to win: A new era for sport*. London: DCMS.

Department for Culture, Media and Sport (DCMS) (2010). *Plans for the legacy from the 2012 Olympic and Paralympic games*. London: DCMS.

Department for Culture, Media and Sport (DCMS) (2012). *Creating a sporting habit for life: A new youth sport strategy*. London: DCMS.

DeSensi, J.T. and Rosenberg, D. (eds.) (2003). *Ethics and morality in sport management* (2nd edn). Morgantown, WV: Fitness Information Technology.

Deutsch, M.U., Kearney, G.A and Rehrer, N.J. (2006). Time-motion analysis of professional rugby union players during match play. *Journal of Sports Sciences*, 25: 461–472.

Dirix, A., Knuttgen, H.G. and Tittel, K. (eds.) (1988). *The Olympic book of sports medicine*. Oxford: Blackwell Publishing.

Dishman, R.K. (1983). Identity crises in North American sport psychology: Academics in professional issues. *Journal of Sport Psychology*, 5: 123–134.

Drewe, S.B. (2000). Coaches, ethics and autonomy. *Sport, Education and Society*, 5(2): 147–162.

Dvorak, J. and Junge, A. (2000). Football injuries and physical symptoms: A review of the literature. *American Journal of Sports Medicine*, 28: suppl 5, S3–S9.

Eady, J. (1993). *Practical sports development*. London: Hodder and Stoughton.

Ebbeck, V. and Becker, S.L. (1994). Psychosocial predictors of goal orientations in youth soccer. *Research Quarterly for Exercise and Sport*, 65: 355–362.

Edwards, K. and Ridgewell, M. (2011, November). Audit of injuries sustained by elite sportsmen. Poster presented at the *UKSEM Conference*, London, UK.

Ekstrand, J. and Gillquist, J. (1983). The avoidability of soccer injuries. *International Journal of Sports Medicine*, 2: 124–128.

Epstein, J. (1989). Family structures and student motivation: A developmental perspective. In C. Ames and R. Ames (eds.), *Research on motivation in education*: Vol.3. New York: Academic Press. pp. 259–295.

Faigenbaum, A.D., Kraemer, W.J., Blimkie, C.J.R, Jeffreys, I., Mitchell, L.J., Mitka, M. and Rowland, T.W. (2009). Youth resistance training: Updated position statement paper from the National Strength and Conditioning Association. *Journal of Strength and Conditioning Research*, 23: S60–S79.

Farooq, S. and Parker, A. (2009). Sport, physical education and Islam: Muslim independent schooling and the social construction of Masculinities. *Sociology of Sport Journal*, 26(2): 277–295.

Fasting, K. and Brackenridge, C. (2009). Coaches, sexual harassment and education. *Sport, Education and Society*, 14(1): 21–35.

Faull, A. and Cropley, B. (2009). Reflective learning in sport: A case study of a senior level tri-athlete. *Reflective Practice*, 10: 325–339.

Feltz, D.L. and Kontos, A.P. (2002). The nature of sport psychology. In T. Horn (ed.), *Advances in sport psychology* (2nd edn). Champagne, IL: Human Kinetics. pp. 3–19.

Ferrall, C. (2011). C.L.R. James and the dialectics of cricket. In D. Carnegie, P. Millar, D. Norton, H. Ricketts (eds.), *Running writing robinson*. Wellington: Victoria University Press. pp. 256–269.

Filby, W.C.D., Maynard, I.W. and Graydon, J.K. (1999). The effect of multiple-goal strategies on performance outcomes in training and competition. *Journal of Applied Sport Psychology*, 11: 230–246.

Finch, C.F. (1997). An overview of some definitional issues for sports injury surveillance. *Sports Medicine*, 24(3): 157–163.

Finch, C. (2006). A new framework for research leading to sports injury prevention. *Journal of Science and Medicine in Sport*, 9: 3–9.

Fitts, P.M. and Posner, M.I. (1967). *Human performance*. Belmont, CA: Brooks/Cole.

Flanagan, O. (1991). *Varieties of moral personality: Ethics and psychological realism*. Boston: Harvard University Press.

Fleming, S. (1995). *Home and away: Sport and South Asian male youth*. Aldershot: Avebury.

Fletcher, D. and Hanton, S. (2003). Sources of organizational stress in elite sports performers. *The Sport Psychologist*, 17: 175–195.

Fletcher, D., Hanton, S. and Mellalieu, S.D. (2006). An organizational stress review: Conceptual and theoretical issues in competitive sport. In S. Hanton and S.D. Mellalieu (eds.), *Literature reviews in sport psychology*. Hauppauge, NY: Nova Science.

Fong, D.T., Hong, Y., Chan, L., Yung, P.S. and Chan, K. (2007). A systematic review of ankle injury and ankle sprain in sports. *Sports Medicine*, 37(1): 73–94.

Ford, P., Hodges, N.J. and Williams, A.M. (2005). Online attentional-focus manipulations in a soccer dribbling task: Implications for the proceduralization of motor skills. *Journal of Motor Behavior*, 37(5): 386–394.

Ford, P.R., Yates, I. and Williams, A.M. (2010). An analysis of practice activities and instructional behaviours used by youth soccer coaches during practice: Exploring the link between science and application. *Journal of Sports Science*, 28(5): 483–495.

Fosnot, C.T. (1996). Constructivism: A psychological theory of learning. In C.T. Fosnot (ed.), *Constructivism: Theory, perspectives and practice*. New York: Teachers College, Columbia University. pp. 103–119.

Fraleigh, W. (1995). Why the good foul is not good. In Morgan and Meir (eds.), *Philosophical inquiry sport* (2nd edn). Champaign, IL: Human Kinetics. pp. 185–187.

Franks, I.M. (1997). Use of feedback by coaches and players. In T. Reilly, J. Bangsbo and M. Hughes (eds.), *Science and football 3*. London: E and FN Spon. pp. 267–278.

Fry, J. (2000). Coaching a kingdom of ends. *Journal of the Philosophy of Sport*, 27(1): 51–62.

Fuller, C.W., Ekstrand, J., Junge, A., Andersen, T.E., Bahr, R., Dvorak, J., Hägglund, M., McCrory, P. and Meuwisse, W.H. (2006). Consensus statement on injury definitions and data collection procedures in studies of football (soccer) injuries. *Scandinavian Journal of Medicine and Science in Sports*, 16(2): 83–92.

Fuller, C.W., Molloy, M.G., Bagate, C., Bahr, R., Brooks, J.H.M., Donson, H., Kemp, S.P.T., McCrory, P., McIntosh, A.S., Meeuwisse, W.H., Quarrie, K.L., Raftery, M. and Wiley, P. (2007). Consensus statement on injury definitions and data collection procedures for studies of injuries in rugby union. *British Journal of Sports Medicine*, 41: 328–331.

Gabbett, T.J. (2004). Reductions in pre-season training loads reduce training injury rates in rugby league players. *British Journal of Sports Medicine*, 38: 743–749.

Gallagher, J.D. and Thomas, J.R. (1980). Effects of varying post-kr intervals upon children's motor performance. *Journal of Motor Behavior*, 12(1): 41–46.

Gallagher, S.S., Finison, K., Guyer, B. and Goodenough, S. (1984). The incidence of injuries among 87,000 Massachusetts children and adolescents: Results of the 1980–81 Statewide Childhood Injury Prevention Program Surveillance System. *American Journal of Public Health*, 74(12): 1340–1347.

Gardner, H. (1993). *Multiple intelligences*. New York: Basic Books.

Gentile, A.M. (1972). A working model of skill acquisition with application to teaching. *Quest (Monograph XVII)*: 3–23.

Gentile, A.M. (2000). Skill acquisition: Action, movement, and neuromotor processes. In J.H. Carr and R.B. Shepherd (eds.), *Movement science: Foundations for physical therapy* (2nd edn). Rockville, MD: Aspen. pp. 111–187.

Gibbs, G. (1988). *Learning by doing: A guide to teaching and learning methods*. London: Further Education Unit.

Gilbert, W. and Trudel, P. (1999). Framing the construction of coaching knowledge in experiential learning theory. *Sociology of Sport Online*, 2(1). Retrieved from http://physed.otago.ac.nz/sosol/v2i1/v2i1s2.htm.

Gilbert, W. and Trudel, P. (2001). Learning to coach through experience: Reflection in model youth sport coaches. *Journal of Teaching in Physical Education*, 21: 16–34.

Gilbert, W. and Trudel, P. (2004). Role of the coach: How model youth team sport coaches frame their roles. *The Sport Psychologist*, 18: 21–43.

Gilbert, W. and Trudel, P. (2005). Learning to coach through experience: Conditions that influence reflection. *Physical Educator*, 62(1): 32–43.

Gilbert, W. and Trudel, P. (2006). The coach as a reflective practitioner. In R.L. Jones (ed.), *The sports coach as educator*. London: Routledge. pp. 113–127.

Gilbourne, D. and Richardson, D. (2006). Tales from the field: Personal reflections on the provision of psychological support in professional soccer. *Psychology of Sport and Exercise*, 7: 325–337.

Gilligan, C. (1982). *In a different voice: Psychological theory and women's development*. Cambridge: Harvard University Press.

Gilligan, S.G. and Bower, G.H. (1983). Reminding and mood-congruent memory. *Bulletin of the Psychonomic Society*, 21(6): 431–434.

Gittoes, M.R.J, Brewin, M.A. and Kerwin, D.G. (2006). Soft tissue contributions to impact forces using a four-segment wobbling mass model of forefoot-heel landings. *Human Movement Science*, 25(6): 775–787.

Giulianotti, R. (ed.) (2004). *Sport and modern social theorists*. Basingstoke, Hants: Palgrave Macmillan.

Glaister, M. (2005). Multiple sprint work: Physiological responses, mechanisms of fatigue and the influence of aerobic fitness. *Sports Medicine*, 35: 757–777.

Gleim, G.W. and McHugh, M. (1997). Flexibility and its effects on sports injury and performance. *Sports Medicine*, 24: 289–299.

Glynn, J., King, M. and Mitchell, S. (2006). Determining subject-specific parameters for a computer simulation model of a one handed tennis backhand. In H. Schwameder, G. Strutzenberger, V. Fastenbauer, S. Lindinger and E. Muller (eds.), *Proceedings of XXIV International Symposium on Biomechanics in Sports*, Salzburg, Austria: 766–769.

Goldberg, A.S., Moroz, L., Smith, A. and Ganley, T. (2007). Injury surveillance in young athletes: A clinician's guide to sports injury literature. *Sports Medicine*, 37(3): 265–278.

Gottwald, V.M., Lawrence, G.P. and Khan, M.A. (2010). Can learning under an external focus of attention counteract the negative effects of choking under pressure? *Journal of Sport and Exercise Psychology*, 32: S82.

Gould, D., Dieffenbach, K. and Moffett, A. (2002a). Psychological characteristics and their development in Olympic champions. *Journal of Applied Sport Psychology*, 14: 172–204.

Gould, D., Giannina, J., Krane, V. and Hodge, K. (1990). Educational needs of elite U.S. National team, Pan America, and Olympic coaches. *Journal of Teaching in Physical Education*, 9: 332–344.

Gould, D., Greenleaf, C., Chung, Y. and Guinan, D. (2002b). A survey of U.S. Atlanta and Nagano Olympians: Variables perceived to influence performance. *Research Quarterly for Exercise and Sport*, 73: 175–186.

Green, M. (2009). Podium or participation? Analysing policy priorities under changing modes of sport governance in the United Kingdom. *International Journal of Sport Policy and Politics*, 1(2): 121–144.

Griffin, J. and Harris, M.B. (1996). 'Coaches' attitudes, knowledge, experiences and recommendations regarding weight control'. *The Sport Psychologist*, 10(2): 180–194.

Guadagnoli, M.A., Holcomb, W.R. and Weber, T.J. (1999). The relationship between contextual interference effects and performer expertise on the learning of a putting task. *Journal of Human Movement Studies*, 37(1): 19–36.

Hall, K.G., Domingues, D.A. and Cavazos, R. (1994). Contextual interference effects with skilled baseball players. *Perceptual and Motor Skills*, 78(3): 835–841.

Hamill, J. and Knutzen, K.M. (2009). *Biomechanical basis of human movement*. London: Lippincott Williams and Wilkins.

Hamill, J., Haddad, J.M. and McDermott, W.J. (2000). Issues in quantifying variability from a dynamical systems perspective. *Journal of Applied Biomechanics*, 16: 407–418.

Hanton, S. and Jones, G. (1997). Antecedents of intensity and direction dimensions of competitive anxiety as a function of skill. *Psychological Reports*, 81: 1139–1147.

Hanton, S. and Jones, G. (1999a). The acquisition and development of cognitive skills and strategies: Making the butterflies fly in formation. *The Sport Psychologist*, 13: 1–21.

Hanton, S. and Jones, G. (1999b). The effects of a multimodal intervention program on performers: II. Training the butterflies to fly in formation. *The Sport Psychologist*, 13: 22–41.

Hanton, S., Cropley, B. and Lee, S. (2009). Reflective practice, experience and the interpretation of anxiety symptoms. *Journal of Sports Sciences*, 27(5): 517–534.

Hanton, S., Cropley, B., Neil, R., Mellalieu, S.D. and Miles, A. (2007). Experience in sport and its relationship with competitive anxiety. *International Journal of Sport and Exercise Psychology*, 5: 28–53.

Hanton, S., Neil, R. and Mellalieu, S.D. (2008). Recent developments in competitive anxiety direction and competition stress research. *International Review of Sport and Exercise Psychology*, 1: 45–57.

Hanton, S., Thomas, O. and Maynard, I. (2004). Competitive anxiety responses in the week leading up to competition: The role of intensity, direction and frequency dimensions. *Psychology of Sport and Exercise*, 5: 169–181.

Hardman, A., Jones, C. and Jones, R.L. (2010). Sports coaching, virtue ethics and emulation. *Physical Education and Sports Pedagogy*, 15(4): 345–359.

Hardy, L. (1990). A catastrophe model of anxiety and performance. In J.G. Jones and L. Hardy (eds.), *Stress and performance in sport*. Chichester: Wiley. pp. 81–106.

Hardy, L., Jones, G. and Gould, D. (1996a). *Understanding psychological preparation for sport: Theory and practice of elite performers*. Chichester: Wiley.

Hardy, L., Mullen, R. and Jones, G. (1996b). Knowledge and conscious control of motor actions under stress. *British Journal of Psychology*, 87: 621–636.

Hardy, S. (2003). *How Boston played: Sport, recreation, and community, 1856–1915*. Knoxville, TN: University of Tennessee Press.

Hargreaves, J. (1994). *Sporting females: Critical issues in the history and sociology of women's sports*. London: Routledge.

Harter, S. (1978). Effectance motivation reconsidered: Toward a developmental model. *Human Development*, 1: 661–669.

Harvey, A. (2005). *Football: The first 100 years*. London: Routledge.

Hassan, M.F. (2011). *Motivational climate in sports coaching*. Unpublished doctoral thesis. University of Wales Institute, Cardiff.

Hay, J.G. (1994). *The biomechanics of sports techniques*. Englewood Cliffs, NJ: Prentice Hall.

Hays, K., Maynard, I., Thomas, O. and Bawden, M. (2007). Sources and types of confidence identified by world class sport performers. *Journal of Applied Sport Psychology*, 19: 434–456.

Hays, K., Thomas, O., Maynard, I. and Bawden, M. (2009). The role of confidence in world-class sport performance. *Journal of Sports Sciences*, 27: 1185–1199.

Hebert, E.P. and Landin, D. (1994). Effects of a learning-model and augmented feedback on tennis skill acquisition. *Research Quarterly for Exercise and Sport*, 65(3): 250–257.

Hebert, E.P., Landin, D. and Solmon, M.A. (1996). Practice schedule effects on the performance and learning of low- and high-skilled students: An applied study. *Research Quarterly for Exercise and Sport*, 67(1): 52–58.

Helgerud, J., Høydal, K., Wang, E., Karlsen, T., Berg, P., Bjerkaas, M., Simonsen, T., Helgesen, C., Hjorth, N., Bach, R. and Hoff, J. (2007). Aerobic high-intensity intervals improve $V^{\bullet}O_{2max}$ more than moderate training. *Medicine and Science in Sports and Exercise*, 39: 665–671.

Hemmestad, L.B., Jones, R.L. and Standal, Ø.F. (2010). Phronetic social science: A means of better researching and analysing coaching? *Sport, Education and Society*, 15(4): 447–459.

Henry, F.M. (1968). Specificity vs. generality in learning motor skill. In G.S. Brown and R.C. Kenyon (eds.), *Classical studies on physical activity*. Englewood Cliffs, NJ: Prentice Hall. pp. 331–340.

Henry, I. (2001). *The politics of leisure policy* (2nd edn). Basingstoke: Palgrave.

Hiley, M.J. and Yeadon, M.R. (2005). The margin for error when releasing the asymmetric bars for dismounts. *Journal of Applied Biomechanics*, 21: 223–235.

Hill, J. and Williams, J. (eds.) (1996). *Sport and identity in the North of England*. Keele: Keele University Press.

Hobsbawm, E. (1983a). Introduction: Invented traditions. In E. Hobsbawm and T. Ranger (eds.), *The invention of tradition*. Cambridge: Cambridge University Press. pp. 1–14.

Hobsbawm, E. (1983b). Mass-producing traditions: Europe, 1870–1914. In E. Hobsbawm and T. Ranger (eds.), *The invention of tradition*. Cambridge: Cambridge University Press. pp. 263–307.

Hobsbawm, E. (1992). *Nations and nationalism since 1790: Programme, myth, reality*. Cambridge: Cambridge University Press.

Hodge, K., Lonsdale, C. and Ng, J.Y.Y. (2008). Burnout in elite rugby: Relationships with basic psychological needs fulfilment. *Journal of Sports Sciences*, 26: 835–844.

Hollembeak, J. and Amorose, A.J. (2005). Perceived coaching behaviours and college athletes' intrinsic motivation: A test of self-determination theory. *Journal of Applied Sport Psychology*, 17: 20–36.

Hollman, W. (1988). The definition and scope of sports medicine. In A. Dirix, H.G. Knuttgen and K. Tittel (eds.), *The Olympic book of sports medicine*. Oxford: Blackwell.

Home Office (2010). The Equality Act. London: The National Archives. Available: http://www.homeoffice.gov.uk/equalities/equality-act/

Horne, J., Tomlinson, A. and Whannel, G. (1999). *Understanding sport: An introduction to the sociological and cultural analysis of sport*. London: E and FN Spon.

Horne, T. and Carron, A. (1985). Compatibility in coach-athlete relationships. *Journal of Sport Psychology*, 7: 137–149.

Houlihan, B. and White, A. (2002). *The politics of sports development: Development of sport or development through sport*. London: Routledge.

Hubbard, M. and Alaways, L.W. (1987). Optimum release conditions for the new rules javelin. *International Journal of Sport Biomechanics*, 3: 207–221.

Hughes, M. (1998). The application of notational analysis to racket sports. In A. Lees, I. Maynard, M. Hughes and T. Reilly (eds.), *Science and racket sports 2*. London: E and FN Spon pp. 211–220.

Hughes, M. (2008). Notational analysis for coaches. In R.L. Jones, M. Hughes and K. Kingston (eds.), *An introduction to sports coaching: From science and theory to practice* (2nd edn). London: Routledge. pp. 101–113.

Hylton, K. and Totten, M. (2008). Community sports development. In K. Hylton, and P. Bramham (eds.), *Sports development: Policy, process and practice*. London: Routledge.

Iachini, A., Amorose, A. and Anderson-Butcher, D. (2010). Exploring high school coaches' implicit theories of motivation from a self-determination theory perspective. *International Journal of Sports Science and Coaching*, 5(2): 291–308.

Intiso, D., Santilli, V., Grasso, M.G., Rossi, R. and Caruso, I. (1994). Rehabilitation of walking with electromyographic biofeedback in foot-drop after stroke. *Stroke*, 25(6): 1189–1192.

Irwin, G., Hanton, S. and Kerwin, D. (2004). Reflective practice and the origins of elite coaching knowledge. *Reflective Practice*, 5: 425–442.

Irwin, G., Hanton, S. and Kerwin, D.G. (2005). The conceptual process of progression development in artistic gymnastics. *Journal of Sports Sciences*, 23(10): 1089–1099.

Irwin, G. and Kerwin, D. (2001). Use of 2D-DLT for the analysis of longswings on high bar. In J. Blackwell (ed.), *Proceedings of XIX International Symposium on Biomechanics in Sports*, San Francisco: 315–318.

Irwin, G. and Kerwin, D.G. (2005). Biomechanical similarities of progressions for the longswing on high bar. *Sports Biomechanics*, 4(2): 164–178.

Irwin, G. and Kerwin, D.G. (2006). Musculoskeletal work in the longswing on high bar. In E.F. Moritz and S. Haake (eds.), *The Engineering of Sport 6, Volume 1*. New York, USA: Springer LLC. pp. 195–200.

Irwin, G. and Kerwin, D.G. (2007a). Musculoskeletal work of high bar progressions. *Sports Biomechanics*, 6(3): 360–373.

Irwin, G. and Kerwin, D.G. (2007b). Inter-segmental co-ordination of high bar progressions. *Sports Biomechanics*, 6(2): 129–142.

Irwin, G. and Kerwin, D.G. (2009). The influence of the vaulting table on the handspring front somersault. *Sports Biomechanics*, 8(2): 114–128.

Jackson, R.C., Ashford, K.J. and Norsworthy, G. (2006). Attentional focus, dispositional reinvestment, and skilled motor performance under pressure. *Journal of Sport and Exercise Psychology*, 28: 49–68.

James, C.L.R. (1994). *Beyond a boundary*. London: Serpents' Tail.

Janelle, C.M., Kim, J.G. and Singer, R.N. (1995). Subject-controlled performance feedback and learning of a closed motor skill. *Perceptual and Motor Skills*, 81(2): 627–634.

Jarvie, G. (1990a). Towards an applied sociology of sport. *Scottish Journal of Physical Education*, 18: 11–12.

Jarvie, G. (1990b). The sociological imagination. In F. Kew (ed.), *Social perspectives on sport*. Leeds: British Association of Sports Sciences and National Coaching Foundation.

Jarvie, G. (ed.) (1991). *Sport, racism and ethnicity*. London: Falmer Press.

Jarvie, G. (2006). *Sport, culture and society: An introduction*. London: Routledge.

Jarvie, G. and Maguire, J. (1994). *Sport and leisure in social thought*. London: Routledge.

Jenkins, R.E., Morgan, L. and O'Donoghue, P.G. (2007). A case study into the effectiveness of computerized match analysis and motivational videos within the coaching of a league netball team. *International Journal of Performance Analysis of Sport-e*, 7(2): 59–80.

Johns, C. (1994). Guided reflection. In A. Palmer, S. Burns and C. Bulman (eds.), *Reflective practice in nursing*. Oxford, UK: Blackwell Science. pp. 110–130.

Jones, G. (1991). Recent issues in competitive state anxiety research. *The Psychologist*, 4: 152–155.

Jones, G. (1995). More than just a game: Research developments and issues in competitive anxiety in sport. *British Journal of Psychology*, 86: 449–478.

Jones, G., Hanton, S. and Connaughton, D. (2002). What is this thing called mental toughness? An investigation of elite sport performers. *Journal of Applied Sport Psychology*, 14: 205–218.

Jones, G., Hanton, S. and Connaughton, D. (2007). A framework of mental toughness in the world's best performers. *The Sport Psychologist*, 21: 243–265.

Jones, L., Evans, L. and Mullen, R. (2007). Multiple roles in an applied setting: Trainee sport psychologist, coach and researcher. *The Sport Psychologist*, 21: 210–226.

Jones, N.P., James, N. and Mellalieu, S.D. (2008). An objective method for depicting team performance in elite professional rugby. *Journal of Sports Sciences*, 26: 691–700.

Jones, R.L. (2000). Toward a sociology of coaching. In R.L. Jones and K.M. Armour (eds.), *The sociology of sport: Theory and practice*. London: Addison Wesley Longman. pp. 33–43.

Jones, R.L. (2006a). How can educational concepts inform sports coaching? In R.L. Jones (ed.), *The sports coach as educator: Reconceptualising sports coaching*. London: Routledge.

Jones, R.L. (2006b). Dilemmas, maintaining 'face' and paranoia: An average coaching life. *Qualitative Inquiry*, 12(5): 1012–1021.

Jones, R.L., Armour, K.M. and Potrac, P. (2002). Understanding the coaching process: A framework for social analysis. *Quest*, 54(1): 34–48.

Jones, R.L. and Standage, M. (2006). First among equals: Shared leadership in the coaching context. In R.L. Jones, (ed.), *The sports coach as educator: Reconceptualising sports coaching*. London: Routledge. pp. 65–76.

Jones, R.L., Armour, K.M. and Potrac, P. (2003). Constructing expert knowledge: A case study of a top-level professional soccer coach. *Sport, Education and Society*, 8(2): 213–229.

Jones, R.L., Armour, K.M. and Potrac, P. (2004). *Sports coaching cultures: From practice to theory*. London: Routledge.

Jones, R.L., Glintmeyer, N. and McKenzie, A. (2005). Slim bodies, eating disorders and the coach-athlete relationship: A tale of identity creation and disruption. *International Review for the Sociology of Sport*, 40(3): 377–391.

Jones, R.L., Potrac, P., Cushion, C. and Ronglan, L.T. (eds.) (2011). *The sociology of sports coaching*. London: Routledge.

Junge, A., Dvorak, J., Graf-Baumann, T. and Peterson, L. (2004). Football injuries during FIFA tournaments and the Olympic Games 1998–2001 – Development and implementation of an injury-reporting system. *American Journal of Sports Medicine*, 32(1) suppl 80S–89S.

Junge, A., Engebretsen, L., Mountjoy, M., Alonso, J.M., Renström, Per, A.F.H., Aubry, M.J. and Dvorak, J. (2009). Sports injuries during the summer Olympic Games 2008. *American Journal of Sports Medicine*, 37(11): 2165–2172.

Kavussanu, M. and Roberts, G.C. (1996). Motivation in physical activity contexts: The relationship of perceived motivational climate to intrinsic motivation and self-efficacy. *Journal of Sport and Exercise Psychology*, 18: 264–280.

Kay, T. (2000). Sporting excellence: A family affair? *European Physical Education Review*, 6: 151–169.

Kernodle, M.W. and Carlton, L.G. (1992). Information feedback and the learning of multiple-degree-of-freedom activities. *Journal of Motor Behavior*, 24(2): 187–196.

Kerwin. D.G. and Irwin, G. (2010). Musculoskeletal work preceding the outward and inward Tkachev on uneven bars in artistic gymnastics. *Sports Biomechanics*, 9(1): 16–28.

Kerwin, D.G., Yeadon, M.R. and Sung-Cheol, L. (1990). Body configuration in multiple somersault high bar dismounts. *International Journal of Sport Biomechanics*, 6: 147–156.

Khan, M.A. and Franks, I.M. (2000). The effect of practice on component submovements is dependent on the availability of visual feedback. *Journal of Motor Behavior*, 32(3): 227–240.

Kidman, L. (2001). *Developing decision makers: An empowerment approach to coaching*. Christchurch, NZ: Innovative Print Communications.

Kingston, K. and Hardy, L. (1997). Effects of different types of goals on processes that support performance. *The Sport Psychologist*, 11: 277–293.

Kingston, K.M., Harwood, C.G. and Spray, C.M. (2006). Contemporary approaches to motivation in sport. In S. Hanton and S.D. Mellalieu (eds.), *Literature Reviews in Sport Psychology*. Hauppauge, NY: Nova Science. pp. 159–197.

Kingston, K., Lane, A. and Thomas, O. (2010). A temporal examination of elite performers sources of sport-confidence. *The Sport Psychologist*, 18: 313–332.

Kirkbride, A.N. (in press). Media applications of performance analysis. In McGarry, T., O'Donoghue, P.G. and Sampaio, J. (eds.), *The Routledge handbook of sports performance analysis*. London: Routledge.

Knowles, Z. and Gilbourne, D. (2010). Aspiration, inspiration and illustration: Initiating debate on reflective practice writing. *The Sport Psychologist*, 24: 504–520.

Knowles, Z., Borrie, A. and Telfer, H. (2005). Towards the reflective sports coach: Issues of context, education and application. *Ergonomics*, 48(11–14): 1711–1720.

Knowles, Z., Gilbourne, D., Borrie, A. and Nevill, A. (2001). Developing the reflective sports coach: A study exploring the processes of reflective practice within a higher education coaching programme. *Reflective Practice*, 2(2): 185–207.

Knowles, Z., Gilbourne, D., Tomlinson, V. and Anderson, A. (2007). Reflections on the application of reflective practice for supervision in applied sport psychology. *The Sport Psychologist*, 21: 109–122.

Knuttila, M. (1996). *Introducing sociology: A critical perspective.* Oxford: Oxford University Press.

Komi, P.V., Linnamo, P., Silventoinen, M. and Sillanpaa, M. (2000). Force and EMG power spectrum during eccentric and concentric actions. *Medicine and Science in Sports and Exercise*, 32(10): 1757–1762.

Kowal, J. and Fortier, M.S. (2000). Testing relationships from the hierarchical model of intrinsic and extrinsic motivation using flow as a motivational consequence. *Research Quarterly for Exercise and Sport*, 71: 171–181.

Kraemer, W.J., Patton, J.F., Gordon, S.E., Harman, E.A., Deschenes, M.R., Reynolds, K., Newton, R.U., Triplett, N.T. and Dziados J.E. (1995). Compatibility of high intensity strength and endurance training on hormonal and skeletal muscle adaptations. *Journal of Applied Physiology*, 78: 976–989.

Kraemer, W.J., Adams, K., Cafarelli, E., Dudley, G.A., Dooly, C., Feigenbaum, M., Fleck, S., Franklin, B., Fry, A., Hoffman, J.R., Newton, R.U., Potteiger, J., Stone, M.H., Ratamess, N.A. and Triplett-McBride, T. (2002). American College of Sports Medicine position stand on progression models in resistance training for healthy adults. *Medicine and Science in Sports and Exercise*, 34: 364–380.

Kreider, R.B., Fry, A.C. and O'Toole, M.L. (1998). *Overtraining in sport.* Champaign, IL: Human Kinetics,

Kretchmar, R.S. (1994). *Practical philosophy of sport.* Leeds: Human Kinetics.

Kristjánsson, K. (2005). Smoothing it: Some Aristotelian misgivings about the phronesis-praxis perspective on education. *Educational Philosophy and Theory*, 37(4): 455–473.

Lago, C. and Martin, C. (2007). Determinants of possession of the ball in soccer. *Journal of Sports Sciences*, 25: 969–974.

Laird, P. and Waters, L. (2008). Eye-witness recollection of sports coaches. *International Journal of Performance Analysis of Sport*, 8(1): 76–84.

Lampton, C.C., Lambert, M.E. and Yost, R. (1993). The effects of psychological factors in sports medicine rehabilitation adherence. *Journal of Sports Medicine and Physical Fitness*, 33(3): 292–299.

Lave, J. and Wenger, E. (1991). *Situated learning: Legitimate peripheral participation.* Cambridge: Cambridge University Press.

Lawrence, G.P., Beattie, S.J., Woodman, T., Khan, M.A., Hardy, L., Gottwald, V.M. and Cassell, V.E. (in press). Practice with anxiety improves performance, but only when anxious: Evidence for the specificity of practice hypothesis. *Journal of Sport and Exercise Psychology, S*.

Lawrence, G.P., Gottwald, V.M., Hardy, J. and Khan, M.A. (2010). Internal and external focus of attention in a novice form sport. *Research Quarterly for Exercise and Sport*, 82(3): 431–441.

Lawrence, G.P., Khan, M.A., Mourton, S. and Bernier, P.M. (2011). The reliance on visual feedback for online and offline processing. *Motor Control*, 15(2): 232–246.

Lazarus, R. S. (1999). *Stress and emotion: A new synthesis.* London: Free Association.

Lazarus, R.S. and Folkman, S. (1984). *Stress, appraisal and coping.* New York: Springer.

Lee, M. (1988). Values and responsibilities in children's sport. *Physical Education Review*, 11: 19–27.

Lee, T.D. and Magill, R.A. (1983). The locus of contextual interference in motor-skill acquisition. *Journal of Experimental Psychology: Learning Memory and Cognition*, 9(4): 730–746.

Lee, T.D. and Magill, R.A. (1985). Can forgetting facilitate skill acquisition? In D. Goodman, R.B. Wilberg and I.M. Franks (eds.), *Differing perspectives in motor learning, memory and control*. Amsterdam: Elsevier. pp. 3–22.

Lee, T.D., White, M.A. and Carnahan, H. (1990). On the role of knowledge of results in motor learning: Exploring the guidance hypothesis. *Journal of Motor Behavior*, 22(2): 191–208.

Lees, A., Vanrenterghem, J. and Dirk, D.C. (2004). Understanding how an arm swing enhances performance in the vertical jump. *Journal of Biomechanics*, 37(12): 1929–1940.

Lemert, C. (1997). *Social things: An introduction to the sociological life*. New York: Rowan and Littlefield.

Liao, C. and Masters, R.S.W. (2002). Self-focused attention and performance failure under psychological stress. *Journal of Sport and Exercise Psychology*, 24: 289–305.

Lian, O.B., Engebretsen, L. and Bahr, R. (2005). Prevalence of jumper's knee among elite athletes from different sports: A cross-sectional study. *American Journal of Sports Medicine*, 33(4): 561–567.

Light, R. (2008). Complex learning theory – Its epistemology and its assumptions about learning: Implications for physical education. *Journal of Teaching in Physical Education*, 27: 21–37.

Light, R. and Wallian, N. (2008). A constructivist-informed approach to teaching swimming. *Quest*, 60: 387–404.

Loland, S. (2011). The normative aims of coaching. In A. Hardman and C.R. Jones (eds.), *The ethics of sports coaching*. London: Routledge.

Long, J. and Spracklen, K. (eds.) (2011). *Sport and challenges to racism*. Basingstoke: Palgrave Macmillan.

Louw, R. with John Cameron-Dow (1987). *For the love of rugby*. Melville: Hans Strydom Publishers.

Lowenthal, D. (1985). *The past is a foreign country*. Cambridge: Cambridge University Press.

Lyle, J. (2002). *Sports coaching concepts: A framework for coaches' behaviour*. London: Routledge.

Lyle, J. (2008). Sports development and sports coaching. In K. Hylton and P. Bramham (eds.), *Sports development: Policy, process and practice*. London: Routledge.

McDonald, I. (1995). 'Sport for all – RIP?' In S. Fleming, M. Talbot and A. Tomlinson (eds.), *Physical education policy and politics in sport and leisure* (LSA publication no. 55). Eastbourne: Leisure Studies Association.

McFee, G. (1998). Are there philosophical issues with respect to sport (other than ethical ones)? In M. J. McNamee and S. J. Parry (eds.), *Ethics and sport*. London: Routledge. pp. 3–18.

McGarry, T. and Franks, I.M. (1994). Stochastic approaches to predicting competition squash match play. *Journal of Sports Sciences*, 12: 573–584.

MacIntyre, A.C. (1984). *After virtue*. London: Duckworth.

Macionis, J. (2007). *Sociology* (11th edn). New Jersey: Pearson Education International.

McKay, G.D., Payne, W.R., Goldie, P.A., Oakes, B.W. and Stanley, J.J. (1996). A comparison of the injuries sustained by female basketball and netball players. *The Australian Journal of Science and Medicine in Sport*, 28(1): 12–17.

237

Mackrous, I. and Proteau, L. (2007). Specificity of practice results from differences in movement planning strategies. *Experimental Brain Research*, 183(2): 181–193.

MacLean, M. (2010). Ambiguity within the boundary: Re-reading C. L. R. James's *Beyond a Boundary. Journal of Sport History*, 37(1): 99–117.

MacLean, M (2011). Artificially natural: A brief history of modern sport. In C. Anxo, Roibas, E. Stamtakis and K. Black (eds.), *Design for sport*. Aldershot: Ashgate. pp. 13–32.

McNamee, M.J. (1995). Sporting practices, institutions and virtues: A critique and a restatement. *Journal of the Philosophy of Sport*, 22: 61–82.

McNamee, M.J. (1997). Values in sport. In D. Levinson and K. Christenson (eds.), *Encyclopedia of world sport*. Oxford: ABC-Clio Inc.

McNamee, M. (1998). Celebrating trust: Virtues and rules in the ethical conduct of sports coaches. In M. McNamee and J. Parry (eds.), *Ethics and Sport*. London: Routledge.

McNamee, M.J. and Parry, S.J. (1990). Notes on the concept of 'health'. In J. Long (ed.), *Leisure, health and well-being*. Brighton: LSA Publications.

McNevin, N.H., Shea, C.H. and Wulf, G. (2003). Increasing the distance of external focus of attention enhances learning. *Psychological Research*, 67: 22–29.

MacPhail, A., Lyons, D., Quinn, S., Hughes, A-M. and Keane, S. (2010). A framework for lifelong involvement in sport and physical activity: The Irish perspective. *Leisure Studies*, 29(1): 85–100.

Mageau, G.A. and Vallerand, R.J. (2003). The coach-athlete relationship: A motivational model. *Journal of Sport* Sciences, 21: 883–904.

Magill, R.A. (2010). *Motor learning and control: Concepts and applications* (9th edn). New York: McGraw-Hill.

Magill, R.A. and Hall, K.G. (1990). A review of the contextual interference effect in motor skill acquisition. *Human Movement Science*, 9: 241–289.

Magill, R.A. and Schoenfelder-Zohdi, B. (1996). A visual model and knowledge of performance as sources of information for learning a rhythmic gymnastics skill. *International Journal of Sport Psychology*, 27(1): 7–22.

Malmerg, E. (1978). Science innovation and gymnastics in the USSR, *International Gymnast*, 20: 63.

Marqusee, M. (2005). *Anyone but England: An outsider looks at English cricket* (3rd edn). London: Aurum Press.

Marsh, I., Keating, M., Eyre, A., Campbell, R. and McKenzie, J. (1996). *Making sense of society: An introduction to sociology*. London: Longman.

Martens, R. (2004). *Successful coaching*. Champaign, IL: Human Kinetics.

Martens, R., Burton, D., Vealey, R.S., Bump, L.A. and Smith, D.E. (1990). Development and validation of the Competitive State Anxiety Inventory-2 (CSAI-2). In R. Martens, R.S. Vealey and D. Burton (eds.), *Competitive anxiety in sport*. Champaign, IL: Human Kinetics. pp. 117–213.

Martindale, A. and Collins, D. (2005). Professional judgement and decision making: The role of intention for impact. *The Sport Psychologist*, 19: 303–317.

Maslovat, D. and Franks, I.M. (2008). The need for feedback. In M. Hughes and I.M. Franks (eds.), *Essentials of performance analysis: An introduction*. London: Routledge. pp. 1–7.

Masters, R.S.W. (1992). Knowledge, knerves and know-how: The role of explicit versus implicit knowledge in the breakdown of a complex motor skill under pressure. *British Journal of Psychology*, 83: 343–358.

Masters, R.S.W. (2000). Theoretical aspects of implicit learning in sport. *International Journal of Sport Psychology*, 31: 530–541.

Mawer, M. (1995). *The effective teaching of physical education*. Essex: Longman.

Maxwell, J.P. and Masters, R.S.W. (2008). The theory of reinvestment. *International Review of Sport and Exercise Psychology*, 1(2): 160–183.

Mayes, A., O'Donoghue, P.G., Garland, J. and Davidson, A. (2009). The use of performance analysis and internet video streaming during elite netball preparation. *3rd International Workshop of the International Society of Performance Analysis of Sport*. Lincoln, UK, 6–7 April 2009.

Maynard, I.W. and Cotton, P.C.J. (1993). An investigation of two stress management techniques in a field setting. *The Sport Psychologist*, 6: 357–387.

Mazur, J. (1990). *Learning and behaviour* (2nd edn). Englewood Cliffs, NJ: Prentice-Hall.

Mellalieu, S.D., Hanton, S. and Fletcher, D. (2006). A competitive anxiety review: Recent directions in sport psychology research. In S. Hanton and S.D. Mellalieu (eds.), *Literature reviews in sport psychology*. Hauppauge, NY: Nova Science.

Metzler, M. (2000). *Instructional models for physical education*. Boston: Allyn & Bacon.

Mirwald, R.L., Baxter-Jones, A.D.G., Bailey, D.A. and Beunen, G.P. (2002). An assessment of maturity from anthropometric measurements. *Medicine and Science in Sports and Exercise*, 34: 689–694.

Mitchell, M. and Kernodle, M. (2004). Using multiple intelligences to teach tennis. *Journal of Physical Education, Recreation and Dance*, 75(8): 27–32.

Mohr, M., Krustrup, P., Nybo, L., Nielsen, J.J. and Bangsbo, J. (2004). Muscle temperature and sprint performance during soccer matches – beneficial effect of re-warm-up at half time. *Scandinavian Journal of Medicine and Science in Sports*, 14: 156–162.

Moore, W.E. and Stevenson, J.R. (1994). Training for trust in sport skills. *The Sport Psychologist*, 8: 1–12.

Morgan, K. (2011). *Athletics challenges* (2nd edn). London: Routledge.

Morgan, K. and Carpenter, P.J. (2002). Effects of manipulating the motivational climate in physical education lessons. *European Journal of Physical Education*, 8: 209–232.

Morgan, K. and Kingston, K. (2008). Development of a self-observation mastery intervention programme for teacher education. *Physical Education and Sport Pedagogy*, 13(2): 1–28.

Morgan, K. and Kingston, K. (2010). Promoting a mastery motivational climate in a higher education sports class. *Journal of Hospitality, Leisure, Sport and Tourism Education. Practical paper*, 9(1): 73–84.

Morgan, K., Sproule, J., Weigand, D. and Carpenter, P. (2005a). Development of a computer-based measure of teacher behaviours related to motivational climate in physical education. *Physical Education and Sport Pedagogy Journal*, 10: 113–135.

Morgan, K., Sproule, J. and Kingston, K. (2005b). Teaching styles, motivational climate and pupils' cognitive and affective responses in physical education. *European Physical Education Review*, 11(3): 257–286.

Morgan, L. and Fleming, S. (2003). The development of coaching in Welsh Rugby Union Football. *Football Studies*, 6(2): 39–51.

Morgan, W.J. (2003). Why the 'view from nowhere' gets us nowhere in our moral considerations of sports. *Journal of the Philosophy of Sport*, 30(1): 51–67.

Morgan, W.J. (2004). Moral antirealism, internalism and sport. *Journal of the Philosophy of Sport*, 31: 161–183.

Morris, L., Davis, D. and Hutchings, C. (1981). Cognitive and emotional components of anxiety: Literature review and revised worry-emotionality scale. *Journal of Educational Psychology*, 75: 541–555.

Mosston, M. (1966). *Teaching physical education*. Columbus, Ohio: Merrill Publishing Co.

Mosston, M. (1981). *Teaching physical education* (2nd edn). Columbus, Ohio: Merrill Publishing Co.

Mosston, M. and Ashworth, S. (2002). *Teaching physical education* (5th edn). Columbus, Ohio: Merrill Publishing Co.

Mullen, R. and Hardy, L. (2000). State anxiety and motor performance: Testing the conscious processing hypothesis. *Journal of Sport Science*, 18: 785–799.

Murias, J.M., Lanatta, D., Arcuri, C.R. and Laino, F.A. (2007). Metabolic and functional responses playing tennis on different surfaces. *Journal of Strength and Conditioning Research*, 21: 112–117.

Nash, C. and Sproule, J. (2009). Career development of expert coaches. *International Journal of Sport Science and Coaching*, 4(1): 121–138.

Nash, C. and Sproule, J. (2011). Insights into experiences: Reflections of an expert and novice coach. *International Journal of Sport Science and Coaching*, 6(1): 149–161.

Nash, C., Sproule, J. and Horton, P., (2011). Excellence in coaching: The art and skill of elite practitioners. *Research Quarterly for Exercise and Sport*, 82(2): 229–238.

Neil, R., Hanton, S., Mellalieu, S.D. and Fletcher, D. (2011). Competition stress and emotions in sport performers: The role of further appraisals. *Psychology of Sport and Exercise*, 12: 460–470.

Nelson, L.J. and Cushion, C.J. (2006). Reflection in coach education: The case of the national governing body coaching certificate. *The Sport Psychologist*, 20: 174–183.

Nesti, M. (2001). Working in sports development. In K. Hylton, P. Bramham, D. Jackson and M. Nesti (eds.), *Sports development: Policy, process and practice*. London: Routledge.

Newell, K.M. and Walter, C.B. (1981). Kinematic and kinetic parameters as information feedback in motor skill acquisition. *Journal of Human Movement Studies*, 7(4): 235–254.

Ng, J.Y.Y., Lonsdale, C. and Hodge, K. (2011). The basic needs satisfaction in sport scale (BNSSS): Instrument development and initial validity evidence. *Psychology of Sport and Exercise*, 12: 257–264.

Nicholls, A., Polman, R.C.J. and Levy, A.R. (2012). A path analysis of stress appraisals, emotions, coping and performance satisfaction among athletes. *Psychology of Sport and Exercise*, 13: 263–270.

Nicholls, J.G. (1989). *The competitive ethos and democratic education*. Cambridge, MA: Harvard University Press.

Nissinen, M.A, Preiss, R. and Brüggemann, P. (1985). Simulation of human airborne movements on the horizontal bar. In D.A. Winter and R. Norman (eds.), *Biomechanics IX-B*. Champaign, IL: Human Kinetics. pp. 373–376.

Ntoumanis, N. and Biddle, S.J.H. (1998). The relationship between competitive anxiety, achievement goals and motivational climate. *Research Quarterly for Exercise and Sport*, 69: 176–187.

O'Donoghue, P.G. (2005). Normative profiles of sports performance. *International Journal of Performance Analysis of Sport*, 5(1): 104–119.

O'Donoghue, P.G. (2006). The use of feedback videos in sport. *Performance analysis of sport 7* (eds. H. Dancs, M. Hughes and P.G. O'Donoghue), 23–26 August 2006, Szombathely, Hungary, Cardiff: CPA UWIC Press, pp. 126–137.

O'Donoghue, P.G. (2010). *Research methods for performance analysis*. London: Routledge.

O'Donoghue, P.G. and Cullinane, A. (2011). A regression-based approach to interpreting sports performance. *International Journal of Performance Analysis in Sport*, 11: 295–307.

240

O'Donoghue, P.G. and Longville, J. (2004). Reliability testing and the use of statistics in performance analysis support: A case study from an international netball tournament. In P.G. O'Donoghue and M. Hughes (eds.), *Performance analysis of sport 6*. Cardiff: CPA Press, UWIC. pp. 1–7

O'Donoghue, P.G., Mayes, A., Edwards, K.M. and Garland, J. (2008). Performance norms for British National Super League netball. *International Journal of Sports Science and Coaching*, 3: 501–511.

Olsen, E. and Larsen, O. (1997). Use of match analysis by coaches. In T. Reilly, J. Bangsbo and M. Hughes (eds.), *Science and Football III*. London: E&FN Spon. pp. 209–220.

Ommundsen, Y., Roberts, G.C. and Kavussanu, M. (1998). Perceived motivational climate and cognitive and affective correlates among Norwegian athletes. *Journal of Sport Sciences*, 16: 153–164.

Ost, L.G. (1988). Applied relaxation: Description of an effective coping technique. *Scandinavian Journal of Behaviour Therapy*, 17: 83–96.

Oudejans, R.R.D. (2008). Reality-based practice under pressure improves handgun shooting performance of police officers. *Ergonomics*, 51(3): 261–273.

Oudejans, R.R.D. and Pijpers, J.R. (2009). Training with anxiety has a positive effect on expert perceptual-motor performance under pressure. *Quarterly Journal of Experimental Psychology*, 62(8): 1631–1647.

Oudejans, R.R.D. and Pijpers, J.R. (2010). Training with mild anxiety may prevent choking under higher levels of anxiety. *Psychology of Sport and Exercise*, 11(1): 44–50.

Papaioannou, A. (1997). Perceptions of the motivational climate, beliefs about the causes of success and sportsmanship behaviours of elite Greek basketball players. In R. Lidor and M. Bar-Eli (eds.), *Innovations in sport psychology: Linking theory and practice*. Proceedings of the IX World Congress in Sport Psychology: Part II. Netanya, Israel: Ministry of Education, Culture and Sport. pp. 534–536.

Partington, M. and Cushion, C. (2011). An investigation of the practice activities and coaching behaviours of professional top-level youth soccer coaches. *Scandinavian Journal of Medicine and Science in Sports*: 1–9.

Patel, D.R., Greydanus, D.E., Pratt, H.D. and Phillips, E.L. (2003). Eating disorders in adolescent athletes. *Journal of Adolescent Research*, 18(3): 280–296.

Pearson, P. and Webb, P. (2006). Improving the quality of games teaching to promote physical activity. *Journal of Science and Medicine in Sport*, 9(6): 9–18.

Pelletier, R.L., Montelpare, W.J. and Stark, R.M. (1993). Intercollegiate ice hockey injuries: A case for uniform definitions and reports. *American Journal of Sports Medicine*, 21: 78–81.

Perez, C.R., Meira, C.M. and Tani, G. (2005). Does the contextual interference effect last over extended transfer trials? *Perceptual and Motor Skills*, 100(1): 58–60.

Perkins, D. (1999). The many faces of constructivism. *Educational Leadership*, 57(3): 6–11.

Perkins-Ceccato, N., Passmore, S.R. and Lee, T.D. (2003). Effects of focus attention depend on golfer's skill. *Journal of Sports Sciences*, 21: 593–600.

Pigott, R.E. and Shapiro, D.C. (1984). Motor schema: The structure of the variability session. *Research Quarterly for Exercise and Sport*, 55(1): 41–45.

Pitchford, A. and Collins, M. (2010). Sports development as a job, a career and training. In M. Collins (ed.), *Examining sports development*. London: Routledge.

Polley, M. (2011). *The British Olympics: Britain's Olympic heritage 1612–2012*. London: Played in Britain/English Heritage.

Poolton, J.M., Maxwell, J.P., Masters, R.S.W. and Raab, M. (2006). Benefits of an external focus of attention: Common coding or conscious processing? *Journal of Sports Sciences*, 24: 89–99.

Porter, J.M. and Magill, R.A. (2010). Systematically increasing contextual interference is beneficial for learning sport skills. *Journal of Sports Sciences*, 28(12): 1277–1285.

Potrac, P. and Jones, R.L. (1999). The invisible ingredient in coaching knowledge: A case for recognising and researching the social component. *Sociology of Sport Online*, 2(1). Available: http://physed.otago.ac.nz/sosol/v2i1/v2i1a5.htm

Potrac, P. and Jones, R.L. (2009a). Micropolitical workings in semi-professional football. *Sociology of Sport Journal*, 26: 557–577.

Potrac, P. and Jones, R.L. (2009b). Power, conflict and co-operation: Towards a micro-politics of coaching. *Quest*, 61(2): 223–236.

Potrac, P., Jones, R.L. and Armour, K.M. (2002). 'It's all about getting respect': The coaching behaviours of an expert English soccer coach. *Sport, Education and Society*, 7(2): 183–202.

Potrac, P., Jones, R.L. and Cushion, C. (2007). Understanding power and the coach's role in professional English soccer: A preliminary investigation of coach behaviour. *Soccer and Society*, 8(1): 33–49.

Powell, J.W. and Barber-Foss, K.D. (1999). Injury patterns in selected high school sports: A review of the 1995–1997 seasons. *Journal of Athletic Training*, 34(3): 277–284.

Powers, C.H. (2004). *Making sense of social theory: A practical introduction*. Lanham, MD: Rowan and Littlefield.

Premack, D. (1965). Reinforcement theory. In D. Levine (ed.), *Nebraska symposium on motivation*. Lincoln: University of Nebraska Press. pp. 123–180.

Pribram, K.H. and McGuinness, D. (1975). Arousal, activation and effort in the control of attention. *Psychological Review*, 82: 116–149.

Prinz, W. (1997). Perceptions and action planning. *European Journal of Cognitive Psychology*, 9: 129–154.

Proteau, L. and Marteniuk, R.G. (1993). Static visual information and the learning and control of a manual aiming movement. *Human Movement Science*, 12(5): 515–536.

Purdy, L.G. (2006). Coaching in the 'current': Capturing the climate in elite rowing training camps. Unpublished PhD dissertation, University of Otago, New Zealand.

Reinboth, M. and Duda, J.L. (2006). Perceived motivational climate, need satisfaction and indices of well-being in team sports: A longitudinal perspective. *Psychology of Sport and Exercise*, 7: 269–286.

Richards, A. (2002). *Carwyn: A personal memoir*. Swansea: Christopher Davies.

Riess, S. (1991). *City games: The evolution of American urban society and the rise of sports*. Urbana-Champaign, IL: University of Illinois Press.

Robbins, J.E. and Rosenfeld, L.B. (2001). Athletes' perceptions of social support provided by their head coach, assistant coach and athletic trainer, pre-injury and during rehabilitation. *Journal of Sport Behavior*, 24: 277–297.

Roberts, G.C. (2001). Understanding the dynamics of motivation in physical activity: The influence of achievement goals on motivational processes. In G.C. Roberts (ed.), *Advances in motivation in sport and exercise*. Champaign, IL: Human Kinetics. pp. 1–50.

Roberts, K. (2004). *The leisure industries*. Basingstoke, Hants: Palgrave Macmillan.

Roberts, T. (1995). Sport and strong poetry. *Journal of the Philosophy of Sport*, 23: 94–107.

Robertson, G., Caldwell G., Hamill, J., Kamen, G. and Whittlesey, S. (2004). *Research methods in biomechanics*. Champaign, IL: Human Kinetics.

Robinson, L. (2004). *Managing public sport and leisure services*. London: Routledge.

242

Rodano, R. and Tavana, R. (1995). Three-dimensional analysis of instep kicks in professional soccer players. In T. Reilly, J. Clays and A. Stibbe (eds.), *Science in Football II*. London: E & FN Spon. pp. 357–361.

Rogers, C.A. (1974). Feedback precision and post-feedback interval duration. *Journal of Experimental Psychology*, 102(4): 604–608.

Rothstein, A.L. and Arnold, R.K. (1976). Bridging the gap: Application of research on videotape feedback and bowling. *Motor Skills: Theory into Practice*, 1: 36–61.

Ryall, E, (2010). *Critical thinking for sports students*. Exeter: Learning Matters.

Ryan, R.M. and Deci, E.L. (2000). Self-determination theory and the facilitation of intrinsic motivation, social development and well-being. *American Psychologist*, 55: 68–78.

Salmoni, A.W., Schmidt, R.A. and Walter, C.B. (1984). Knowledge of results and motor learning: A review and critical reappraisal. *Psychological Bulletin*, 95(3): 355–386.

Sarrazin, P., Boiché, J. and Pelletier, L. (2007). A self-determination theory approach to dropout in athletes. In M. Hagger and N. Chatzisarantis (eds.), Intrinsic motivation and self-determination in exercise and sport. Champaign, IL: Human Kinetics.

Saury, J. and Durand, M. (1998). Practical knowledge in expert coaches: On-site study of coaching in sailing. *Research Quarterly for Exercise and Sport*, 69(3): 254–266.

Schmidt, R.A. (1975). Schema theory of discrete motor skill learning. *Psychological Review*, 82(4): 225–260.

Schmidt, R.A. (1991). Frequent augmented feedback can degrade learning: Evidence and interpretations. In J. Renquin and G.E. Stelmach (eds.), *Tutorials in motor neuroscience*. Dordrecht, The Netherlands: Kluwer Academic Publishers. pp. 59–75.

Schmidt, R.A. and Lee, T.D. (2011). *Motor control and learning: A behavioural emphasis* (5th edn). Champaign IL: Human Kinetics.

Schmidt, R.A. and Wrisberg, C.A. (2000). *Motor learning and performance* (2nd edn). Champaign, IL: Human Kinetics.

Schmikli, S.L., Backx, F.J.G., Kemler, H.J. and Mechelen, W. (2009). National survey on sports injuries in the Netherlands: Target populations for sports injury prevention programs. *Clinical Journal of Sport Medicine*, 19(2): 101–106.

Schön, D.A. (1983). *The reflective practitioner: How professionals think in action*. New York: Basic Books.

Schön, D.A. (1987). *Educating the reflective practitioner*. San Francisco: Jossey-Bass.

Schunk, D. (1999). Social self interaction and achievement behaviour. *Educational Psychologist*, 26: 207–231.

Scuderi, G.R. and McCann, P.D. (2005). *Sports medicine: A comprehensive approach*. Philadelphia, PA: Elsevier Mosby Books.

Shaheen, R. (2010). Creativity in education. *Creative Education*, 1(3): 166–169.

Sharpe, T. and Koperwas, J. (1999). *BEST: Behavioral Evaluation Strategy and Taxonomy software*. Thousand Oaks, CA: Sage Publications.

Shea, C.H. and Kohl, R.M. (1990). Specificity and variability of practice. *Research Quarterly for Exercise and Sport*, 61(2): 169–177.

Shea, C.H. and Kohl, R.M. (1991). Composition of practice: Influence on the retention of motor skills. *Research Quarterly for Exercise and Sport*, 62(2): 187–195.

Shea, J.B. and Morgan, R.L. (1979). Contextual interference effects of the acquisition, retention and transfer of a motor skill. *Journal of Experimental Psychology*, 5(2): 179–187.

Shea, J.B. and Zimny, S.T. (1983). Context effects in memory and learning in movement information. In R.A. Magill (ed.), *Memory and control of action*. Amsterdam: North-Holland. pp. 345–366.

Shoenfelt, E.L., Snyder, L.A., Maue, A.E., McDowell, C.P. and Woolard, C.D. (2002). Comparison of constant and variable practice conditions on free-throw shooting. *Perceptual and Motor Skills*, 94(3): 1113–1123.

Shumway-Cook, A., Anson, D. and Haller, S. (1988). Postural sway biofeedback: Its effect on re-establishing stance stability in hemiplegic patients. *Archives of Physical Medicine and Rehabilitation*, 69(6): 395–400.

Sicilia-Camacho, A. and Brown, D. (2008). Revisiting the paradigm shift from the versus to the non-versus notion of Mosston's Spectrum of teaching styles in physical education pedagogy: A critical pedagogical perspective. *Physical Education and Sport Pedagogy*, 13(1): 85–108.

Siedentop, D. (1994). *Sport education*. Champaign, IL: Human Kinetics.

Simon, R.L. (1991). *Fair play: Sports, values and society*. Boulder, CO: Westview.

Slavin, R. (2003). *Educational psychology: Theory and practice* (7th edn). Boston: Allyn & Bacon.

Smith, C.A. (1994). The warm-up procedure to stretch or not to stretch: A brief review. *Journal of Orthopaedic Sports Physiotherapy*, 19: 12–17.

Smolevskij, V. (1969). *Masterstvo gimnastov*. Moscow.

Smyth, J. and Shacklock, G. (1998). *Re-making teaching: Ideology, policy and practice*. New York: Routledge.

Soligard, T., Myklebust, G., Steffen, K., Holme, I., Silvers, H., Bizzini, M., Junge, A., Dvorak, J., Bahr, R. and Andersen, T.E. (2008). Comprehensive warm-up programme to prevent injuries in young female footballers: Cluster randomised controlled trial. *British Medical Journal*, 337: a2469.

Solmon, M.A. (1996). Impact of motivational climate on students' behaviors and perceptions in a physical education setting. *Journal of Educational Psychology*, 88: 731–738.

Spielberger, C.D. (1966). Theory and research on anxiety. In C.D. Spielberger (ed.), *Anxiety and behavior*. New York: Academic Press. pp. 3–20.

sports coach UK (2004). *UK coaching certificate monitoring study: Learning from the early stages of implementation: Phase 2 report*. Leeds: sports coach UK.

sports coach UK (2006). *UK action plan for coaching: Consultation draft*. Leeds: sports coach UK.

sports coach UK (2008). *The UK Coaching Framework: a 3-7-11 year action plan*. Leeds: sports coach UK.

sports coach UK (2011a). *The UK Coaching Certificate Support Guide Levels 1–3*. Leeds: Coachwise Ltd.

sports coach UK (2011b). *Sports Coach UK Annual Review 2010–2011*. Leeds: sports coach UK.

Spray, C.M. (2002). Motivational climate and perceived strategies to sustain pupils' discipline in physical education. *European Physical Education Review*, 18: 5–20.

Sproule, J., Ollis, S., Gray, S., Thorburn, M., Allison, P. and Horton, P. (2011). Promoting perseverance and challenge in physical education: The missing ingredient for improved games teaching. *Sport, Education and Society*, 16(5): 665–684.

Standage, M., Duda, J.L. and Ntoumanis, N. (2003). Predicting motivational regulations in physical education: The interplay between dispositional goal orientations, motivational climate and perceived competence. *Journal of Sports Sciences*, 21: 631–647.

Standahl, Ø.F and Hemmestad, L. (2011). Becoming a good coach: Coaching and phronesis. In A. Hardman and C.R. Jones (eds.), *The ethics of sports coaching*. London: Routledge. pp.45–55.

Steele, M.K. (1996). *Sideline help: A guide for immediate evaluation and care of sports injuries*. Champaign, IL: Human Kinetics.

Stones, R. (1998). Tolerance, plurality and creative synthesis in sociological thought. In R. Stones (ed.), *Key sociological thinkers*. Basingstoke, Hants: Macmillan Press.

Suinn, R.M. (1987). Behavioural approaches to stress management in sports. In J.R. May and M.J. Asken (eds.), *Psychology of motor behaviour and sport*. Champaign, IL: Human Kinetics. pp. 54–72.

Suits, B. (1995). The elements of sport. In W.P. Morgan and K.V. Meier (eds.), *Philosophic inquiry in sport*. Leeds: Human Kinetics.

Swain, A.B.J. and Jones, G. (1993). Intensity and frequency dimensions of competitive state anxiety. *Journal of Sport Sciences*, 11: 533–542.

Swinnen, S.P., Schmidt, R.A., Nicholson, D.E. and Shapiro, D.C. (1990). Information feedback for skill acquisition: Instantaneous knowledge of results degrades learning. *Journal of Experimental Psychology: Learning, Memory and Cognition*, 16(4): 706–716.

Szymanski, S., Kruger, A., Riess, S. and MacLean, M. (2008). Forum: Associativity and modern sport. *Journal of Sport History*, 35(1): 1–64.

Taimela, S., Kujala, U.M. and Osterman, K. (1990). Intrinsic risk factors and athletic injuries. *Sports Medicine*, 9: 205–215.

Targett, S.G.R. (1998). Injuries in professional rugby union. *Clinical Journal of Sport Medicine*, 8(4): 280–285.

Taylor, B. and Garratt, D. (2011). The professionalisation of sports coaching: Definitions, challenges and critique. In J. Lyle and C. Cushion (eds.), *Sports coaching: Professionalisation and practice*. London: Elsevier. pp. 99–117.

Taylor, J.B., Mellalieu, S.D., James, N. and Shearer, U.A. (2008). The influence of match location, quality of opposition and match status on technical performance in professional association football. *Journal of Sports Sciences*, 26: 885–895.

Taylor, M. (2005). *The leaguers: The making of professional football in England, 1900–1939*. Liverpool: Liverpool University Press.

Tenga, A., Holme, I., Ronglan, L.T. and Bahr, R. (2010a). Effect of playing tactics on goal scoring in Norwegian professional soccer. *Journal of Sports Sciences*, 28: 237–244.

Tenga, A., Holme, I., Ronglan, L.T. and Bahr, R. (2010b). Effect of playing tactics on achieving score-box possessions in a random series of team possessions from Norwegian professional soccer matches. *Journal of Sports Sciences*, 28: 245–255.

Thomas, J.R., Launder, A.G. and Nelson, J.K. (2001). *Play practice: The games approach to teaching and coaching sports*. Champaign, IL: Human Kinetics.

Thomas, O., Lane, A. and Kingston, K. (2011). Defining and contextualizing robust sport-confidence. *Journal of Applied Sport Psychology*, 23: 189–208.

Thomas, O., Maynard, I. and Hanton, S. (2004). Temporal aspects of competitive anxiety and self-confidence as a function of anxiety perceptions. *The Sport Psychologist*, 18: 172–187.

Thomas, O., Maynard, I. and Hanton, S. (2007). Intervening with athletes during the time leading up to competition: Theory to practice II. *Journal of Applied Sport Psychology*, 19: 398–418.

Tinning, R. (1997). Performance and participation discourses in human movement: Toward a socially critical physical education. In J.M. Fernadex-Balboa (ed.), *Critical post-modernism in human movement, physical education and sport*. Albany, NY: SUNY. pp. 99–119.

Tinning, R., Kirk, D. and Evans, J. (1993). *Learning to teach physical education*. London: Prentice Hall.

Tod, D. (2007). The long and winding road: Professional development in sport psychology. *The Sport Psychologist*, 21: 94–108.

Tom, A.R. (1984). *Teaching as a moral craft*. New York: Longman.

Torkildsen, G. (2011). Torkildsen's sport and leisure management (6th edn). In P. Taylor (ed.), *Torkildsen's sport and leisure management*. London: Routledge.

Totsika, V. and Wulf, G. (2003). An external focus of attention enhances transfer to novel situations and skills. *Research Quarterly for Exercise and Sport*, 74: 220–225.

Tracey, J. (2003). The emotional response to the injury and rehabilitation process, *Journal of Applied Sport Psychology*, 15(4): 279–293.

Treasure, D. (1993). A social-cognitive approach to understanding children's achievement behavior, cognitions and affect in competitive sport. *Unpublished doctoral dissertation*. University of Illinois, Urbana-Champaign, IL.

Tremblay, L. and Proteau, L. (1998). Specificity of practice: The case of power-lifting. *Research Quarterly for Exercise and Sport*, 69(3): 284–289.

Tremblay, L. and Proteau, L. (2001). Specificity of practice in a ball interception task. *Canadian Journal of Experimental Psychology-Revue Canadienne De Psychologie Experimentale*, 55(3): 207–218.

Turner, D. and Nelson, L.J. (2009). Graduate perceptions of a UK university based coach education programme and impacts on development and employability. *International Journal of Coaching Science*, 3(2): 3–28.

Tuxhill, C. and Wigmore, S. (1998). 'Merely meat'? Respect for persons in sport and games. In M.J. McNamee and S.J. Parry (eds.), *Ethics and sport*. London: Routledge.

Vallerand, R.J. (1997). Toward a hierarchical model of intrinsic and extrinsic motivation. In M.P. Zanna (ed.), *Advances in experimental sport psychology* (Vol. 29). San Diego: Academic Press. pp. 271–360.

Vallerand, R.J. (2007). Intrinsic and extrinsic motivation in sport and physical activity: A review and a look at the future. In G. Tenenbaum and R.E. Eklund (eds.), *Handbook of sport psychology* (3rd edn). New York: John Wiley. pp. 49–83.

Vallerand, R.J. and Losier, G. F. (1999). An integrative analysis of intrinsic and extrinsic motivation in sport. *Journal of Applied Sport Psychology*, 11: 142–169.

van Emmerik, R.E.A and van Wegen, E.E.H. (2000). On variability and stability in human movement, *Journal of Applied Biomechanics*, 16: 394–406.

Van Mechelen, W., Hlobil, H. and Kemper, H.C. (1992). Incidence, severity, aetiology and prevention of sports injuries: A review of concepts. *Sports Medicine*, 14(2): 82–99.

Vealey, R.S. (1986). Conceptualization of sport-confidence and competitive orientation: Preliminary investigation and instrument development. *Journal of Sport Psychology*, 8: 221–246.

Vealey, R.S. (2001). Understanding and enhancing self-confidence in athletes. In R.N. Singer, H.A. Hausenblas and C.M. Janelle (eds.), *Handbook of sport psychology* (2nd edn). New York: Wiley. pp. 550–565.

Vealey, R.S. and Chase, M.A. (2008). Self-confidence in sport: Conceptual and research advances. In T.S. Horn (ed.), *Advances in sport psychology* (3rd edn). Champaign, IL: Human Kinetics. pp. 65–97.

Vealey, R.S., Hayashi, S.W., Garner-Holman, M. and Giacobbi, P. (1998). Sources of sport-confidence: Conceptualization and instrument development. *Journal of Sport and Exercise Psychology*, 20: 54–80.

Vealey, R.S. and Knight, B.J. (2002, September). *Multidimensional sport-confidence: A conceptual and psychometric extension*. Paper presented at the Association for the Advancement of Applied Sport Psychology Conference, Tucson, AZ.

Vilwock, M.R., Meyer, E.G., Powell, J.W., Fonty, A.J. and Haut, R.C. (2009). Football playing surface and shoe design affect rotational traction. *American Journal of Sports Medicine*, 37(3): 518–525.

Viru, A., Loko, J., Harro, M., Volver, A., Laaneots, L. and Viru M. (1999). Critical periods in the development of performance capacity during childhood and adolescence. *Physical Education and Sport Pedagogy*, 4: 75–119.

Vygotsky, L.S. (1978). *Mind in society: The development of higher psychological processes*. Cambridge, M.A: Harvard University Press.

Walker, J. and O' Shea, T. (1999). *Behaviour management: A practical approach for educators* (7th edn). Upper Saddle River, NJ: Prentice Hall.

Walling, M.D., Duda, J.L. and Chi, L. (1993). The perceived motivational climate in sport questionnaire: Construct and predictive validity. *Journal of Sport and Exercise Psychology*, 15: 172–183.

Watkins, J. (2007). *An introduction to biomechanics of sport and exercise*. Edinburgh, UK: Elsevier.

Watkins, C. and Mortimore, P. (1999). Pedagogy: What do we know. In P. Mortimore (ed.), *Understanding pedagogy and its impact on learning*. London: Paul Chapman. pp. 1–19.

Watson, A.W.S. (1997). Sports injuries: Incidence, causes, prevention. *Physical Therapy Reviews*, 2(3): 135–151.

Weinberg, D.R., Guy, D.E. and Tupper, R.W. (1964). Variation of post-feedback interval in simple motor learning. *Journal of Experimental Psychology*, 67: 98–99.

Whannel, G. (1992). *Fields in vision: Television sport and cultural transformation*. London: Routledge.

Whannel, G. (2002). *Media sport stars: Masculinities and moralities*. London: Routledge.

Whannel, G. (2008). *Culture, politics and sport: Blowing the whistle revisited*. London: Routledge.

White, A. and Bailey, J. (1990). Reducing disruptive behaviour of elementary physical education students with sit and watch. *Journal of Applied Behaviour Analysis*, 3: 353–359.

Williams, J. (2003). *A game for rough girls? A history of women's football in Britain*. London: Routledge.

Williams, J.M. and Straub, W.F. (2005). Sport psychology: Past, present, future. In J.M. Williams (ed.), *Applied sport psychology: Personal growth to peak performance* (5th edn). Mountain View, CA: Mayfield.

Williams, K. (3 April 2012). Aspel & Co Show, BBC [online:youtube.com/watch?v=CdDt wc9HA7s&feature=player_detailpage 1987]

Wilson, C., King, M.A. and Yeadon, M.R. (2006). Determination of subject-specific model parameters for visco-elastic elements. *Journal of Biomechanics*, 39: 1883–1890.

Winkler, W. (1988). A new approach to the video analysis of tactical aspects of soccer. In T. Reilly, A. Lees, K. Davids and W. Murphy (eds.), *Science and football*. London: E & FN Spon. pp. 368–372.

Winstein, C.J. and Schmidt, R.A. (1990). Reduced frequency of knowledge of results enhances motor skill learning. *Journal of Experimental Psychology: Learning Memory and Cognition*, 16(4): 677–691.

Wolf, B.R., Ebinger, A.E., Lawler, M.P. and Britton, C.L (2009). Injury patterns in division I collegiate swimming. *American Journal of Sports Medicine*, 37(10): 2037–2042.

Woodcock, C., Richards, H. and Mugford, A. (2008). Quality counts: Critical features for neophyte professional development. *The Sport Psychologist*, 22: 491–506.

Woodman, T. and Hardy, L. (2001a). Stress and anxiety. In R. Singer, H.A. Hausenblas and C.M. Janelle (eds.), *Handbook of research on sport psychology* (2nd edn). New York: Wiley. pp. 290–318.

Woodman, T. and Hardy, L. (2001b). A case study of organizational stress in elite sport. *Journal of Applied Sport Psychology*, 13: 207–238.

Woollard, J. (2010). *Psychology for the teacher: Behaviourism*. London: Routledge.

Wright Mills, C.W. (1959). *The sociological imagination*. New York: Oxford University Press.

Wulf, G. (2007). Attentional focus and motor learning: A review of 10 years of research. *Bewegung Und Training*, 1: 1–11.

Wulf, G., Höβ, M. and Prinz, W. (1998). Instructions for motor learning: Differential effects of internal versus external focus of attention. *Journal of Motor Behavior*, 30: 169–179.

Wulf, G., Lauterbach, B. and Toole, T. (1999). Learning advantages of an external focus of attention in golf. *Research Quarterly for Exercise and Sport*, 70: 120–126.

Wulf, G., McNevin, N.H., Fuchs, T., Ritter, F. and Toole, T. (2000). Attentional focus in complex skill learning. *Research Quarterly for Exercise and Sport*, 71: 229–239.

Wulf, G., McNevin, N. and Shea, C.H. (2001). The automaticity of complex motor skill learning as a function of attentional focus. *The Quarterly Journal of Experimental Psychology*, 54(4): 1143–1154.

Wulf, G. and Schmidt, R.A. (1994). Contextual interference effects in motor learning: Evaluating a KR-usefulness hypothesis. In J.R. Nitsch and R. Seiler (eds.), *Movement and sport: Psychological foundations and effects* (Vol. 2. Motor control and learning). Sankt Augustin, Germany: Acedemia Verlag. pp. 304–309.

Wulf, G. and Su, J. (2007). An external focus of attention enhances golf shot accuracy in beginners and experts. *Research Quarterly for Exercise and Sport*, 78(4): 384–389.

Wulf, G., Zachry, T., Granados, C. and Dufek, J.S. (2007). Increases in jump-and-reach height through an external focus of attention. *International Journal of Sports Science and Coaching*, 2: 275–284.

Young, D.E. and Schmidt, R.A. (1992). Augmented kinematic feedback for motor learning. *Journal of Motor Behavior*, 24(3): 261–273.

Zachry, T., Wulf, G., Mercer, J. and Bezodis, N. (2005). Increased movement accuracy and reduced EMG activity as the result of adopting an external focus of attention. *Brain Research Bulletin*, 67: 304–309.

Zimmerman, B.J. and Kitsantas, A. (1996). Self-regulated learning of a motoric skill: The role of goal setting and self-monitoring. *Journal of Applied Sport Psychology*, 8: 60–75.

Zinkovsky, A.V., Vain, A.A. and Torm, R.J. (1976). Biomechanical analysis of the formation of gymnastic skill. In P.V. Komi (ed.), *Biomechanics V-B*. Baltimore, MD: University Park Press.

Zinsser, N., Bunker, L. and Williams, J.M. (2001). Cognitive techniques for building confidence and enhancing performance. In J.M. Williams (ed.), *Applied sport psychology: Personal growth to peak performance*. Mountain View, CA: Mayfield. pp. 284–297.

Zuber-Skerritt, O. (1996). Emancipatory action research for organisation change and management development. In O. Zuber-Skerritt (ed.), *New directions in action research*. London: Falmer. pp. 83–105.

INDEX